DEVELOPMENT ST

Bureaucracy
*Its Role in Third World
Development*

Vivien
Lowndes
1990

Bureaucracy
Its Role in Third World Development

Malcolm Wallis

**MACMILLAN
PUBLISHERS**

First published 1989

Published by *Macmillan Publishers Ltd*
London and Basingstoke
Associated companies and representatives in Accra,
Auckland, Delhi, Dublin, Gaborone, Hamburg, Harare,
Hong Kong, Kuala Lumpur, Lagos, Manzini, Melbourne,
Mexico City, Nairobi, New York, Singapore, Tokyo

ISBN 0–333–44068–4

Printed in Hong Kong

A CIP Catalogue record for this book is available from
the British Library.

Contents

Biographical Note

Malcolm Wallis was born in Hertford in 1945 and educated in England and Kenya. He studied at Southampton University as an undergraduate and then at London and Manchester Universities. Much of his early working life was spent in Africa, as a lecturer at the Universities of Zambia and Lesotho and, between 1973 and 1975, as a Research Fellow at the University of Nairobi. His earlier book, *Bureaucrats, Politicians and Rural Communities in Kenya*, was published by the University of Manchester in 1982.

He is at present a lecturer in the Institute of Local Government Studies at the University of Birmingham, England, and he lists his personal interests as jazz, sport, family life and enjoying the company of friends.

Acknowledgements

A number of people helped in the preparation of this book. What follows may seem like a long list but could easily have been trebled. The idea for this book emerged from the ten years I spent teaching introductory courses on public administration in Lesotho. Numerous colleagues and students during that period should be thanked for their help, notably David Hirschmann, James Katorobo, Ron Cadribo, Chris Goldman, Henk Brasz, Roeland Van de Geer, Sophie Hoohlo, Pontso Sekatle and Tseli Mapetla. Bill Tordoff and Martin Minogue both made valuable comments on the text, whilst the editorial contributions of Liz Paren and Janey Fisher cannot be allowed to pass without mention. Michelle Archer and Paulette Lowe found time to type the text as well as carry out a multitude of other tasks. The assistance provided by the staff of Birmingham University's Local Government library is also greatly appreciated. Finally, the support and encouragement of my wife, Ruth, and daughter, Rebecca, meant more than a formal note of this sort can easily express.

1 Bureaucracy and Development Administration

Introduction

'Bureaucracy' is a word which in ordinary use conjures up negative images in people's minds. It suggests a slow-moving organisation, usually associated with government, which serves the public with a mixture of arrogance, deliberate obstruction and incompetence. The word is often employed as an insult, whilst 'bureaucrats' (the members of bureaucracies) are sometimes seen as figures of fun. This picture is a caricature. Whilst it contains a grain of truth, as most caricatures do, it obscures a great deal of reality. In that sense, it is an unfortunate image and is in urgent need of correction.

This book attempts to present a somewhat more balanced picture, based on academic uses of the term. It focuses on bureaucracy in what many writers have called the 'Third World'. Others use the term 'less developed countries' instead, and still others speak of 'developing countries', but these differences of expression are the subject of debates which need not be entered into here. We are concerned with those parts of the world which are relatively impoverished and where there is urgent need for progress so as to improve the welfare of the inhabitants. Many of the countries which concern us are in Africa and Asia, but many are in other areas (e.g. Latin America, the South Pacific, the Caribbean).

In most of these countries, efforts to bring about improvement in people's lives depend heavily on government administrators or bureaucrats. Foreign aid is channelled through their offices and taxation creates domestic financial resources which they control. In return, they are expected to provide services, run projects, design regulations and carry out numerous other tasks in order to make development possible. This book explores what is involved when bureaucrats go about these demanding tasks in various parts of the world. Many examples are drawn from English-speaking Africa as a result of the author's personal experience, but other parts of the world are not ignored, and a large number of Asian illustrations are also provided.

1

Weber's analysis of bureaucracy

The term 'bureaucracy' has been used by numerous writers on public administration. However, its precise meaning has varied, depending on the particular approaches and emphases of different authors. It is generally agreed that the work of the German social scientist, Max Weber, was particularly important in introducing the concept of bureaucracy into the study of organisations. Writing towards the end of the nineteenth century, Weber observed a growing trend in Europe and North America, the emergence of a new form of organisation which he termed 'bureaucracy'.[1] To him, this trend was a distinctive characteristic of the modernisation process, and in particular was closely associated with the development of Western capitalism. His central argument, reflected in various writings, was that a process of change was occurring in which older types of organisation (most of which he called traditional or customary) were being displaced. Thus, the days of rule by such figures as chiefs, kings and emirs (based on the traditional principles of inheritance) were fading away, as were the 'charismatic' forms of rule exercised by religious figures and war heroes, for example, to be replaced by a new system of a more efficient kind, in which the dominant position would be occupied by the 'bureau' or 'office'. To some extent, Weber was correct in arguing that this trend would prove unstoppable, even though it is true that tradition and charisma still remain important factors in many countries, most of them in the less developed world.

In contrast to earlier forms of administration, bureaucracy is based upon what Weber terms *legal rational authority*. In more detailed terms, this means a set of rules and administrative structures which closely control the action of the employees of the organisation. In turn, Weber assumes that the 'bureaucrats' (or employees) share a common belief in the importance of obedience to the organisation's requirements. Thus, for Weber:-

(1) Bureaucracy is based upon *rules* which are accepted (in broad terms) by the members of the organisation.

(2) Bureaucracy is relatively *continuous* in its operation. For example, although governments may change as one set of political figures is replaced by another, bureaucracy tends to remain. It is thus not a temporary or *ad hoc* form of organisation created merely to achieve short-term goals. There are many examples of this principle operating in practice. Uganda has had many different political leaders since the 1960s but its bureaucracy has maintained a high level of continuity throughout.

(3) *The spheres of competence* of bureaucratic administration are

2

specified (generally in written documents such as laws or constitutions). The specifications normally set out the sorts of authority bureaucracy possesses and may also document obligations to carry out certain functions (e.g. a ministry of agriculture usually has both the *authority* to control farming activities and the *obligation* to assist farmers in their endeavours).

(4) An important feature of bureaucracy is that it is based upon the idea of *hierarchy*. This means that there are various layers of administration with lower positions under the control and supervision of higher ones. There can be a large number of different levels within a hierarchy, especially in very large organisations such as central government ministries.

(5) Legal rational authority needs to have the services of officials who are *trained* so that the structures can function in the ways intended.

(6) Officials in bureaucracy are not themselves owners of the means of production (other than of their own labour power).

(7) *Officials do not 'own' their jobs*, that is, the job itself belongs to the organisation, not to the individual who happens to be occupying a particular position in the hierarchy at any point in time.

(8) The successful and continuing operation of bureaucracy depends to a large extent upon *written records*. The keeping of records by means of files has historically been the main way in which decisions and processes have been made available for administrators to trace precedents and to check the facts in a particular case. Nowadays, the computer is, of course, a growing resource for the keeping of administrative records, particularly regarding staffing and financial matters.

• *The bureaucrats*
From our discussion so far it will be clear that the operations of bureaucracy depend to a considerable extent upon officials or bureaucrats. A few points about their positions may be made in addition to those already noted:-

  i) Weber stresses that bureaucrats are *personally free* in the sense that they are only subject to legal rational authority with respect to their impersonal official obligations. Thus, a head of department in the civil service would normally have a clear schedule of duties for which he is responsible and this would normally exclude activities outside those listed. Thus, a clear distinction is made between 'official' and 'private' life.

  ii) Individuals occupy positions *within the hierarchy*, and they are normally expected to 'know their place'.

  iii) Bureaucrats are expected to know with reasonable clarity what their *legal position* is, (i.e. the rules governing their authority and obligations).

3

iv) There is a *contractual arrangement* whereby bureaucrats agree to perform certain tasks in return for payments made by the organisation.

v) Officials are appointed on the basis of their *qualifications and experience*, rather than because of considerations such as family connections or political affiliation. This is sometimes known as the principle of 'merit recruitment'. In many developing countries its application has proved to be a controversial matter, as we shall see later.

vi) Bureaucratic officials are paid at *standard rates* linked to the rank they occupy in the hierarchy. Payments are generally made at regular intervals and through the use of money.

vii) To Weber the official should be primarily occupied *as such*, meaning that any other positions he may occupy external to the bureaucracy should be subordinated to the official tasks required of him.

viii) Bureaucrats are normally placed *within a career structure*, involving clearly defined possibilities for promotion.

ix) Weber stressed that officials are subject to control and discipline in the conduct of their work.

● *The growth of bureaucracy*

Although his work has been subjected to considerable criticism, Weber's ideas are nevertheless helpful because they help us to observe ways in which the world of organisation has changed over the past hundred years or so. When we use the concept of bureaucracy to study the Third World's experience, two broad points of significance emerge. Firstly, most countries have tended to become more and more bureaucratic. In the sphere of government, a network of ministries has developed, such as agriculture, finance, commerce and industry, etc. All of these are to some extent organised along the lines Weber described as are the numerous 'para-statal' bodies (e.g. development corporations) found in many countries. Secondly, it is clear that non-bureaucratic elements remain highly relevant to the study of administration in many states. For example, customary or traditional administration in the form of chieftainship still plays an important role in various parts of the world (e.g. Swaziland, Thailand). Also, the Weberian principle of merit recruitment is not always fully applied in practice, despite the provisions made by formal rules and regulations. Family relationships, political affiliations and other factors apart from qualification and experience still count for a great deal. Thus, bureaucracy has not totally displaced other forms of administration throughout the world.

To the advocates of bureaucracy, there is little doubt that it possesses

4

significant advantages over other forms of administration. Because it is relatively precise, stable and reliable it is seen as a highly efficient way of performing many of the tasks needed by society. It was largely because of this that Weber saw as inevitable the growth of bureaucracy not just in government, but also in private enterprise (e.g. industry) and even in churches and voluntary associations of different kinds. He thought that all this would happen regardless of the beliefs (or ideologies) pursued by the political leaders in control of governments. Thus, whether a given state was proclaimed socialist or liberal-democratic was to Weber unlikely to alter its need for a bureaucratic style of administration. He saw bureaucracy emerging as part and parcel of the growth of Western capitalism but nevertheless thought that societies which adopted the socialist path would be obliged to follow the same style of administration. This was because such states would also require the efficient provision of services for their citizens, and to him this meant that there was no real alternative to bureaucratic administration.

Bureaucracy and colonialism

Weber was a European and his ideas about bureaucracy reflect the trends he was most readily able to observe at the turn of the century. He was by no means uninterested in non-Western societies (he wrote a great deal, for example, about social organisation and religion in China), but he did not have a great deal to say about another significant trend of the nineteenth century — the spread of colonial rule. It would not be appropriate to discuss in any detail here the various undercurrents and forces which led certain European nations — notably Britain and France — to become the rulers of large slices of the world during the nineteenth and early twentieth centuries. However, this major change in the existence of so much of mankind had enormous implications, one of which was the spread of bureaucracy from Europe into other parts of the world.

● *Different approaches to colonial rule*
The process by which this happened was a complex one. It is too simple merely to state that Western administration or bureaucracy was imposed upon the colonised peoples. In the case of India, for example, the imposition of colonial rule initially occurred through the British East India company which did not simply introduce British administration but rather developed a model which owed something to an already existing Indian pattern dominated by the old Moghul Empires.

This is important not only because of the size of India, but also because the structures which were created there (in particular the administrative district) were subsequently transplanted by the British to other parts of Asia (e.g. Malaysia), Africa, the Caribbean and the South Pacific. Thus, whilst it may be said that the British imposed bureaucratic forms of administration it cannot be claimed that *British* bureaucracy in all its features as experienced in the 'home country' was imposed. After all, that crucial figure in many a British colony, the District Commissioner, has no counterpart in the history of Britain itself.[2]

In contrast, the French tended to transfer their own models to their colonies.[3] Thus domestic and colonial administration had more in common with one another in the French than in the British case, reflecting perhaps a more rigid adherence to administrative theory on the part of the French.

These two colonial powers also differed as far as relations with 'customary' administration were concerned. By and large, the British were inclined to allow a much more substantial role for customary rulers than were the French. In 1917 the Governor-General of French West Africa wrote a circular which came to be regarded as the basis of France's 'native policy'.[4] He was at pains to draw a sharp contrast with 'certain colonial powers', by which he apparently had mainly Britain in mind. His approach was that, where French colonialism came into contact with 'veritable sovereigns', their states should be recognized, examples being Cambodia in Asia, Tunisia and Morocco in Africa. In most instances, however, he argued that:-

> The role which determines the powers of native chiefs must therefore be as follows: they have no power of any sort in their own right, for there are not two authorities in the *Cercle* (district), French authority and native authority — there is only the one! Only the *commandant de cercle* (equivalent of District Commissioner) commands; only he is responsible. The native chief is only an instrument, an auxiliary. It is true that this auxiliary is not a mere transmission agency, and that he puts at the service of the *commandant de cercle* not only his loyalty and his energies, but his knowledge of the country, and the genuine influence which he may have over its inhabitants. The native chief never speaks or acts in his own name, but always in the name of the *commandant de cercle*, and by formal or tacit delegation of his authority.[5]

Whilst it is true that the views expressed in this document came to be somewhat modified by subsequent administrations, this passage sums up well the general approach of the French to colonialism — to incorporate the indigenous population into the bureaucratic model as it existed in France leaving behind mere remnants of customary authority. This is not to say that the policy altogether succeeded since customary systems often continued to function regardless of colonial edicts and the French did on occasion use traditional leaders, as in Upper Volta (now Burkina-Faso).

The approach of the British meant there were large parts of the British Empire where the customary rulers remained as important components of colonial administration. The doctrine known as 'Indirect Rule' was applied in a number of British-ruled territories, the most notable example being Northern Nigeria. Lord Lugard, who became Governor-General of Nigeria, spelt out the policy as follows:

> ... Liberty and self-development can be best secured to the native population by leaving them free to manage their own affairs through their own rulers, proportionately to their degree of advancement, under the guidance of the British staff, and subject to the laws and policy of the administration.[6]

He justified this policy by three specific arguments:-

a) The Political Staff available for the administration of so vast a country, inhabited by many millions, must always be inadequate for complete British administration in the proper sense of the word, and it was, therefore, imperative to utilise and improve the existing machinery.

b) Referring to the example of the loyalty and progress made in the Protected States of India under the sympathetic guidance and control of Residents — though it will be noted that the status of the Chief in Nigeria differs fundamentally from the Independent Native States in India.

c) By the obvious folly of attempting any drastic reform which would cause a dislocation of methods which, however faulty, have the sanction of traditional usages, are acquiesced in by the people, until we had an increased knowledge both of Moslem method, of rule and of Native law and custom.[7]

In summary, Lugard argued that Indirect Rule was a policy that could be defended because it economised on scarce (British) bureaucratic resources, it had succeeded in India (albeit in somewhat different form), and it maintained continuity and was therefore more likely to be accepted by the indigenous population.

The British could not apply this policy everywhere; they recognized the need for flexibility in the light of local conditions. However, the idea was to implement it where practicable and sometimes disciples of Lugard (e.g. Cameron in Tanganyika — now mainland Tanzania) tried enormously hard to demonstrate that the requisite traditional structures of authority existed. On the other hand, in Kenya, for example, the conclusion reached by the colonial government was that Indirect Rule could not be sensibly applied in view of the way existing societies were organised (they were mostly chiefless) and a situation quite similar to that of French-ruled Africa came into being instead.

• The purposes of colonial administration

These contrasts and complexities aside, however, the bureaucratic model of administration was introduced *via* colonial rule. Certain questions arise from this fact, one of the main ones concerning the purposes which it served. Colonial administration is often referred to as being mainly aimed at the maintenance of law and order. How far was this true? Clearly colonial administrations were instrumental in the economic exploitation of the empires for which they possessed responsibility. In this sense, they may even be said to have participated in the process of underdevelopment which colonial rule brought in its train.[8] Their role was to facilitate the exploitation of the colonies by businessmen, traders, settler-farmers, mining companies and so on. The administrative role, therefore, was not confined to a mere keeping of the peace.

Through the implementation of tax systems colonial administrators played a direct role in ensuring a regular supply of labour for various economic interests — in order to pay the 'hut' or 'poll' taxes introduced by the colonial administrators it became necessary for men to obtain employment in mines, farms, etc.[9] This role often transcended the formal colonial boundaries. Thus administrators in Basutoland (now Lesotho) played a crucial role in ensuring that the mines in neighbouring South Africa had a sufficiency of Basotho labour.

• Post-1940 trends

Before 1940, there were only isolated instances of development (e.g. the Gold Coast in the 1920s). Following the Second World War, attempts were made to promote patterns of development which would be of some benefit to indigenous populations. Under the Colonial Development Welfare Act of 1940, the British, for example, embarked upon rudimentary forms of economic planning, generally aimed at benefiting colonised peoples. Although it may be said that discernible changes occurred in some localities, e.g. in education and the provision of infrastructure, little of significance was achieved in many areas for the duration of colonial rule. The ending of that rule came soon after the war in Asia (India's independence came in 1947). It was subsequently pursued in Africa and other parts of the world.

'Development Administration', then, was a part of the colonial record, but it was nevertheless very much secondary to the political and economic considerations which were mainly exploitative. Although 'colonial development' was insignificant in many territories, it did mean that some administrators had to reorientate themselves to meet new requirements, e.g. co-ordinating the work of specialists (agriculturalists, veterinary officers etc.).

Administrative institutions were built up during colonial rule, supplying a framework for what was to follow. In various ways, the structures established could be described as bureaucracies in the sense Weber had used the expression at the turn of the century. Thus, the major colonial powers (Britain and France in particular) introduced into the countries of the Third World types of organisation which had marked similarities to those which had been created in Europe at an earlier period. These structures were inherited by the various independent regimes which entered the world stage from the mid-1940s onward.

Effects of independence

The transfer of political power posed two important questions as far as bureaucracy was concerned. First, was the colonial model suitable for the new initiatives which incoming governments wanted to take? Many countries wanted radical changes, which involved dismantling the old system. To think in such terms was an understandable reaction, given the nature of the colonial past, but it was not always easy to suggest alternatives which would be as stable and efficient as the colonial model. The notion of 'Development Administration' came to the fore. There was to be a new dawn in which the cobwebs of colonialism would be swept aside and radical new initiatives taken. The problem was that the advocates of major change were remarkably vague about what exactly this should mean in practice.[10]

● *Localisation*
The second question concerned the bureaucrats themselves. In many areas under colonial rule the structures of administration had tended to be racially stratified (in itself a notable departure from Weber's model). What should be done about the 'expatriates' (normally whites), who occupied so many of the important bureaucratic positions? In such colonial territories as Swaziland and Botswana even quite junior positions (e.g. roads foreman, mechanic) were occupied by whites. In these circumstances, there was an understandable concern that the public services should be 'localised', and various programmes aimed at replacing foreign incumbents were launched.[11]

9

'Localisation', as it became known, proceeded at varying paces throughout the ex-colonial countries. The speed of change depended on three main factors:

a) the attitudes of the political leadership in a particular country (Malawi's Banda and Ivory Coast's Houphouet-Boigny were in less of a hurry than Kenya's Kenyatta and Zambia's Kaunda);

b) the availability of suitable human resources (the Philippines and India, for example, were better endowed with pools of educated manpower than were the new African states);

c) the extent of localisation pre-independence (countries such as India, Sri Lanka, Ghana and Nigeria had begun this process before becoming independent — some 60 per cent of senior administrative posts in Ghana were localised before 1957).

Alternative views of bureaucracy

Before exploring in more detail the experience of Third World states, it is necessary to stress that bureaucracy has had its critics. Not everyone has agreed with Weber's view of it as a particularly efficient form of administration. Although these critics have mostly based their ideas on the European and North American experience, a review here is appropriate because such criticisms have some relevance to Third World conditions.

●Robert Merton

The American sociologist, Robert Merton, can be cited as one important critic of bureaucracy who has suggested a new dimension to its study.[12] As already noted, Weber regarded bureaucracy as an efficient way of achieving goals. To Merton this is not necessarily the case because the discipline required of bureaucrats by its structures and rules may in fact lead to what he calls 'trained incapacity', a rigidity of approach which makes it difficult to adjust to altered circumstances. He argues that this may lead to a situation where the achievement of organisational goals may be undermined — what he terms the 'displacement of goals'. Thus, a ministry of agriculture, for example, may commit time and resources to the detailed enforcement of farming regulations to the point where it may lose sight of its basic task of aiding farmers. This argument is contrary to the view that hierarchy and discipline are key requirements for development administration.

For our present purposes, Merton's work is useful for two main reasons. Firstly, he showed that the advantages of bureaucracy may be rather more limited than suggested by Weber's analysis. In a sense, he

10

conferred a measure of academic respectability upon the derogatory use of the word 'bureaucracy'. Secondly, he highlights a factor Weber tended to ignore — the need to focus on reactions of bureaucrats as human beings to the structures of which they are members. Weber, on the other hand, rather assumed that bureaucrats would behave in ways which ultimately would serve organisational purposes effectively.

• Elton Mayo and Peter Blau

Others have also drawn attention to the human factor in administration, and in so doing have, at least implicitly, criticised Weber's framework not so much for what he put into it, as for what he omitted. The contributions of Elton Mayo[13] and Peter Blau[14] may be briefly mentioned in this connection.

Mayo is often described as the 'founding father' of the 'human relations' school of management. His studies of American industry in the 1920s and 1930s brought to the fore some factors in organisations which Weber's structural approach had largely ignored. Mayo's work is particularly important because it brings out the need to study human beings in organisations not as isolated individuals but as part of a wider social context in which membership of groups is an important feature. These ideas, which also influenced a number of scholars of development administration, are based on the work he carried out at the Hawthorne industrial plant in the USA. Although carried out in American industry, the implications of his work are important for the study of public bureaucracies, even those in less developed countries.

The purpose of this research was to examine working conditions (notably lighting) and see how far they were related to output. Essentially the initial approach adopted was closely related to that of Frederick Taylor's 'Scientific Management' school which, as its name implied, was based upon a close study of the physical dimensions of work situations in order to see how best to generate higher levels of productivity. As a result of his studies, Mayo came to argue that social organisation within the plant had a great deal more to do with determining output than had hitherto been realized. He drew attention to *informal groups* as playing a major role in determining the behaviour of individuals. Thus, the worker came to be seen not as an *isolated individual* but as a *group member* with his behaviour determined to a large extent by the group.

It is important to understand the distinction between formal and informal groups. *Formal* groups are those of which individuals are members because the official structures of the organisation determine that they should be. There are many examples that may be given: agricultural extension teams, for instance; or task forces appointed to

11

look into a particular problem. But in addition to such formal structures, individuals are often part of groups which are not a part of the official organisational structure but which may play a major role in controlling output. These are termed *informal groups* and usually consist of a number of individuals who frequently consult one another about aspects of work. Typically, they are groups of colleagues who discuss various matters over coffee or eat lunch together.

Mayo's work gave rise to an influential school of thought which departed quite substantially from the more mechanistic approaches which had prevailed hitherto. Essentially his philosophy was that management should integrate informal groups as far as possible into the life of the organisation; thus, he argued, a more harmonious and productive outcome would result. In Mayo's own words, the Hawthorne study 'first enabled us to assert that the third major preoccupation of management must be that of organising teamwork, that is to say, of developing and sustaining cooperation'.[15]

Blau's work attempted to apply the idea of informal groups to public bureaucracy in the USA. He carried out a detailed study of a tax enforcement agency and was able to establish that a considerable amount of decision-making was carried out *via* informal rather than formal channels. Thus, both Blau and Mayo highlighted factors within organisations which Weber's approach, being based much less on detailed field research, had neglected.

• *Observers of Third World bureaucracy*
Finally, we should note that bureaucracy has often come under fire from observers of the Third World scene. There have been those such as Bernard Schaffer who have suggested that, because bureaucracy and efficiency may not be so very closely linked after all (a view similar to Merton's) it is not a suitable vehicle for the tasks of development:

> So, with the development agenda in mind, the following points can be made about the costs of bureaucracy. The bureaucratic model is not really an *efficiency* or 'output' model. The emphasis is on repetition and reiteration rather than on innovation. Inevitable tensions of administration are solved by personality bureaucratisation and institutionalisation. The prime concern is not the product but the value of certainty. Certainty requires controls.[16]

Whilst some writers still share this type of perspective and argue for administrative changes which would avoid the pitfalls of bureaucracy, others are rather more pessimistic about the prospects for meaningful reforms, given prevailing political and social conditions.[17] Still others have been critical of the performance of bureaucracy because it contributes to the processes of class formation in society.[18] The work of Issa Shivji in the 1970s on Tanzania is a case in point. He sees the emergence of social class inequalities in that country as being closely connected with the growth of public bureaucracy which enables those in senior bureaucratic and political positions to have access to wealth and power, and become what he terms a 'bureaucratic bourgeoisie'. The members of this class are seen as a small privileged minority situated within a wider setting of considerable poverty.

Bureaucrats and the development crisis

During the last ten years or so, much literature on the 'development crisis' has appeared.[19] In particular, there has been a growing concern with drought-stricken parts of Africa such as Sudan and Ethiopia, about which there have, of course, also been very significant and dramatic demonstrations of public concern in Western countries. For example, the activities of the 'Band Aid' organisation have heightened public awareness in Britain of the problems of poverty and famine. The problems being faced, however, go beyond these two African countries and, indeed, affect other continents also. Our task in the rest of this chapter is not to discuss this crisis in detail but to consider a few points which specifically concern bureaucratic performance. Before doing so, we shall go back to the period when most Third World states acquired their independence — the late 1950s and early 1960s.

In the early years after independence the populations of most countries were optimistic about the future. Having been released from the shackles of foreign political domination, the peoples of Africa and Asia had high expectations of their new rulers. This outlook had been encouraged by emerging political leaders who had a vested interest in promising to deliver higher living standards. Governments throughout the Third World therefore found themselves faced with largely impoverished populations which had participated in the electoral process often on the assumption that concrete material rewards would be on offer once the 'colonial masters' had departed from the scene. In retrospect, it can be said that these expectations were unrealistically high because the transfer of power in itself was not development. Nevertheless, they were real perceptions at the time and constituted a tremendous pressure on the new governments, which were soon to see that the symbolism of independence could not sustain them politically in the absence of concrete material benefits for their supporters. The latter were by no means an undifferentiated mass. A diversity of elements existed — the urban and the rural, the educated and the uneducated, a variety of ethnic groups, the old and the young, the

13

trade unions, the military, the party workers, the bureaucrats, and so on. All had their particular demands for a better life and looked to those holding the reins of power to provide it. Thus, the scene was set for the post-independence 'struggle for development', within already quite complex social systems in which different groups were competing for scarce resources.

- ● *The State and development*
What is particularly notable is that in most countries development was seen as the specific responsibility of such state institutions as government ministries and public corporations. This was to have far-reaching implications for the role of public bureaucracy, the arm of the State which was expected to carry out the wishes of the political leaders who found themselves occupying such positions as Prime Minister, President, Minister of Agriculture, Minister of Industry, and so forth. This emphasis on the State, as opposed to the often foreign-dominated private sector, arose from three principal factors. Firstly, there were the politically inspired and nurtured expectations which we have already noted. Although tempered in some cases by a pragmatic assessment of the situation (as perhaps in Kenyatta's Kenya), the broad assumption was that the newly created political institutions — bureaucracy included — emerging out of the struggle for independence would provide the instruments required for success.

Secondly, institutions outside of the state machinery did not appear to offer very much hope. For example, the alternative of relying on the owners of private capital to bring about development was largely ignored, the problem being that this capital was often in foreign hands. What have been termed 'multinational corporations' had often been involved in colonial economies some time before independence. In some states it was the foreign merchants and settlers (European and otherwise) who dominated the private sector (e.g. in Kenya, Zimbabwe and Uganda). During colonial rule indigenous capital ownership had been given relatively little scope, especially in Africa. This was reinforced by the restrictive use of the colonial state structures (e.g. racial discrimination in legislation on trade or agriculture). Foreign domination of capital thus made it more likely that governments would pursue what may be termed an interventionist role. They were faced with demands for a more equitable distribution of economic opportunity, demands which were all the stronger because existing inequalities were frequently also racial in nature. There was little confidence in the private sector's commitment to the needs of the indigenous peoples. Thus foreign economic interests could not be left to their own devices. The only alternative, so it seemed to most of the new rulers, was to stress the economic role of the state machine.[20] Of course, there were varied responses. Some, such as Houphoeut-Boigny in the Ivory Coast, emphasised the role of the State much less than others, such as Guinea's Sekou Touré — to use two 'francophone' examples.

Thirdly, there was the aid dimension. The early years of independence saw many countries and institutions 'queuing up' to provide aid to the Third World. Under colonial rule the possibilities for this kind of donor involvement had been restricted. However, after independence many new states adopted virtually an 'open door' policy. The aid came from a variety of sources. As well as the former colonial powers, the governments of other countries played a major role (e.g. the United States Agency for International Development — USAID, the Swedish International Development Authority, etc.), whilst international bodies such as the United Nations and the World Bank also entered the picture much more fully than had been possible earlier. There was seen to be very little alternative but to channel this aid through the state machinery of the recipient countries. Thus, even donor governments which were strongly pro-private enterprise, as was that of the USA, were obliged to operate through such channels and to bolster the role of the State in the poorer countries.

The performance of bureaucracy: an overview

How well equipped to carry this load were the various emerging bureaucracies? In reviewing the experience of the past two or three decades it is difficult to evade the conclusion that bureaucracies have found extreme difficulty in 'delivering the goods'. The reasons for this are complex. Certainly, there were difficulties which were beyond the control of both bureaucrats and politicians. Fitch and Oppenheimer have, for example, chronicled how Ghana's economy was adversely affected by the collapse of the world market for her principal commodity, cocoa[21] whilst other Third World economies faced similar problems, especially where they were dependent on a vulnerable single export commodity. Examples are Zambia's copper industry and various economies (e.g. Mauritius, Trinidad and Tobago, and Fiji) which historically have relied heavily on sugar production. Even less amenable to state intervention have been problems associated with drought (e.g. Sudan and Ethiopia) or floods (as in Bangladesh). Economies may be diversified away from dependence on a single commodity, albeit perhaps only in the long term and with some difficulty, but conditions of drought are not so obviously soluble by policy intervention, although this is not to excuse many governments which might have responded more effectively than they have done. A further complication has

15

arisen because of international conflicts (e.g. Southern Africa, the Middle East, the Horn of Africa, and South-east Asia in the 1960s and 1970s). Faced with these obstacles, the effectiveness of bureaucracy is bound to be limited.

● *The question of 'absorptive capacity'*
These external circumstances facing government have not made life easy, it is true, but nevertheless it is necessary to look at bureaucracy itself to see how well it has performed within the various constraints faced. Let us take the use of aid as an example. The term 'absorptive capacity' has often been used to help explain why aid is sometimes misused or underutilised.[22] It refers to the technical and managerial capacities of the governments receiving aid to utilise it in the ways intended at the time of drawing up and signing agreements with donors. The frequently disappointing records of programmes and projects funded by aid have highlighted the need to strengthen these capacities to use assistance effectively.

This is not to say that the problem of aid utilisation is always the responsibility of the indigenous bureaucracy because the donors are often partly to blame. For example, the donors can sometimes be criticised for imposing upon governments activities and commitments which may not be justified. Examples of this abound — agricultural marketing facilities are set up which are irrelevant to farmers because they can sell produce more profitably elsewhere; technology is used which is not suitable and projects are recommended which require non-available skills.

Nevertheless the concept of absorptive capacity is a helpful one. It must be broken down into its various components to identify what is required to improve it. For example, is there a particular shortage of middle-level technical staff such as mechanics or does the problem lie more with the clerical cadres? Bearing in mind that absorptive capacity is not merely a matter of staff but also of organisational structures and methods of working, questions may also be asked about such super-ficially minor factors as the design of forms, the sequencing (or phasing) of activities, job descriptions, and the allocation of resources within projects (e.g. such issues as whether transport provision or office space is sufficient).

Some critics of bureaucratic performance

Much recent discussion of development has looked in some detail at bureaucracy. Because it is so influential and important, the World

Bank's views are particularly worth reviewing.[23] In the course of the present decade it has published several reports on Africa in which a number of the continent's development problems were discussed, including a hard and critical look at bureaucracy. By and large, the Bank's views represent an attack on bureaucracy from a stance that is broadly anti-public sector and pro-private enterprise.[24] In many ways the views expressed in its reports, policy statements and the like, are close to those of the governments of the UK and USA. The emphasis is placed upon giving as much scope as possible to the private sector, whilst downgrading the role of the State. This idea is based on the view that the governments of Third World countries have over-extended their capacities to the point where organisational resources are simply not available to carry the burdens required. To sum up, the State should do less, the private sector should be given the opportunity to do more. This strategy is often referred to as 'privatisation', and will be discussed in more detail in later chapters of the book.

Bureaucrats, however, have also been the recipients of criticism from quite a different quarter. From what may be broadly termed the political 'left', a series of writers have launched attacks on bureaucrats for failing to reverse patterns of colonial exploitation of Third World resources by the West and for using their own privileged positions to gain access to business opportunities denied to the 'common man'. It has been argued that bureaucrats do not promote development, rather they reinforce longstanding tendencies towards dependence on the West and underdevelopment, the origins of which can be traced to the colonial past.[25] These writers vary in their views but they tend to see an alternative to bureaucracy in more socialist forms of organisation, although they shun the highly centralised model of the Eastern bloc countries such as the USSR. China, for some, has seemed to be a possible model,[26] whilst others have looked to other socialist regimes such as Cuba.[27] They also advocate breaking the ties of dependence which link the Third World to the international capitalist economies. These viewpoints will also be mentioned again in later chapters.

● *Growth and development*
A feature of much of the latter kind of writing is the clear distinction between 'growth' and 'development'. Economists such as Seers and Seidman, for example, have argued that much depends on how development is defined.[28] Many earlier authors tended to assume that if a country's per capita income (income per head) was becoming greater then it could be said to be developing. This position, however, overlooked the very real possibility that the wealth of a country might be increasing because a small minority was achieving economic success —

17

in terms of profits, salaries, etc. — whilst the standard of living of most people remained static or was even declining. Thus, Seidman comments that Edozien, in an article on the development decade in Africa, was primarily concerned with the growth of Gross Domestic Product and capital formation 'rather than an analysis of the spread of productivity and increasing levels of living of the broad masses of the population'.[29] Her own approach, reflected in a variety of writings, would be to regard a country as truly developing only if the 'levels of living' of the 'broad masses' were genuinely undergoing improvement. Seers had a similar concern when he wrote:

> The starting point in discussion of the challenges we now face is to brush aside the web of fantasy we have woven around 'development' and decide more precisely what we mean by it. 'Development' is inevitably a normative term and we must ask ourselves what are the necessary conditions for a universally acceptable aim — the realisation of the potential of human personality.[30]

Seers' article remains a useful source on the concept of development, not because he produces a neat and concise definition (he does not) but because he points to a complexity of meaning which goes well beyond the much narrower idea of mere growth. By way of illustration, he points to the case of Trinidad where, between 1953 and 1968, per capita income rose by 5 per cent but unemployment rose steadily. Would it be sensible to describe the country as 'developing' in this period? Probably not, especially if the welfare of the poor was not advancing significantly in other ways (e.g. education and health). Bureaucrats may be contributing to the state of affairs Seers and Seidman describe, one in which little meaningful development is in evidence. Seidman, for example, argues that civil servants and politicians provide the core of an emerging domestic capitalist class with close ties to international capitalism (in the form of major foreign-owned companies such as Shell and Lonrho). Their interests may thus be directly opposed to a development strategy which she would regard as being a just one:

> The African civil servants and politicians who took over the top offices from the former-colonialists are more likely to use a considerable share of increased tax revenues to expand the administrative bureaucracy, pay higher salaries, construct prestigious infrastructure and provide other 'fringe' benefits. They may use their positions to facilitate their own — or relatives' expansion in profitable private business ventures within the inherited economic structure.[31]

These processes, she argues, are reinforced by the roles played by the foreign-owned companies. The conclusion pointed to here is that development, to be meaningful, must be more than a mere improvement in the lot of bureaucrats and politicians. Rather, the welfare of the relatively poor or 'marginal' groups in society must also be advanced before the term 'developing' can properly be applied.

Thus, starting from politically quite different points of view, the World Bank/Western bloc perspective and that of the radicals sympathetic to socialism reach at least one common conclusion: both camps see bureaucracies as obstacles in the way of development and/or growth, rather than as potential instruments by which progress can be made. Whilst it is true that bureaucracy has a lot to answer for, since it has indeed not been particularly successful as a developmental institution, much of this sort of criticism is not accompanied by solutions which carry conviction. For example, as we shall see in later chapters, the effect of giving more opportunity to the private sector may be to create more problems than are solved. On the other hand, there has not yet really been any significant evidence to suggest that socialist strategies can be undertaken without spawning further bureaucracy, thus compounding the problem in another way. This has perhaps been the experience of Ethiopia, for example.

This apparent absence of workable solutions suggests that it may be useful to look again at the performance of bureaucracy to see whether there may not be a 'middle ground' to be found between these two broad critiques. Whilst one can accept that much in the 'track record' is negative it is hard to see any real alternative but to build upon institutions such as government ministries, development corporations, and so on, which — as in the West and East — seem destined to be here to stay. By looking at a variety of issues affecting bureaucracy we hope to demonstrate that scope does exist for building up administrative institutions which can be effective agencies for development. This means accepting the bureaucratic model in broad terms whilst also arguing for a more effective and creative approach to management. This may mean, for example, taking a hard look at how efficient the various ministries really are in delivering services or reviewing what sort of co-ordination between them is needed. Numerous questions of this kind will be discussed in the ensuing chapters.

In addition, however, measures may be needed which conflict with the interests of bureaucrats, much as Seidman observes. Whether this is a realistic option is clearly one of a number of complex issues which have to be raised. We are thus not merely concerned with discussions of bureaucratic efficiency, as though civil services were machines, merely requiring the right sort of maintenance service. There has to be a political dimension too, looking at, for example, such issues as bureaucratic privileges (e.g. the provision of housing and high salaries). Thus, whether bureaucracy is effective or not depends not just on the efficiency with which it works but also on the nature of its relationships with society as a whole.

Conclusions

Since Weber's day bureaucracy has spread to all parts of the world. He tended to emphasise the advantages of this style of administration, but did not really see the negative side of the picture, which was later analysed by writers such as Robert Merton. Weber's analysis was a partial one in that he did not consider fully the human factors involved in administration, a factor which Elton Mayo, for example, emphasised. For most Third World countries, colonialism introduced bureaucracy. Following independence, patterns of administration established by the erstwhile colonial rulers continued to operate without a great deal of adaptation. At the same time, however, independence brought pressure to bear on bureaucrats to achieve the various goals of development. How best to improve on bureaucratic performance is thus an extremely challenging question; it is also one to which there is as yet no completely satisfactory answer. The subject is obviously a broad one; our task in the later chapters of this book is to discuss at least a few of the issues involved.

Discussion questions

1   What are the main characteristics of bureaucracy according to Weber? Compare his model with government organisations in your own country. How bureaucratic are they?

2   To what extent did the work of later writers (e.g. Merton, Mayo, Blau) imply the need to revise Weber's work on bureaucracy?

3   How far is it correct to argue that the British and French colonial powers introduced their own versions of bureaucracy to their colonies?

4   Outline the main features of the 'development crisis' with which bureaucrats are faced. Suggest strategies which they might be advised to adopt in tackling this crisis.

2 The Political Environment

Introduction

Those who teach public administration are frequently asked to explain how their subject matter differs from that of their counterparts who teach business or commerce. The latter are often seen as purveyors of a dynamic and forward-looking body of knowledge frequently referred to as 'management'. This is thought to be quite different from the rigidity of the administrative world of civil service bureaucracy. This simplistic distinction misses two vital points. The first is that public servants are often the equal of the business manager in terms of knowledge of management. The second point — and the one with which we are concerned in this chapter — is that the public administrator has a far closer connection with the world of the politician than has the typical manager in private business.

The role of the public servant is performed within a political context (or environment) which has far-reaching effects on what can and cannot be achieved. This is far removed from the problems typically confronting a private firm, in which politics no doubt play a part but more as a side show than as a dominating force.

Perhaps the most significant of these factors is that the processes involved in policy-making are to a large extent political in nature. Determining whether or not to embark on an agricultural development programme is not a purely technical decision to be made with the advice of various qualified experts in agriculture, economics and related disciplines. The politicians know that such programmes can favour some groups or regions within the country more than others. This means, in turn, that they will endeavour to bring pressure to bear on the policy process to ensure that their own political supporters benefit as much as possible. For example, a major programme (as in Kenya in the 1960s) to promote smallholder tea-growing brought in its train demands from politicians that their areas should not be left out. These political concerns, however, do not end once policy has been decided.

All the time that policies are being carried out (or implemented) political interventions are to be expected. Many administrators have found to their cost that to resist these interventions is to invite reprisals harmful to career development. Indeed, dismissal from government employment under such circumstances has been a common fate in several countries. Policy and politics are thus closely interwoven.

In addition, it is important to be aware that bureaucracies have their own 'internal politics'. Civil servants come from a variety of backgrounds and, as a result, may be identified with differing political factions or parties within the country. Family or ethnic rivalries may also be important elements of conflict within ministries and departments. Thus, transfers, promotions and other forms of personnel change frequently take place as an outcome of internal political processes. Often these are of an informal or 'behind the scenes' kind, but they are nevertheless very much part of the reality of administrative life in many countries.

The role of politics in development

The political changes which took place in the Third World from the 1940s onwards led to a transfer of power. Colonialism retreated from the scene and newly independent governments took control. The assumption was widely held by social scientists and other commentators that these changes were necessary if development was to occur. Throughout much of the literature appearing from the late 1950s onwards this kind of assumption is made, whether explicitly or implicitly. Apter's work on the politics of 'modernisation' and Almond and Coleman's on the 'developing areas' are cases in point.[1] Development was seen not purely as a matter of economics, of building of stocks of capital, planning for its use, fixing exchange rates, and so forth. It was thought also to be a matter of the politics of the leaders and the institutions they in theory now controlled. Hence it was hoped and expected that independence would usher in a quite new and developmental style of politics which would be able to alleviate underdevelopment throughout the Third World. Such was the rhetoric, at any rate.

With the benefit of hindsight, it is clear that such expectations were excessively optimistic, for several reasons.

(1) With the possible exception of some communist states, e.g. USSR, there have been few cases where economic development can be traced directly to strong political direction from central government.[2] Since the new states of the Third World did not intend to adopt the communist approach (for a variety of reasons), it follows that to call for a politically directed form of development was to expect of governments achievements which would have been without clear precedent. Historically,

22

some political intervention and regulation can be shown to be necessary for economic development (as in Britain or France, for example) but this was not the same as the central role that was expected of so many new state governments in the early years of independence.

(2) A closely related point is that even in the smallest and most simple societies it is not always possible to ensure compliance with the government's will merely through making a political decision. In fact, power may well be in the hands of a government which can actually accomplish very little, even if coercion is employed. For example, the Tanzanian government in the 1970s adopted what it called the 'ujamaa' policy, by which rural populations were to be moved to villages where services were to be available in a concentrated form. This appeared to be a clearly thought-out central government policy, but it failed; partly because of the resistance and non-compliance of the people who did not see the need to move.[3]

(3) There were numerous obstacles, both internal and external, which political leaders were either not fully aware of, or were reluctant to face. This ignorance or reluctance was undoubtedly encouraged by the rather glib optimism expressed by so many development advisers and analysts at the time. On the internal side, there were numerous weaknesses (infrastructure, education, agriculture, industry, etc.) which were not really amenable to the kind of 'quick fix' approach that was so often thought possible. On the external side, adverse movements in the terms of trade and dependence upon foreign capital and aid were only some of the issues which were not as honestly confronted as they might have been.

(4) Political leaders were often very inexperienced in the management of government. In a few countries (notably Nigeria and Ghana) the leaders in the post-independence era had gained a few years ministerial experience in the colonial government, but even this was very limited. Often, new ministers assumed their positions far too near to independence day to be of any preparatory value. Little by way of preparation for the job of government was done, yet even highly experienced ministers would probably have found the tasks of development leadership on the scale envisaged beyond them. 'Virgin' ministers could hardly be expected to perform with a high level of competence within a few days of raising the flag of the new nation.

(5) Political leaders were not necessarily wholeheartedly committed to the general welfare. On the contrary, they often had quite strong economic and other interests of their own to promote for which political office provided the ideal opportunity. In many cases, activity especially in the field of business (hotels, taxis, property, etc.) constituted the real priority for the new leaders of government and thus the general welfare tended to be ignored or even opposed although the official rhetoric

23

suggested otherwise. Kenya in the 1960s and 1970s was a good example, as Leys has shown, of a situation where political leaders developed economic interests which did not coincide with those of the poorer sections of society.[4]

(6) Many new states were assumed to be politically united when in reality they were deeply divided. Zolberg's work on West Africa in the 1960s illustrates this point well.[5] At the time this writer was considered to be 'going against the grain' somewhat, in two senses. First, by drawing attention to political divisions – whether 'tribal' or otherwise – in West Africa rather than the supposed consensus he was drawing attention to a political reality far removed from the rhetoric being proclaimed by leaders such as Nkrumah of Ghana or Sekou Touré of Guinea. Secondly, his approach stood in quite marked contrast to the ideas held by most of the fellow American political scientists working on Africa and Asia at the time. On the whole, the tendency then was to downplay the conflict and take at face value the rhetoric dispensed by the political leaders. Looking closely at reality, however, Zolberg came to the conclusion that the prospects were for 'a sort of institutionalised instability, just as in Latin America over many decades the 'coup' became an institution'.[6] Thus, whereas the 'ideological maps' of leaders stressed unanimity or consensus, realistic observation suggested something quite different. Zolberg's assessment in the 1960s of the prospects for Africa seem to be substantially justified in the light of the events of the subsequent two decades. Many regimes (e.g. Uganda, Nigeria) have proved to be institutionally unstable, restricting the chances of a unified political leadership emerging which is wholeheartedly committed to national development.

The idea, then, that the political realm could fundamentally change the economic circumstances of Third World countries was a deceptive one, based as it was on misleading assumptions about politics in general and about the particular development problems being experienced. These assumptions, however, were strongly held and persuasively argued by many social scientists concerned with the study of development. Often similar views were held by those responsible for much government policy-making. The performance of bureaucrats in these early years can only be understood and assessed fully in the light of these circumstances.

The relationship between politics and administration

Until recently the view of many commentators has been that the worlds of politics and administration should be kept distinct. It is the politician, and the political leader in particular, who has the task of deciding what policies should be followed in, for example, agricultural or industrial matters, whilst to the administrator is allocated the burden of carrying out those policies. Often the term 'policy formulation' is used to depict the politician's role while 'policy implementation' is used for the administrative function. Thus, the political leader is clearly seen in the role of master whilst the administrator is seen as a kind of servant (hence the term 'civil servant').

Woodrow Wilson, an American scholar who later became President of his country, is perhaps the best known proponent of this view. An article of his, published in 1887, is often cited because of the very clear and persuasive way he drew the distinction between the two spheres of activity.[7] A number of public administration specialists, especially those writing in the first half of the twentieth century, followed Wilson's lead in this matter. In general, these writers adopted a strongly normative or prescriptive tone in the sense that they were trying to argue for what *should* be the case rather than merely observing and trying to understand reality. Thus, we may regard the distinction between politics and administration as a *doctrine* rather than as empirical observation.

The Wilsonian doctrine, however, has frequently come under critical review, especially since the Second World War. Essentially, the criticisms made have been directed both at the idea that the worlds of politics and administration *can* be kept wide apart and also at the idea that this *ought* to be the case. These criticisms initially were made by observers of bureaucracies in the industrialised states, but they have subsequently been echoed in writing on the Third World. A good review of the arguments is to be found in a recent book on Nigeria by Adamolekun which begins with a discussion of the Wilsonian doctrine but then goes on to show its limitations in the light of experience, both Nigerian and otherwise.[8] The point that the critics are generally making is that, given the complex realities of political systems, it is very unlikely that the simplicity of the Wilsonian doctrine can make adequate sense, both as a way of describing reality and as an administrative doctrine. These complexities need not detain us here at any great length, but certain important features should nevertheless be noted.

In the first place, senior bureaucrats can generally be expected to know more about the subject matter of policy issues than the typical political leader. This generalisation should be qualified by noting that some ministers have had substantial expertise and experience relevant to the work of their ministries (e.g. ministers of finance with advanced degrees in economics), but on the whole it is the senior bureaucrats who have the detailed knowledge needed to make informed policy decisions. This point is particularly relevant to countries such as Uganda and Nigeria where institutional instability at the political level has been combined with a relative continuity in administrative arrangements. Thus, the politicians may come and go but the bureaucrats remain. There is an interesting comparison here with the case of France which has experienced almost two centuries of considerable discontinuity in politics but has had quite a stable and permanent bureaucracy, closely following the Weberian model in terms of both theory and practice.[9]

It follows from this that bureaucratic dominance is likely to arise, but this should not be taken to mean that the political sphere has no relevance whatsoever. Certainly, we are not arguing that bureaucrats should play a dominant role to the extent of excluding the politician altogether. However, it can be argued that circumstances in many Third World states are such that administrators cannot be seen as confined to mere implementation, a point we would make in both normative and empirical terms. It is a normative point in that in most cases it seems desirable that bureaucrats should be able to influence policy, empirical because it can be observed that this is in fact what happens in most cases.

There are other reasons why bureaucrats play a major policy-making role, or at least attempt to do so. Beneath a cloak of knowledgeability, bureaucrats may well in fact be pursuing their own interests, be they political, economic or whatever. Examples of this situation vary a great deal in their nature from country to country. In Uganda in the 1960s for example, the government of President Obote was dominated by certain ethnic groups mainly coming from the north of the country whilst the civil service had been recruited from the more educated Baganda and others from the south. The subsequent political difficulties of that country had a great deal to do with this imbalance since it led to considerable distrust between senior politicians and senior bureaucrats. Nigeria faced similar problems, with ethnic factors playing a major part in generating conflict. In both cases, administrators were perceived by political leaders as pursuing their own interests at the expense of government requirements. It is difficult to establish with any precision whether these perceptions were fair. There is, however, no doubt that relationships between ministers and permanent secretaries were largely devoid of harmony, and that a high level of distrust prevailed.

In other countries circumstances have been different. Although the ethnic element has played little part in the Tanzanian case, for example, there have nevertheless been tensions between politicians and administrators based upon ideological factors. Shivji has argued that a major problem facing the government's socialist policy in the 1960s and 1970s was the less than wholehearted support obtained from administrators, and used the term 'bureaucratic bourgeoisie' to depict a class of people within the administration who were placing their self-interest before the government policies of the time.[10] Shivji actually includes ministers

26

within the 'bureaucratic bourgeoisie'. He would, however, presumably not include all of them since socialist policies were clearly advocated by the senior government ministers. Thus, the tensions existing were between those in the political leadership who took a distinctly socialist 'line' and the emerging bureaucratic bourgeoisie who held strategic positions within the administration, and who, incidentally, had very important international ties.

It appears, then, that the Wilsonian doctrine with which we began this discussion does not work in practice. It should be noted that this discrepancy has by no means only occurred in the Third World. A highly entertaining, but relevant, TV series based on the British experience has been made and shows how relatively inexperienced ministers can be manipulated by wily bureaucrats who wish to pursue objectives of their own (in this case the welfare and status of the bureaucrats themselves).[11] An interesting comparison has been made between Britain, France, and the USA. The conclusion reached was that bureaucrats have considerable scope to manipulate ministers in Britain, relatively little scope in France (despite its record of administrative continuity) while in the USA (home of the Wilsonian doctrine) the situation lies somewhere in between.[12] Comparisons of a number of Third World countries would doubtless reveal similar variations. It seems unlikely that the Wilsonian doctrine could anywhere be confidently applied in its original form.

● *Bureaucracies and legislatures*
The constitutions with which most new states had to set about governing themselves in the first few years after independence were often the outcome of complex and prolonged negotiations with the outgoing colonial governments. These complexities arose not only from a clash of objectives between the nationalist groups and the colonial rulers, but also from the divisions which existed within the ranks of the politicians aiming to take over power. In the circumstances, it was somewhat surprising how closely the legislative arrangements finally arrived at resembled those of the outgoing colonial powers. In Africa, for example, most of the new legislatures bore some resemblance to the British or French arrangements. A fundamental feature of these constitutions was the creation of elected parliaments, or legislatures. In many cases the official term for them was 'National Assembly' (e.g. Kenya, Lesotho).

Detailed discussion of the intended functions of these bodies need not be undertaken here, but certain key points should be noted.
  i) They were to be representative bodies in the sense that the elected members were expected to represent the interests of the

voters. In the ex-British countries the principle followed was generally that of the single member constituency.

ii) It was intended that the formation of governments should be based upon the composition of parliament. Following the British model, the idea was that the party obtaining a majority in parliament should form the government. If no party held a majority, then a coalition (a combination) of parties would assume power. When one bears in mind that most new states in Africa and Asia achieved independence with more than one party possessing a significant body of support, it can be seen why this model seemed so appropriate at the time.

iii) Parliament was expected have some control over the performance of government, which, in turn, was supposed to be accountable to parliament. A crucial role here was to be performed by the ministers responsible for various policy areas (e.g. agriculture, employment, education, health). Thus, parliament could require ministers to explain and justify government performance (i.e. accountability), having the ultimate sanction of being able to vote the government out of office if sufficiently dissatisfied with what it was offered.

These three parliamentary functions − to represent the voters, to provide a mechanism through which governments can be formed, and to control government performance − are crucial to the constitutional theories of parliamentary democracy. The practice, however, has deviated substantially from the theory in many cases. It is of particular importance to record that these deviations have often meant that parliament is not a very effective means of controlling government performance. Thus, bureaucracy has not been exposed to the critical gaze of a lively parliament intent on exposing error, inefficiency, corruption and other faults, and demanding improvement.

It would seem that Weber's view of the European scene almost a hundred years ago also fits circumstances in much of the Third World quite accurately. He was concerned that parliamentary control would not be effective because bureaucrats would become the real masters rather than confining themselves to the more limited service roles required of them by the formal constitutional arrangements.[13]

In practical terms, the performance of parliaments in the Third World has been varied. In some parliaments, a measure of vitality has enabled them to exercise some control over the workings of government. Examples exist in Kenya and India. In spite of being a one-party state, the former's national assembly has until recently been a forum through which elected members have frequently and vigorously pursued answers to the questions they have raised. Many of their questions have been about the quality of bureaucratic performance. Thus, although elected members have from time to time faced disciplinary measures because of the outspoken way they have carried out their functions, the parliament of Kenya has acquired a reputation for its readiness to question the performance of the government, the civil service and the various public corporations.[14] India is a somewhat different case both because it has a multi-party system and also because it has quasi-federal constitutional arrangements. The existence of official opposition parties at both federal and state levels seems to have contributed to a parliamentary vitality which can play a significant part in keeping bureaucrats 'on their toes'. Furthermore, the relatively open nature of India's political system has meant that members of the ruling party are not so inhibited by coercive measures as many of their counterparts elsewhere.[15]

These two cases, however, are exceptional to the general trend in most of the Third World. One-party states and military regimes, in particular, tend to regard parliamentary criticism as highly undesirable and have often concluded that it should not be tolerated. The result is often that parliamentary discussion of government performance is very inhibited. In a sense, governments have used a 'carrot and stick' approach to achieve this state of affairs. On the one hand, members may be concerned for their own career ambitions. Criticism of government may have markedly negative consequences on a member's ambitions for ministerial office. On the other, there is the fear of being punished through 'preventive detention' or in other ways if an outspoken position is adopted. If, in addition, there is no opposition party represented in parliament there is very little chance of any tough questions being brought forward. The bureaucracy, in these circumstances, is not likely to be worried about parliamentary control. So long as the ministers are satisfied all is well: and it may not be difficult to achieve this aim if the minister is content to remain ill-informed and preoccupied with personal matters (as has often been the case). Further, there has been a growing trend towards presidentialism in which strong heads of state are in direct contact with senior civil servants and outsiders, largely ignoring parliament itself.

Parallel to the weaknesses of parliament has been the performance of the equivalent institutions at local level — the local authorities.[16] Thus, as we shall see in a later chapter, bureaucrats posted by central government to work at the local level (e.g. districts, regions, divisions, locations) have generally operated independently of legislative control at that level. In most countries there have been elected local authorities, established before independence, with certain specified powers and duties. Although these bodies mostly have survived, their resource base and their powers have been substantially reduced primarily because of greater central control; that is, what has been termed 'centralisation'.

A broad conclusion may thus be drawn: power at the local level tends to be in the hands of bureaucrats whose main task is to represent the interests of central government, rather than in the hands of locally elected bodies such as district, county or town councils.

● Bureaucracy under military rule

Many states in the Third World are ruled by the military. This was not anticipated at the time when colonial rule was ending. It was expected that elected political leaders would take control and that the soldiers, airmen and other servicemen, would follow the normal Western pattern and confine themselves to being the instruments of civilian authorities. It was, perhaps, naive to expect this to happen since the history of Latin America suggested otherwise. Several countries in that part of the Third World have been independent for over 150 years: during that time they have experienced very marked institutional instability with the military heavily involved in politics and often assuming the reins of power. During the 1980s a trend towards civilian rule could be observed in Latin America as military governments gave way to civilian in countries such as Argentine and Brazil, but the overall historical tendency has been for the military to be very active in politics and not merely available for use by civilian governments.

The British and French ex-colonies of Africa and Asia have often followed the Latin American trend. Within Africa, the western part of the continent (e.g. Nigeria, Ghana, Liberia, Burkina Faso − previously Upper Volta − and Benin) has been most affected, but there are also examples of military rule in the centre (Zaire), east (Uganda until 1986) and south (Lesotho 1986). In Asia, Pakistan has been ruled by the military for more years than it has been by civilians whilst other countries have experienced military government periodically (e.g. Burma in 1958 and many countries in the Middle East).

Military intervention in politics is not confined to the seizing of power. There are a number of cases of what Ferrel Heady terms 'tacit coercion' where the soldiers decide not to take power but are such a major element in politics that the civilian authorities are compelled to behave according to their wishes. He quotes the examples of Indonesia, Brazil, Iran, Ecuador, Jordan and the Dominican Republic.[17] As far as Africa is concerned, the examples of Lesotho pre-1986 and Kenya during the late 1970s may also be given. In these instances the military has operated as a particularly powerful pressure group because it possesses the ultimate sanction in the form of its control over the use of violence in society. Faced with this threat, civilian governments may feel that it is necessary to make concessions to the military (often in

30

terms of wages, conditions of service, etc.) in order to divert them from staging a *coup d'état*.

There has been much debate about the reasons for a high level of military intervention in politics. The complex issues involved are not really relevant here except to note that the military often seem to combine two rather contrasting motives. On the one hand, they act to promote and protect their own positions. On the other, they often claim to be motivated by the desire to save their countries from the chaos and ruin they accuse the civilian rulers of creating. In the rhetoric of the *coup d'état* it is often the latter that is given prominence, but the former, being based on self-interest, may be closer to the real motive.

For our present purposes what is more important are the ways the military go about governing once they have assumed power. Generalisation is again difficult but a few key points seem to emerge from the evidence available.

(1) In many countries the military have tended to assume that their hierarchical authority structures, linked with an emphasis on discipline, can make an important contribution to development administration by improving upon the laxities of their predecessors. These assumptions, however, have generally proved unrealistic since the administrative skills and structures called for in development administration are of a different order, requiring as they do the attributes of flexibility and responsiveness to public opinion.

(2) As Odetola has noted for Africa, the military and bureaucracy find they have a lot in common:

> Because both the bureaucracy and military were organised in relatively rigid hierarchies with limited scope for initiative and relatively ordered promotion, they have conservative attitudes. They both show firm interest in ordered modernisation and economic growth, and both are well placed to get what the politicians have often failed to get.[18]

Factors such as these have resulted in the military regarding bureaucrats as natural allies in pursuit of a more effective development strategy.

(3) It follows that the bureaucracy may benefit from military rule because the soldiers may well be more prepared to see the bureaucratic point of view than the politicians. The Gowon regime in Nigeria was a case in point.[19] The term 'military-bureaucratic complex' was used to depict the situation which arose there.

(4) Finally, there is only scant evidence to suggest that military-bureaucratic coalitions have been developmentally successful. After

an exhaustive review of the African experience, Odetola draws this apparently paradoxical conclusion:

> The military has probably recorded greater success in their perform-ance in the political sector than in the economic sector. They have built political institutions where the goals and strengths of military leadership permit.[20]

Given that the achievements of the military in terms of political devel-opment have to be treated as marginal, this means that the military have by and large not demonstrated any great capabilities in the field of economic development. From our point of view, it is also perhaps even more significant to observe that bureaucracies do not seem to have made the best of whatever opportunities the military have made available. Thus the evidence not only places in question the effectiveness of the military as economic developers, it also points to the weaknesses of the bureaucratic approach as well. The soldiers and the bureaucrats, acting in concert, do not seem to provide a more appropriate develop-mental model than one in which politicians play a prominent role.

Ideology and administration: African cases

The attainment of independence in Africa was often followed by attempts to formulate 'ideologies' or 'philosophies' upon which devel-opment strategy could be based. Frequently the ideas which emerged were referred to as 'African Socialism', a useful term because it high-lights two central issues which political leaders felt were important — the need for an ideology which was both authentically African in kind (rooted both in tradition and in current realities) and also in some ways linked to the body of thought which had come to be known as socialism. (This latter owed much to Marxism but also to other schools of thought such as British Fabianism.) It was thus 'non-aligned' in the sense that its character distinguished it from both the West and the East. 'Rural populism' may be seen as in some ways a variant of 'African Socialism', although it has sometimes been used to depict opposition to government, based on the idea of a rural 'mass' being squeezed or exploited by a central government dominated by the urban elite. 'African Socialism' has generally been an ideology 'pro-claimed from above', closely linked to the interests of those holding power at the centre.

Not all African states have shown these ideological concerns, but most have done so. Three will be reviewed as case-studies here: Kenya, Tanzania and Zambia. Although only Kenya adopted the term 'African Socialism', all three offered variations of that type of thinking.

● *Kenya — 'African Socialism'*

The doctrine was spelt out in detail in a document which was produced in 1965, and which is still commonly referred to in policy papers, circulars, and the like (also known as Sessional Paper no. 10 of 1965).[21] It is often claimed that American planning advisers played a major role in preparing this document, which outlines the main elements of the doctrine as being:

a) political democracy;
b) mutual social responsibility;
c) various forms of ownership;
d) a range of controls to ensure that property is used in the mutual interests of society and its members;
e) diffusion of ownership to avoid concentration of economic power;
f) progressive taxes to ensure an equitable distribution of wealth and income.[22]

The assumption is made that European styles of socialism do not apply to Kenya. It is argued that:

> The sharp class divisions that once existed in Europe have no place in African Socialism and no parallel in African society. No class problem arose in the traditional African society and none exists today among Africans.[23]

There is also a heavy emphasis upon African traditional beliefs which is worth quoting at length:

> There are two African traditions which form an essential basis for African Socialism — political democracy and mutual social responsibility. Political democracy implies that each member of society is equal in his political rights and that no individual or group will be permitted to exert undue influence on the policies of the state. The state, therefore, can never become the tool of special interests, catering to the desires of a minority at the expense of the needs of the majority. The state will represent all of the people and will do so impartially without prejudice.[24]

These general assumptions lead to specific policy statements. For example, nationalisation is seen as a 'useful tool' but one that is to be used very sparingly. Private enterprise, on the other hand, is strongly advocated as a means by which greater 'Africanisation' of the economy may be achieved. What really is being advocated here is a 'mixed economy' approach, rather than a Marxist or radical version of socialism. As such, it has come under criticism from those on the Left who advocate a more explicitly anti-capitalist ideology. Sometimes these criticisms take a rural populist form as, for example, when it is argued that the 'rural masses' are the victims of exploitation under present

33

structures. The assumption here is that there is an undifferentiated rural mass which is supposedly the victim of policies pursued by an urban elite aiming to accumulate wealth for itself in the name of socialism.

• *Tanzania — 'Ujamaa Socialism'*

In 1967 President Nyerere made a speech which became known as the 'Arusha Declaration' (named after the town in Northern Tanzania where the speech was delivered). It leans much more heavily upon socialist ideas of European origin than was the case in Kenya. For example, Nyerere argued that:

> A truly socialist state is one in which all people are workers and in which neither capitalism nor feudalism exists. It does not have two classes of people, a lower class composed of people who work for their living, and an upper class of people who live on the work of others. In a really socialist country no person exploits another; everyone who is physically able to work does so; every worker obtains a just return for the labour he performs; and the incomes derived from different types of work are not grossly divergent.[25]

To achieve this sort of society, he advocated the substantial nationalisation of industry (reference being made here to the 'commanding heights' of the economy). This contrasted sharply with the Kenyan approach.

An even more distinctive feature of Nyerere's view of development was the element of 'rural populism' which it contained. Under the heading 'we have put too much emphasis on industries' he argued that a big mistake had been made in thinking that industrialisation was the priority. A shift was needed in order to bring the rural areas much more into the development picture, otherwise 'we might get to the position where the real exploitation in Tanzania is that of the town dwellers exploiting the peasants' (p. 28). Following on from this came the 'ujamaa' approach which entailed organising rural dwellers to live in villages based on co-operative principles. A clear link with African tradition was brought in as part of the justification for such measures.

Unlike Kenya, the official ideology in Tanzania was attacked from both right and left. The latter argued that Nyerere's approach did not go far enough, that it was essentially 'reformist', falling well short of the revolutionary transformation that was needed. Views such as these were particularly associated with academics at the University of Dar es Salaam (many of whom were expatriates). From the other side of the political spectrum came the view that socialism in an underdeveloped

34

country such as Tanzania simply does not work because it imposes too great a managerial planning burden upon the State. In recent years, it is this view that has come to dominate, a shift of opinion strongly influenced by the donor community within which the World Bank has played a particularly significant role.

• *Zambia – 'Zambian Humanism'*
There are rather more parallels with Tanzania than Kenya in this case. For example, the head of state's own ideas clearly led the way in both Zambia and Tanzania. President Kaunda's speeches are thus our main source, in much the same way as President Nyerere's are for Tanzania. There is also in the Zambian case a closer link with radical versions of socialism; the state takeover of a large part of the copper industry is an obvious example of this.

Kaunda, however, began with a model of African traditional society which is reminiscent of Kenya's case:

> The traditional community was a mutual aid society. It was organised to satisfy the basic human needs of all its members and, therefore, individualism was discouraged...... Human need was the supreme criterion of behaviour.[26]

A great deal of attention was given to the roles played by social institutions such as the chieftainship and the extended family in African tradition, which are contrasted sharply with social structures found in Europe and North America. This is what he meant by 'humanism'. (It is worth noting that he used the word quite differently from the way it is used in the West, where it is generally taken to mean scepticism regarding the existence of God.) He envisaged a link between tradition and the modern era:

> This high valuation of MAN and respect for human dignity which is a legacy of our tradition should not be lost in the new Africa. However 'modern' and 'advanced' in a Western sense this young nation of Zambia may become, we are fiercely determined that this humanism will not be obscured... We in Zambia intend to do everything in our power to keep our society man centred. For it is in this that what might be described as African civilisation is embodied and indeed if modern Africa has anything to contribute to this troubled world, it is in this direction that it should.[27]

It is through the State that this continuity of 'man centredness' was to be achieved. Accordingly, a variety of measures were taken, many of them involving state ownership of the means of production to reverse trends in the direction of capitalism:

35

It is clear to all of us, that ever since we took over we have been working hard to change from a capitalist system to a socialist one. It must be emphasised once again that this can never be a seven-day-wonder job. Capitalism has been entrenched in this country whether you look at it from an economic, sociological, cultural or, indeed, political angle.[28]

Numerous industries (particularly copper) were consequently earmarked for state ownership (some of them in combination with private enterprise, others 100 per cent state-owned).

Again, the ideology has had its critics. Broadly speaking, the pattern has been similar to the Tanzanian case, the Left seeing Zambian Humanism as being in reality a lukewarm version of socialism. Occasionally the expression 'state capitalism' has been used by such critics to make the point that state intervention does not necessarily bring about socialism. On the right, there has been concern at the management and planning problems which such a large sector brings in its train.

• *Some general comments*

These three examples illustrate that in Africa a quest has been going on for a set of ideas which can serve as the guiding principles of development. There was a need for such a quest because of what appeared to be the inappropriateness of foreign ideologies and because traditional values were regarded as far too important to be discarded. Thus, there was a desire to build a view of the world which was authentically African and thus capable of motivating members of society towards development goals. All three countries reviewed had this desire to find a distinctive set of beliefs, even though the precise content of their ideologies varied.

With hindsight, it has become possible to look back over the twenty or so years since these ideas surfaced and make some comments about them.

(1) There have clearly been major implementation problems. In Tanzania and in Zambia it now seems to be recognized that the State cannot handle the burdens imposed; the difficulty now is to find alternatives to heavy state intervention which do not lean too strongly in the capitalist direction previously rejected. Kenya is perhaps a rather more successful case; it could be argued that much of Sessional Paper No. 10 of 1965 has been put into practice through the 'mixed economy' approach. The question which arises in this case, though, is whether the term 'socialism' should really be used at all.

36

(2) None of the ideologies really come to grips with the class issue. This is understandable in a sense because during the 1960s significant class differences had yet to emerge or else had largely coincided with racial differences. The passage of years, however, has seen the development of a much more stratified social order for which some sort of class analysis (not necessarily Marxist) is relevant. 'Rural populism' has been one response to this, but it is an inadequate one because it assumes that the key differences can be viewed in rural-urban terms without adequately taking into account class differences within both urban and rural settings. Blurring of these differences obscures an important feature of the emerging reality.

(3) This discussion perhaps means that the 'age of ideology' is past and that the time has come for pragmatism to dominate the scene. There are many who take this view. It should, however, be borne in mind that pragmatic policy-making also has social consequences, some of which may be viewed as undesirable, and is therefore in a sense also ideological. What is needed may be, however, a set of beliefs grounded in African reality, which are both pragmatic and at the same time linked to the values of humanity and brotherhood which political leaders in all three countries have so eloquently expounded.[29]

Administration and the politics of dependency

In many Third World countries, there is debate as to whether development is really possible given that there is so much reliance on foreign capital and aid for the undertaking of economic activities on any scale. In recent years, this dependence has in some ways increased as bodies like the International Monetary Fund and the World Bank have come to play a growing role in influencing patterns of development by providing (or withholding) support to countries which face severe financial problems. In this section, we note some of the issues involved without, however, putting forward conclusions, as this would require far lengthier treatment.

The debates that take place involve various contrasting positions.[30] First, there are those who argue that economic development is virtually impossible unless this dependence ends. Foreign involvement in the economy has effects that are seen as largely harmful and which result in underdevelopment rather than development. This pattern is said to date from colonial days when the foreign economic presence made itself felt with damaging consequences for indigenous forms of production. The only solution, in this view, is a severing of the links between the Third World and the forces of international capitalism.

Another view taken is that foreign finance and capital, though

37

influential factors which can have negative effects, do not necessarily obstruct domestic economic activity. In this view, then, development can still be meaningfully achieved despite the penetration of foreign forces, if effectively managed.

Still another school of thought sees no real alternative to dependence and thus accepts foreign capital, credit and aid regardless of the negative effects this may have upon the indigenous economy. Such an approach, of course, is likely to be bitterly opposed by those who argue for a severing of links.

The first of these positions is seen as compatible with radical or socialist political viewpoints in that it often contains an anti-capitalism element. The second position is more difficult to categorise in these terms. Some of its advocates see possibilities for the development of indigenous capitalism despite the strong presence of foreign capital whilst others see some form of socialism as being ultimately possible even within such a framework. The third position may be described as a conservative one, involving an acceptance of the existing distribution of economic power in the world. In essence, it means going along with whatever trends are dictated by those who do possess economic power — the USA, Japan, West Germany, the IMF and others.

These arguments have been going on with varying degrees of intensity in many countries for some years now. In Latin-America, for example, dependency was a theme of passionate debate long before most African countries became independent. In practice, very small countries have often perceived there to be no real choice other than dependence (e.g. several states in Southern Africa) whilst some states such as Brazil and South Korea seem to have demonstrated that there is an alternative to dependence. The latter are often referred to as newly industrialising countries (NICs). In between these two categories are states such as Kenya[31] and Malaysia where the pattern seems to involve foreign economic involvement being counterbalanced by increasingly strong indigenous economic forces.

On a political level, questions of dependency are of some significance to administrators. Firstly, they may well have pronounced views of their own about the nature of the economies of their countries and what might be done about dependency. Kitching, for example, notes that Tanzanian civil servants often expressed views on these issues similar to those of President Nyerere and the intelligentsia.[32] Thus, civil servants themselves contribute to the debate, especially in countries where ideological concerns are considered to be of high priority. The advice which they present to politicians is bound to be coloured by their personal views. The preparation of project proposals, for example, is very likely to be affected in this way.

Many governments emphasise that political independence does not necessarily also mean economic independence. Arguments of this sort have led to policies which can be called 'economic nationalism', involving as they do a strengthening of such national economic forces as businessmen, public corporations, banks, and so on. These policies obviously require supportive administrative action if they are to be implemented effectively. In turn, this places considerable pressure on civil servants to achieve results under conditions of great difficulty, given that the overwhelming strength of foreign capital is often found in conjunction with very weak national economic institutions. Indeed, many civil servants, under these conditions, find themselves obliged to advise on, and apply, policies which they may well feel are not realistic.

Senior administrators also spend a great deal of time in negotiation with the representatives of foreign companies, aid agencies and other such bodies. A feature of dependence is that foreign elements of this sort can play a political role within a country by exercising influence within the policy process itself. This is especially likely to happen in weaker countries where dependency is often a particularly important factor. Administrators thus are placed very much in the front line because they are expected to resist foreign influence where it may be harmful without going to the other extreme and driving capital and aid away. The considerable difficulties involved here are always likely to be compounded by the temptation of the 'back handers' or 'under the counter' payments with which foreign firms may try to persuade civil servants to look favourably upon their proposals. This is, of course, particularly likely to occur where the award of lucrative contracts is concerned.

A further possibility is that civil servants may be drawn into involvement with foreign firms in their individual capacities. The Latin-American expression 'comprador' has been used to describe this phenomenon. In many countries, this is not contrary to the law but it does have the effect of giving senior officials a stake in foreign capital interests which will often influence the manner in which they approach questions of policy. Indeed, they may even go beyond what are usually the legal limits and fail to declare their personal interests in the award of contracts to foreign firms with which they are associated.

This brief account of dependency has not aimed to present a full picture. More modestly, it has shown that the political environment within which administrators operate has an international element to it. Administrators are often intricately involved in questions arising from the relationships between foreign economic forces and the economies of the countries for whose governments they work.

Conclusions

Perhaps the central conclusion to be derived from this chapter is that politics and administration are inevitably inter-related. The notion that politicians can somehow be removed from the area of administration and leave the field open to the administrator is an impossibility in the real world. Whether they like the idea or not, administrators have to deal with politicians. Even in military regimes, political activity does not end. Accordingly, administrators need to accept this fact and perceive their managerial roles accordingly. It is in this particular sense that a sharp distinction can be drawn between public and private administration; the latter is not necessarily more dynamic than the former, but it is usually a good deal less political in nature. At the same time administrators are drawn into the arena of the politician. Whether or not this is regarded as desirable, it is a fact of life which the student of public administration has to acknowledge.

Discussion questions

1   What is meant by the 'Wilsonian' doctrine? Why has it been criticised?
2   How successful have military regimes been in harnessing bureaucratic resources to achieve development?
3   Review the case-studies of ideology outlined in this chapter. What do these cases imply for the practice of administration in the states discussed? Using these three examples as a model, prepare a case-study of your own state's experience.
4   Outline *four ways* in which the politics of dependency may affect administrative performance.

3 Development Planning

Introduction

In most Third World countries, governments have tended to assume that development planning is a necessity, without which development is unlikely to be achieved. India led the way by its adoption of development planning a few years after independence. It thus set a precedent for those countries which subsequently became independent. Indeed, to have a development plan came to be a symbol of freedom, along with the national flag and the renaming of streets and cities. It was, however, more than just a symbol because it was seen as a crucial means by which governments could improve the living standards of their people. In broad terms, these hopes and expectations have not been realized in practice. The task of this chapter is to examine some of the reasons for the rather disappointing record that exists. First, however, some theoretical points need to be made.

Planning is a basic function of any organisation. All organisations have to be able to forecast the various circumstances they are likely to face in the future, and make arrangements to deal with them. Thus, a small firm in the private sector has to carry out some sort of planning, even if no formal plan document is actually produced. Part of this exercise may well involve the setting of goals to be reached within a certain period, for example to increase profits by 10 per cent by 1995. Planning at this level may, of course, be quite unscientific and based upon unreliable information, but it is nevertheless an attempt to forecast the future and plan accordingly.

The complexity of planning

The planning done by government goes some way beyond the type of planning usually carried out by small firms. In the first place, a government plan does not usually just look at the future requirements, circumstances and goals of its own component parts (e.g. the ministries);

it has to look at the future of the whole public sector. For example, in most Third World countries a major concern of planners is the improvement of agriculture, an economic activity usually dominated by people who are not part of the government itself — smallholders, landlords, plantation owners, co-operatives, large-scale ranchers, and so on. Similarly, the planners have to be concerned with employment in industry. Normally, the task of the planners is not only to find ways to increase the number of people employed in the public sector; it is also concerned with what can be done to provide more jobs in privately owned industrial firms, such as motor car assembly plants, hotels and breweries. This broader dimension of government planning gives it a greater complexity than is the case with small firms which are normally only responsible for their own future welfare.

Another difference is that development planning tends to require a high level of technical expertise. The preparation of development plans required a good deal of information about a nation's economy. Thus, the services of statisticians are crucial in order to collect and present data about such topics as agricultural production, income levels, unemployment, industrial output and productivity, population (often a census is held at periodic intervals), male-female ratios within the population, and so on. The collection of all these figures is a complex and expensive business but it is essential because planning becomes largely meaningless without a reasonable base of statistical information. It is obviously important for planners to know the present state of the economy in fairly precise quantified terms if they are to determine sensible goals at which to aim in the future. The planners of many newly independent countries lacked this kind of information, when they began planning. Under such circumstances, it was possible to prepare plans of some sort, but their usefulness was greatly reduced by this deficiency.[1] Indeed, some plans have been so general in tone that it has been almost impossible to judge whether they have been successful or not. This weakness has now been remedied in most countries as a result of improved statistical services.

The techniques of the statistician, however, are less important than those of the economist, whose task it is to analyse the data provided by the statistician and write plans on that basis. The techniques of economic analysis, often quite sophisticated in kind, have to be used in this exercise. The theory of planning is that targets can be indicated which are realistic in view of the economic circumstances of the country. Thus, the economists have two central concerns. One is that there has to be an analysis of the present performance of the economy. This often involves a review of what took place in the previous plan period of five years (or whatever it may have been) in order to identify problems (often termed 'bottlenecks') to be faced in the future. At the

42

same time, the idea of such a review is to identify possible opportunities for the future of the economy (perhaps export markets are available for certain agricultural products, for instance, but have so far not been pursued vigorously enough). The analysis of the present is then combined with a forecast of the future to arrive at meaningful targets to be achieved during the forthcoming plan period. Forecasting involves numerous topics. In most countries, among the most important are figures for the numbers of school leavers expected to be looking for jobs, likely population trends and levels of agricultural production. Forecasting is, of course, a hazardous undertaking because so many uncertainties exist. However, it is a fundamental requirement of planning.

Many countries were short of qualified statisticians and economists when they began to plan. A high priority was to train people in these fields of expertise. In the meantime it was necessary to employ expatriates if planning was to make any headway at all. As a result, many countries' first plans had a strong foreign input whilst some countries still draw on expatriate sources to provide the specialised knowledge and techniques required.

Along with the economists and statisticians, representatives of other disciplines should also participate in the preparation of plans. Waterston lists accountants, agronomists, architects, engineers, physical and social scientists, lawyers, educational experts, mathematicians, even physicians and dentists. All these specialisations provide technical information and appraisal of proposals in ways that can greatly benefit planning.[2]

Many organisations need to be involved in development planning. There are the numerous government ministries and departments, all of which can play a part. Each ministry, for example, is expected to have some ideas about what it wants to achieve in the forthcoming plan period. For example, the ministry responsible for the development of small-scale commercial activity may wish to launch a training scheme for businessmen, or a ministry of works may wish to build a major road. Ideas such as these can be regarded as 'inputs' to the planning process since they are attempts to put into the national plan proposals for specific developmental activities. It is generally the ministries and/or departments which are required to carry out or 'implement' the plans that are made. The ministry of works in our earlier example would be expected to carry out the proposals it had made to construct a major road, or at least, arrange for someone else (e.g. a construction company) to do the work involved.

In addition to the ministries and departments, there are other organisations which are likely to be associated with development planning in some way. Many countries have large 'para-statal' sectors (i.e. owned by the State) which are not, strictly speaking, part of government but which still require the attention of planners. For example, an electricity supply corporation carries out certain functions vital to the functioning of the economy of which it is part. It is natural, therefore, that planners will be interested in how well it performs as a supplier of crucial energy requirements for industry, commerce and other customers.

Other organisations, which have no connection with government at all, also enter into the planning picture. Many of them are directly involved in development. For example, the Red Cross organisation might be building rural health clinics, or one of the churches might be trying to assist with education. Such initiatives, although not coming from government, still require some planning. This should be done in such a way that these organisations are helped to carry out their work successfully, and not discouraged by the imposition of unnecessary controls or obstacles (which, unfortunately, often happens). Then there is also private enterprise to consider. Whether it be an international company, such as Coca Cola, General Motors or Brooke Bond, or a small local firm, planners are bound to be interested in a number of matters. For example, the question of employment creation is highly important everywhere, and so the policies and practices of private enterprise are bound to be of interest. Taxation arrangements are also important. Are companies taxed too much, thus discouraging their expansion or involvement? Or are they undertaxed, depriving the government of badly needed funds? These questions, and many others, should concern the development planners.

Planning has to be concerned, then, with numerous organisations. This makes life complicated for planners in a host of ways. For example, *information* has to be obtained from all types of sources, many of them outside of government. Obtaining this is difficult. Often information will be withheld because of possible disadvantages to the organisation if certain facts are known about its operations. Often the information supplied will be unreliable because it is not collected with sufficient thoroughness, and so on. Yet planning needs co-operation from numerous organisations, many of which may not understand the need for planning, and may even resent what they see as interference in their activities.

Finally, the complexity of planning is increased by political factors. Since governments are inevitably composed of politicians of some description (whether they be military officers or civilians) planning is bound to involve the exercise of political authority. Whatever the precise organisational arrangements are, there is bound to be a political leader (e.g. a minister) in charge of that part of the government bureaucracy which is responsible for planning the economy. The performance of this minister will go a long way towards determining the outcome of planning activities. For instance, the minister might himself be a highly qualified economist with a strong commitment to planning: he will then strongly support what his fellow planning professionals are trying to do. On the other hand, he may not be very interested at all, may provide little or no direction, and may give little support when the planning organisation is under fire in parliament or cabinet. A third possibility is that he will see his position as providing an opportunity to advance his political ambitions. For example, he may try to ensure that close political colleagues are given favourable treatment in the location of new development projects, in return for their support for his political aims. Similarly, he may be worried about the future of his own constituency (in a system based upon election) and endeavour to ensure that his popularity is enhanced by locating attractive projects ('vote winners') within it.

All three of these possible ways of behaving as a minister responsible for planning have been observed in developing countries from time to time. Clearly, then, to understand how planning functions it is important to be able to analyse it within its political context. Because much of the literature on planning has been produced by economists this point has sometimes been neglected. Economists tend to argue that politicians 'interfere' in planning without accepting that what planners do must be understood as a fundamental feature of the political system as a whole and analysed as such. It can certainly be argued that the tools of the political scientist are as relevant to the analysis of planning as those of the economist.[3]

Planning in mixed economies

What follows in this section is a look at some of the issues which have arisen in the various countries which have undertaken planning. Most of them have followed what has been termed the 'mixed economy' approach, meaning that they combine private enterprise with a measure of state ownership and intervention. Thus, they are distinguished on the one hand from the communist states, in most of which private enterprise is negligible, and on the other from the largely unplanned capitalist economies, of which the USA is the best example. In depicting most Third World countries in this way, it should not be concluded that they are all precisely the same. The term 'mixed economy' can be used to describe a variety of mixtures of private enterprise and state involvement. Within East Africa, for example, the economies of both Tanzania and Kenya may be described as 'mixed' but Tanzania's state sector has tended to play a significantly more dominant role than it has in Kenya, where private enterprise (foreign and indigenous) has been of more importance. Every country is unique. Even where two or more countries have very similar ideological orientations, individual economic circumstances are likely to vary. Zimbabwe presents a good example of a government with a socialist ideology which, however, inherited a large private sector which is likely to remain for some considerable time. Tanzania's socialist approach, on the other hand, is set within a framework of a relatively underdeveloped private sector.

The significant point as far as planning in mixed economies is concerned is that direct control over the private sector cannot be readily achieved. This differs from the socialist approach whereby, in theory, the whole economy can be directly planned because government owns all the crucial institutions. In practice, even the USSR has had problems in trying to exercise this sort of control. It is all the more difficult where the economy is dominated by international companies with allegiance to their shareholders in London, New York and other cities, and whose plans are more directed towards providing profits than to the interests of the country in which they are operating. Even where private enterprise is to a considerable extent in local hands (e.g. in Kenya where such ownership is considerable, although not yet dominant), planners do not have direct control over the activities of private companies.

● *The options*

What are the options for governments in these circumstances? There are several, of which just a few will be noted here.

   i)   Large chunks of the private sector may be transferred to the public sector. Such measures — often known as nationalisation — were taken in Tanzania from the late 1960s onward. The policy there was to take over the 'commanding heights' of the economy (banking, insurance, the larger industries, etc.) in order to give the government more control (a hope which was disappointed, but that is another story).
   ii) Another option is to try to influence the private sector by indirect means. For example, the taxation system may be manipulated to encourage private investment in certain activities. Indeed, companies may be given the opportunity to invest without being obliged to pay tax at all, thus creating investment incentives for them. Lesotho, for example, operates a 'tax holiday' scheme for this purpose.
   iii) Another indirect form of influence may be through the provision of facilities to encourage private sector involvement in certain parts of the country (e.g. the provision of ready built and serviced factories).

46

In most countries, the inclination has been to follow the second, indirect approach. Most planning in such circumstances tends to focus on the public sector itself. Sometimes this means, in effect, screening individual projects proposed by various bodies within government or the para-statals. Alternatively an attempt may be made to integrate public investment activities as closely as possible. These two approaches, which were first identified by Waterston some years ago,[4] are still common features of planning in Third World mixed economies. More ambitious types of planning (e.g. so-called 'comprehensive' planning) have been attempted, especially in the more socialist-oriented countries (e.g. Tanzania). Generally, however, such efforts have been abandoned because the effort put into their preparation did not justify the results achieved. Thus, in most mixed economies the approaches followed may be described as 'partial planning', usually meaning that an attempt is made to plan for the various public sector's activities in a reasonably integrated (or linked) way, in the hope that the private sector will respond positively to such incentives and guidelines as may be provided for it.

The integration of public investment is in itself a considerable advance upon the approach which merely looks at development in terms of individual projects. This is because various development activities may be so closely related to one another that they ought to be planned in an integrated fashion. For example, where resources are limited choices have to be made about where the development priorities lie in a particular country. The acceptance of a large number of enthusiastically proposed educational projects (e.g. university expansion) may mean fewer resources being available for urban sanitation or housing improvement. Thus a country needs to look at all its possible projects and then make decisions which rank (or order) them as priorities.

Certain projects may turn out to be useful only if activities in other sectors are appropriate to them. Universities may again provide an example. A project to increase the number of public administration graduates does not make sense if those receiving this training are subsequently employed in a clerical capacity not involving the use of the knowledge acquired. Plans to build a university medical school similarly need to be linked to the likely capacity of the public and private sectors to absorb qualified practitioners.

The need for integration may also be demonstrated by reference to rural development. A project aiming at promotion of a particular crop should be integrated with all sorts of related concerns: for example, transport must be provided to make markets accessible and credit facilities made available for farmers through the banking system (either public or private banking may be involved, or both).

47

The difficulties of planning

Although the idea of planning seems sensible enough in the form it has been described above, numerous difficulties have occurred and some recent observers have been highly critical of the way many governments have performed. Goran Hyden, in discussing Africa's experience of public management, argues that planning has largely been counter-productive because it has been a waste of scarce resources, rather than a contributor to the development process.[5] Other critics in recent years (most notably the World Bank) have not taken so strong a view, but have argued instead for a concerted effort to strengthen the planning machinery.[6] Any attempt to document all the problems encountered in planning would be doomed to failure as the experiences of different countries inevitably vary a good deal. However, some of the key issues may usefully be highlighted.

• Lack of political commitment

The degree of political commitment in planning has been generally low. Planning is typically conducted in a single department of a large ministry. Alternatively, where planning has a ministry of its own, it is usually a minor one. The minister in charge of planning tends either to be a figure of little significance nationally or else to be pre-occupied with other matters. For example, where planning is part of the office of head of government (which has frequently been the case), it is often a marginal interest, seen as being of much less pressing importance than, for example, national security issues. The problem is compounded by the fact that planners tend as a group to be a mixture of expatriate advisers and the younger generation of civil servant, neither of which usually carries much political weight.

This lack of political commitment is clearly of major importance in at least two ways. In the first place, it makes it much more difficult to secure the co-operation of the political leadership in other ministries, leaving a gap in the network of planning which is hard to overcome. For example, if a minister of agriculture does not believe that planning is an important activity it is unlikely that his civil service staff will feel it important to provide the central planning agency with the assistance they need to prepare a decent section on agriculture in the plan, and link this with targets for other sectors of the economy. In addition lack of political commitment often results in a breakdown of plan discipline at the implementation stage. Obviously, where the political leadership lacks support for planning it is unlikely that there will be much hesitation when opportunities arise to promote economic activity outside of, or even contrary to, planning requirements. There are several ways in

48

which this may happen. For example, a political leader may try to ensure that development projects are located in his constituency in order to boost his chances of re-election. This tends to happen in those countries where reasonably open electoral processes still prevail. Another example is where political leaders have business interests of their own to promote and use their positions in the government hierarchy to do so regardless of what the plan may say. Against forces such as these, the planners are often helpless.

- ## The isolation of planners
A second broad problem area, related to the first, is the relative isolation of the planners within the machinery of government. The status occupied by the planning organisation is often not high in the eyes of the dominant ministries such as finance, office of the President, foreign affairs and the ministries concerned with various key economic sectors such as agriculture and industry. Yet the logic of planning suggests, if not a relationship of authority over such ministries, then at least a degree of influence to ensure that plan discipline prevails, so that co-operation with the planners' requirements is forthcoming. In many states, however, the planners are regarded as rather a nuisance, as a somewhat junior group of people who periodically pester senior civil servants for information which is difficult to pass on (sometimes because it is not available or because it is potentially damaging to those in top positions). In cases such as these, the only value of development plans from the point of view of senior officers and ministers is as a way of providing useful public relations material with which to impress the donor community, which may be more willing to provide aid to projects which have been included in the plan. This is, of course, not the main purpose of planning. However, in practice many governments find it to be its only useful function. This makes it extremely difficult for the planning organisation to carry out one of its major roles, that of monitoring plan progress. It is clear that very often planning is seen as a process which ends when the plan document is published, whilst ideally it should be a continuing exercise: this should involve reviewing the extent to which targets contained in the plan are being achieved, followed by adaptation of them as circumstances are observed to change. Failure to do this is largely a result of the isolation of the planning organisation within the machinery of government as a whole.

- ## Administrative obstacles
Analyses of planning have often drawn attention to the administrative obstacles which have prevented effective implementation of plans.

This third broad problem area was particularly well documented by Waterston in the 1960s but has subsequently been discussed in a number of other studies.[7] In a sense, what such analyses do is to show that the general administrative problems facing developing countries are reflected in their experience of implementing development plans. For example, even if the development planning machinery has a relatively high status, major implementation problems are liable to occur if personnel administration is haphazard and/or corrupt, because the staffing requirements of development activities will probably not be met adequately. A similar point may be made regarding financial administration. If financial control is poor, the money is not likely to flow in a satisfactory manner to the purpose for which it is intended, thus again undermining the purposes of planning.

- *Over-centralised planning*
Planning has also come under attack for being overcentralised. When planning began in most Third World states (i.e. in the 1950s and early 1960s) it was assumed that planning and centralisation of bureaucratic and political power went together, that they complemented one another. Rondinelli and Cheema summarise the general view held at the time:

> Central planning and administration were considered necessary to guide and control the economy and to integrate and unify nations that were emerging from long periods of colonial rule. Moreover, central control was implicit in the requirements of the international assistance agencies that were providing large amounts of capital during the 1950s and 1960s. They insisted that borrowers have comprehensive and long-term plans for the investment of external capital.[8]

Experience demonstrated, however, that these early planning assumptions were wrong because the centralised approach did not succeed. Living standards actually declined in many states. Although to blame this on centralised planning alone would be to distort reality, many observers came to see over-centralisation as one of the reasons for the failure to achieve major development.

In the 1970s there was a growing realisation that highly centralised planning was not working as it gave rise to several problems. One of them concerned support for plans where local communities were expected to participate in implementation of projects. Thus, it was argued that plans were being imposed in 'top-down' fashion on local communities which meant those communities showed little enthusiasm at the crucial implementation stage. Many agricultural projects experi-

50

enced problems of this kind where, for example, centrally based planners might decide on the need to grow certain types of crops in particular areas but without adequate consultation with local farming communities. As development thinking moved towards a greater emphasis on participation and consultation, so it became less appropriate to have a centralised planning structure.

Another criticism was that centralised planning tended to disregard local conditions, a problem which was often exacerbated where plan organisations were dominated by foreigners. Locally based bureaucrats of various kinds tended to be bypassed in plan preparation, together with the local communities with which they worked. This often made planning unrealistic, sometimes to the point of being unimplementable. Part of this problem was that local bureaucrats, even when they might have substantial knowledge of the local environment, lacked the discretion to initiate plans or to administer and co-ordinate their implementation with due flexibility. Local co-ordination, as Conyers and Hills note, is often impossible when a planning system is highly centralised:

> If decision-making is highly centralised, each agency in the area has to seek approval from its headquarters before going ahead with any project or activity; thus coordination at the area level is only possible if there is agreement between the various agencies at the national level, and often such agreement does not occur because each agency has its own priorities and these priorities are not necessarily the same as those at the area level.[9]

Some case-studies

Some of the general issues of planning which have arisen can be well illustrated by looking at the experience of individual states, some of which have clearly been more successful than others in undertaking planning. Four cases will be examined: **Botswana**, a small state in Southern Africa, with a very interesting planning experience; **Malaysia**, a multi-ethnic Asian state; **Tanzania**, an East African state which attempted a socialist approach from the late 1960s onwards; and **Nigeria**, a large federal state in West Africa. All of these cases demonstrate that the political climate affects planning. If this is not favourable, the most sophisticated techniques, operated by highly qualified planning teams, will fall on stony ground. These case-studies are not detailed. Reference is made, however, to sources of further information for those who wish to examine them.

• *Botswana*

Relatively speaking, Botswana's case is a story of success. Beginning from a very modest base at independence in 1966, a planning system has evolved which has worked reasonably well. A World Bank report, produced in 1981, noted that two closely related points had been of crucial significance.[10] First, the Botswana case suggests that political commitment and support for planning makes a substantial difference. The first President (Seretse Khama) and his senior ministers showed greater support for development planning than has often been the case elsewhere. Secondly, planning and budgeting have been closely linked. On the whole, the preparation of the budget takes full account of development plan priorities. This linkage, which is apparently under-pinned by the support political leaders accord to planning, is in many states not as closely made as it needs to be. This point will be discussed further when we turn our attention to financial management.

Several other positive factors about the Botswana experience are noteworthy. Considerable emphasis has been placed upon the recruitment of a highly competent economist cadre for the planning organisation. To this end, there has been a relatively high dependence on expatriates. However, as Raphaeli, Roumani and Mackellar have noted:

> Botswana's human resources at the time of independence in 1966 included very few of the skills necessary to manage its economy. Through effective use of expatriate technical assistance (TA) and steady development of local capabilities, the country has achieved a remarkable record of economic planning and management.[11]

Related to this point was the effort made to ensure that a strong policy-analysis capability was established, together with a planning staff which was continuously involved in budgetary and economic management decisions.[12]

Another way in which Botswana has performed better than most countries is in the decentralisation of planning. Perhaps because it became independent relatively late, it did more to avoid the centralising tendencies which have adversely affected planning elsewhere and was able, albeit haltingly at first, to involve district institutions in the process of preparing the plans. As with central planning this involved an early dependence on expatriates (notably American Peace Corps volunteers) but with the passage of time this has changed. However, the decentralisation of planning achieved so far has had its limitations, notably because it has been largely undertaken by bureaucrats at the district level, with only rather token involvement from the elected councillors. Nevertheless, awareness of this problem exists and greater scope for the elected councillor can be expected in the near future. Certainly Botswana has established an impressive framework for the effective decentralisation of planning.[13] Much of the credit for this must go to the political leadership and especially to Dr Quett Masire, who combined the roles of Minister of Finance and Development Planning until he succeeded Seretse Khama as President.

If Botswana's political climate has the merit of being conducive to effective planning, it none the less has to be said that it is in a vulnerable position internationally.[14] A small state, with a population of less than a million, it has as one of its neighbours the Republic of South Africa, a country determined to create instability where it sees any threats to its 'apartheid' policies. South Africa attacked Botswana in 1985 because of such considerations, clear evidence that it is prepared to use its superior military might to bring such small states to their knees; a strategy which could, *inter alia*, make planning meaningless.

● *Malaysia*
The Malaysian experience of development planning helps demonstrate the importance of two factors. The first of these is that to understand planning properly it is essential to take fully into account the political context. Secondly, it shows the value of establishing a good system for monitoring the planning process so as to check that programmes are moving ahead as originally intended. Some observers have indicated that Malaysia's monitoring system may offer an example from which other countries could usefully learn a great deal.[15]

The essential fact relating to the political context of planning in Malaysia is the plural nature of the society. There are three distinct ethnic groups in the country: a) the Malays who constitute just under half of the population as a whole; b) the Chinese who make up about one-third of the total; c) people of Indian extraction, who make up most of the balance of the population. The differences between these groups are not just those of culture and language. The Malays have a history of being relatively disadvantaged economically by comparison with the other two groups. Figures presented by Davies demonstrate this point well: these show that of all the 'households in poverty' in the country, the Malays comprise 75.5 per cent, the Chinese 15.9 per cent and the Indians 7.8 per cent.[16] Given this information, and the fact that political power has always been in Malay hands since independence in 1957, it is not surprising that the highest priority of the government has been to redress the economic imbalance between the different groups. According to Puthucheary, government policies and programmes are 'distinctly partial towards Malays' to such an extent that civil servants are not expected to be impartial but always to consider the Malays in a favourable manner. This has been particularly the case during the last twenty years.[17]

Planning was introduced at a relatively late stage in Malaysia's history, the early emphasis being on a series of separate departmental programmes operating within the framework of a free enterprise economy. Thus, the first plan was only produced in 1966. The most important development, however, came in 1969, when, following a great deal of political tension, what became known as the 'New Economic Policy' was introduced. It aimed to bring about a better economic balance between the ethnic groups, and to eradicate poverty generally:

> The first prong is to reduce and eventually eradicate poverty by raising income levels and increasing employment opportunities for all Malaysians, irrespective of race. The second prong aims at accelerating the process of restructuring Malaysian society to correct economic imbalance, so as to reduce and eventually eliminate the identification of race with economic function.[18]

That Malaysian planning is thus politically motivated does not mean it is necessarily inefficient. Although a number of criticisms have been made about the performance of the civil service, its record in development administration is by no means a bad one when viewed in comparative terms. In bringing about improvement, a key role was played by the Deputy Prime Minister, Tun Razak, who towards the end of the 1960s identified the 'seven deadly sins' of Malaysian administration: too much departmental separateness; jealousy between departments; lack of co-ordination between officers in the field; lack of co-ordination between departments and agencies; lack of proper planning within departments; the lack of a master plan covering all levels of government; and lack of directive control at the top.[19] Starting from this analysis, the government embarked on a programme of reform, a key aspect of which was the monitoring system referred to earlier.

Crucial to this system has been the 'Operations Room' concept. At all planning levels — federal, state and district — there was introduced an elaborate system of charts, maps and other devices by which every government project could be monitored. Thus, a whole variety of development efforts — roads, irrigation, health, education, and so on, — could be closely monitored. The Operations Room depended, in turn, on effective progress-reporting from the field. This used a standardised form, to be completed on a monthly basis by heads of department with responsibility for particular projects.[20] The system was computerised early in the 1980s, thus bringing to bear some of the advantages of the new information technologies.

Although these concepts sound very simple, they are nevertheless significant because many countries have failed to make suitable arrangements for the performance of these functions. In sum, within a highly charged political atmosphere, Malaysia has managed to develop an administration which may not have fully eliminated Tun Rasak's 'seven deadly sins', but which has nevertheless one of the most effective levels of performance in the Third World.

• *Tanzania*

The choice of Tanzania as a case-study was made because it has attempted to implement a socialist strategy and relied heavily on planning to do so. This approach was not adopted immediately after independence in 1961. The turning point, however, came in 1967 when a policy paper, known as the Arusha Declaration, was adopted by the ruling party. This document committed Tanzania to policies of socialism and self-reliance. Many commercial, financial and industrial concerns in the country passed into state hands through subsequent nationalisations. Ghai notes that:

> The effect of these measures was that the government obtained ownership and control of the major financial institutions and some direct control over the more important industrial and commercial enterprises. State economic enterprises became the most important economic actors.[21]

On the face of it, these measures made life for planners easier because it gave them direct control over key economic actors, with the apparent support of the political leadership and the bureaucracy. In practice, a number of difficulties arose so that by the 1980s the Tanzanian experiment, which had seemed so hopeful in the 1960s and 1970s came to a grinding halt.

Even before the decision to expand the state sector in 1967, Tanzania was finding the administration of development planning difficult. It had more than its fair share of the problems discussed globally by Waterston at around that time.[22] Thus, it already faced critical problems of absorptive capacity, compounded by socialist policies which only added to the planning and administrative burdens. Although the Tanzanian government subsequently became aware of the seriousness of these problems, it found them very hard to solve. Consequently, the expansion of the state sector tended to take an *ad hoc*, unplanned form.

A second, and related, problem in practice concerned the nature of Tanzania's commitment to socialism. Shivji, for example, questioned whether the leaders were genuinely committed to the socialist path in view of the fact that their material interests pointed in another direction.[23] Coulson's work shows a whole range of difficulties which arose through such factors.[24] Although President Nyerere's own socialist views may have been genuinely held, he does not seem to have been able to persuade his countrymen in key positions that his chosen course was correct. In such circumstances, the chances are that plan discipline will not be enforceable except in a somewhat sporadic fashion.

Many early critics of Tanzania, writing in the 1960s and 1970s, held political views basically to the left of those of the Tanzanian government and argued, for example, that more socialist direction would only be possible with a greater measure of disengagement from international capital, which Shivji, for example, saw as a critical problem.[25] In the 1980s, however, a different approach emerged as writers such as Goran Hyden argued that the emphasis placed on the role of the State had been an error.[26] Calls for denationalisation from such quarters as the World Bank seem to have been heeded in the course of the past two or three years.[27] The approach now is not to abandon altogether the idea of planning, but rather to scale down drastically the burden a socialist approach places upon a limited planning and administrative capacity.

• *Nigeria*[28]

As in most countries of the Commonwealth, Nigeria first began planning soon after the Second World War, with the Ten Year Welfare and Development Plan of 1946–1956. This colonial planning, however, had major weaknesses, one of the main ones being the absence of planning skills within the ranks of the generalist administrators ruling Nigeria during that period. Further, there was little consultation with the Nigerian people themselves. By 1955, these difficulties were recognized by the creation of a National Economic Council. However, the inclusion of Nigerian politicians did not really make this body very effective mainly because of serious political differences between them and the colonial administrators, and these undermined the council's planning efforts.

The first post-independence plan covered the period 1962–1968. The absence of planning professionals indigenous to the country necessitated the employment of many foreign staff, who dominated plan formulation to the exclusion of any genuine participation by the Nigerian bureaucracy or the public as a whole. This in turn created serious problems at the implementation stage when the foreigners had departed, leaving behind a Nigerian administration with little sense of involvement in the planning process. Towards the end of the plan period a further political problem arose following a *coup d'état* in 1966 which brought the military to power; later a civil war ensued. In the circumstances, it is understandable that planning took very much a back seat. Planning was, however, resumed during the 1970s under the general guidance of the Supreme Military Council. This renewed effort, however, did not succeed in generating an effective planning system. The poor performance of two federal institutions seems to have been a

56

large part of the problem. The National Manpower Board made manpower forecasts which proved to be very defective; and data provided by the Federal Office of Statistics proved to be inadequate for planning purposes.

A complicating factor in the Nigerian case in the early days was the country's federal constitutional structure, which complicated lines of command and communication. These complications often resulted in virtual paralysis of the system, with planners, politicians and administrators at the various levels all finding it almost impossible to take effective action. There was also a failure to take into account the local authorities. Adamolekun observes:

> Another important deviation in practice at the state level was the failure of practically every state to obtain inputs from the local authorities at the plan preparation stage. Since citizen involvement in both plan preparation and implementation is best carried out at the local level, the failure to involve the local authorities meant that the ordinary citizen was not involved in the planning process.[29]

Under the 1979 constitution a civilian government came to power. There was then a further attempt to institutionalise planning. The new constitution made planning a constitutional obligation for the government. More effective means of eliciting public participation were established.

Although problems were still encountered in the 1980s (including the overthrow of the civilian regime by the army in 1984), planning should not be written off as a total failure. More projects were generated than would probably have happened in the absence of development plans. Nevertheless, there are undoubtedly serious problems which seem likely to persist, notably a political discontinuity which is not conducive to orderly plan formulation and implementation.

Conclusions

The issues discussed in this chapter could obviously have been pursued in greater depth. The various references provided should assist the reader who wishes to do that. Our overview, however, brings out certain salient points:

i)   Planning has proved extremely difficult; few countries can claim a large measure of success;

ii) Third World countries seem to have little choice but to continue trying to develop their economies through planning;

iii) There are various alternative approaches to planning which are worth of consideration. Two examples are: a) to alter the level of

57

direct state intervention; b) to attempt greater decentralisation of planning.

There are thus opportunities for reform, and governments need to think hard about how to exploit them.

Discussion questions

1   List the main obstacles which have hitherto prevented planning being more effective in the less developed countries. Try to include in your list any items you can think of which are *not* discussed in the chapter.

2   Write a brief essay outlining the planning experience of your own country, including some of the issues covered by the case-studies pp. 51–57.

3   What do you consider to be the main arguments *for* and *against* a more decentralised type of planning?

4   Imagine that you have been commissioned to write an advisory paper for the minister in charge of planning in your own country. List the issues you would wish to consider in carrying out such an assignment.

4 Financial Management

Introduction

Finance is of critical importance to development planning and administration. There are few development activities which can entirely depend on voluntary labour, and hence avoid the need for money in some form. Certain basic self-help activities may be possible through labour alone, such as the repair of minor roads, but generally speaking in all countries little can be done without spending money. Many countries have completed projects with high levels of voluntary input, but usually a significant cash element from some source has also been required.

Financial management is best seen as an important tool which governments can use to direct the economy in various ways. This does not mean that it is an effective tool. In fact, much can be said about problems which have arisen in trying to use it. Nevertheless, it remains a crucial element in the development process, and thus requires specific discussion. As will become clear it is of particular importance from the development planning point of view.

Financial scarcity

Poor countries obviously experience financial scarcity. That is their very nature. Money is both hard to obtain and difficult to use in effective ways. Lipton's curt sentence sums it up well: 'Development finance is hard enough to get; it is desperately easy to squander.'[1],

Whilst many countries have been able from time to time to receive financial assistance from outside their borders (i.e. from donors), problems have arisen in the process.

(1) Foreign help with finance is often for specific 'capital' projects (e.g. building an airport) and not for long-term financial needs which are likely to recur. Yet finance is needed for both purposes. Once an airport has been built it has to operate as a going concern. The donors

will rarely be interested in the latter. Whilst they may be willing to provide personnel for a few years (what is known as 'technical assistance'), they would not be interested in longer-term commitments. In short, the building of an airport is a finite exercise, the running of one is not.

(2) Donors often provide loans rather than grants to Third World states. This means that there has to be repayment. The world recession of the last ten years or so has exacerbated the debt problems of many poor countries which have found it impossible to 'service' (repay) these debts. Discussions are now taking place in the world community to see how far 'rescheduling' can be arranged. This means making the debts easier to repay by reducing or eliminating interest charges, or by extending repayment periods. These discussions have also looked at the possibility of 'wiping the slate clean' by writing off the debts completely.

(3) Dependence on the donor community for finance raises the whole question of how far Third World countries can plan their affairs autonomously. There has been a tendency for projects to be undertaken, not because they are judged as desirable by the recipient country, but because of donor priorities. Such projects may thus be imposed on countries not so much against their will as without any real analysis by the recipients of the need for them. The situation is, of course, liable to be exacerbated when the project is funded by a loan which subsequently becomes very hard to pay back. Because money is scarce, however, many countries are reluctant to turn away offers. It is thus easy to see why a strengthening of financial management is of such importance, both to ensure that finance is obtained to meet genuine needs, and also to make sure that when money is received it is used for the intended purposes.

In most Third World countries a crucial area of concern is the low level of private saving. Individuals who are poor do not have much money left after paying for basic necessities such as food, clothing and housing. Thus very little development is possible based directly upon such savings. Instead, public savings have to carry a large part of the burden. The problem is that revenue has first to be obtained, bringing in its train the vexed question of taxation. Governments can only save from the money they receive, which in turn depends to a large extent on the taxes that are paid (this includes income tax, various forms of sales tax, tax on produce — 'cesses', licences, customs duties, and so on). Because people are poor, however, the taxes that can be derived from them are limited. Income tax at a rate of 20 per cent might yield $10,000 per person in a country such as the USA, but in poorer countries the same tax rate might raise a mere $100 per person. This obviously imposes severe limits on how much finance can be obtained through income tax. The situation may be slightly different for taxes on basic consumer goods, such as bread or maize flour, but there are again limits on how far a government can go without making an impoverished people into one in which famine conditions prevail.

An obvious answer here is to argue for higher taxes on the wealthier members of the community but several problems become apparent.

i) It is generally the wealthy who influence the policy-makers, who are often themselves among the wealthiest. There is always likely to be strong resistance to such measures by people in this category. In the early years of independence, it tended to be primarily the expatriates who were wealthy, but now they are often outnumbered by affluent local businessmen, politicians, civil servants and professionals (such as doctors and lawyers).

ii) Where countries have embarked on a capitalist or 'free enterprise' approach there may be some justification for saying that measures which discourage business are illogical. Capitalism depends on private investment by such individuals. Therefore, to deprive them of a large slice of their income will mean that they have less to invest. This argument is beginning to become an influential one as bodies such as the World Bank now try to persuade governments to adopt development strategies of a more capitalistic type. The implication is reduced domestic revenue.

iii) It may be argued that the rich are only a very small section of the community anyhow. Therefore, higher taxes on them will not make much of a difference to the overall financial picture.

iv) The higher taxes are set the more likely it is that people will try to avoid paying them. Enforcement becomes a major problem, depending as it does on already hard-pressed management resources. Tackling such problems requires a highly committed government with clear policies, qualities which are not readily apparent in many countries.

Financial institutions

Our major area of concern is the strength of a country's financial institutions. These may be divided into three types.

● *1 Institutions within government*
These form part of government itself. Of key importance is the ministry with overall financial responsibility, usually known as the ministry of finance (often referred to as the 'treasury' — a throwback to colonial

terminology in countries which experienced British rule). Part of this ministry may include departments specifically for tax collection, for example income tax or sales tax. These departments have a crucial role to play in ensuring that the government receives the revenue due to it. Also within the central financial ministry there will be a section specifically concerned with the preparation of an annual budget for the whole government. This involves matching sources of revenue with various types of expenditure — defence, agriculture, health and so on. The performance of this office is clearly of critical importance for the functioning of the entire government machinery. Another vital institution is that which is concerned with auditing — that is, checking to ensure that money is used correctly and identifying wrongful expenditure wherever in government it may occur. Again, the role of such an office can be vital, especially as a check on the misuse of government funds, a common problem in many countries.

In addition to the finance ministry, there are various other institutions within government, with their own minister, 'Permanent Secretary' and so on, which should be considered as part of the financial network. Every ministry obviously is involved in using money to achieve its goals. The Ministry of Agriculture pays staff with the aim of promoting improved agricultural practice. Similarly, the Health Ministry needs finance to pay doctors, nurses, technicians and other medical personnel. Thus, each ministry has to have arrangements to manage finance. In basic terms, this involves two elements, one being the preparation of estimates of expenditure for the forthcoming year (usually submitted to the central finance ministry), the other accounting for the funds allocated. Both of these are critical and often time-consuming exercises. Accounting, in particular, requires an appropriate level of professional expertise.

• 2 Public enterprises

A second broad type of financial institution is that which has very strong links with government in all sorts of ways, but is nevertheless intended to work somewhat autonomously of it. What are often known as 'para-statals' or 'public enterprises' have been established in many countries to perform specifically financial tasks. Banking is a good example. Sometimes banks are set up by the State to compete with the privately owned commercial banks such as Barclays, Standard, and others. There are also banks which aim to assist the public in particular types of activity, to the exclusion of other types. In most countries there are financial institutions which are intended to help farmers who need investment funds to develop their land. They are unlikely to receive help from the normal commercial banks as these may not be willing to take the risks involved, or may offer loans at interest rates which make them prohibitive from the farmers' point of view. The State is also occasionally involved in the establishment of building societies which help their customers by lending money to build or buy houses. Another example of a para-statal which is involved in financial matters is the type which helps promote industry through credit. Often bodies of this kind are specifically created to help the small business-man who needs funds to get started[2] (e.g. Kenya's Industrial and Commercial Development Corporation; Lesotho's Basotho Enterprises Development Corporation).

• 3 Private institutions

In this category of financial institution banking is crucial because in many countries the large international banks can determine the avail-ability of funds for development in the private sector. Again, credit is involved. A cautious approach by bankers may be a source of frustration to the aspiring businessman, especially if he has nowhere else to go for funds. On the other hand, a willingness to take risks can result in money being made available for unsuitable purposes, other than for the development of the country. For these reasons, governments are very concerned about private banks and may from time to time inter-vene (directly or indirectly, formally or informally) if they feel that banking policies are too much at variance with what is considered to be the 'national interest'.

Also worth considering in the 'private' category are bodies like co-operatives and credit unions.[3] Often such organisations are important mechanisms both for accumulating savings and for giving loans to those who could not normally approach the commercial banks with any hope of success. However, they may be categorised as 'private' (along-side the commercial banks) because they are not owned by the govern-ment in most cases but rather by the members themselves. Government normally enters the picture by advising and controlling these bodies much more than it would in the case of private firms. This has tended to happen because mismanagement has been widespread, making it highly desirable to protect the interests of members whose savings, perhaps accumulated over years of struggle, may otherwise disappear rapidly. Nevertheless, such bodies do fall outside the formal government machinery, and can thus be regarded as belonging to the private sector of the economy.

It is clearly of great importance for development that all these varied institutions — central government ministries, para-statal bodies and private institutions such as banks and co-operatives — perform effectively. They are usefully regarded as channels which link sources of finance with intended purposes. Failure of development projects may often result from poor performance by these channels. Sometimes it is the result of a vacuum existing, i.e. no channels exist. This may happen for example, where no institutional arrangements exist to help people build or buy houses. However, generally the problem is not the absence of institutions but rather their failure to perform in the intended ways.

Aspects of financial management

Rather than trying to provide a comprehensive account of all the problems and issues that have arisen, illustrative material has been selected which provides helpful insights into at least some of the dimensions involved. Budgeting will be analysed, with special reference to attempts at reform. This will be followed by a discussion of auditing which includes a case-study of one country's experience. Next, the general issue of the links between financial management and development planning will be discussed. Finally we will look at donor finance. All of these present significant problems for financial management in less developed countries.

• 1 Budgeting

States which experienced colonialism have generally adopted budgetary practices introduced by their erstwhile colonial masters. Most formerly British-ruled states, for example, have tended to follow the British approach. The idea of government budgeting, in fact, seems to have originated in that country, where its basic principles can be traced back at least 300 years. Essentially a budget is a 'forecast by a government of its expenditure and revenues for a specific period of time'.[4] By a long-established convention the period of time in question has been one year, which, however does not generally coincide with the calendar year.

In those countries which follow the British system, a cabinet minister annually presents his budget to the legislature for approval. In Britain, the minister concerned has always been known as 'Chancellor of the Exchequer'; elsewhere, the more mundane title of 'Minister of Finance' has come into general use. In his budget speech, the minister generally accords a lot of attention to taxation and to other sources of revenue. There is also likely to be some comment on the state of the economy generally and some account given of the intended pattern of government spending in the forthcoming year (normally leaving on one side the donor finance element). In preparing the budget, the Ministry of Finance (or 'Treasury') plays a major role, although it clearly depends on the various spending ministries to submit their estimates in acceptable form and in good time. After the bureaucrats in the finance ministry have scrutinised the various ministry submissions, a budget document is prepared which, if it is found to be acceptable to him, the minister will put to the Cabinet for discussion and approval. Until this is given, the budget is a mere list of submissions with no legal status. As already discussed, legislatures in most states are not likely to enter into conflicts with their national leadership. Because of this, the budget is generally approved without difficulty or major amendments to the government's proposals, although queries may be raised and some criticism voiced.

Few countries have departed in major ways from this traditional model of budgeting. However, a certain amount of innovation has occurred in the USA over the past thirty or so years and some of this has had an influence on Third World countries. A criticism made of the traditional model has been that it does not adequately link finance with programmes of action or performance. The money is voted without any real concern, or analysis, about what it is intended to achieve. In view of this, the Americans initiated 'Programme Performance Budgeting Systems' (PPBS) in the hope that expenditure by government could be more closely related to performance.

Budgeting in Malaysia

Malaysia presents a good example of a country which has tried to change its budgeting system. The traditional system, as derived from the British, was criticised because of its failure to classify the aims behind the money figures or the achievements to be accomplished.[5] Following advice provided through consultants from the USA, a treasury circular in 1968 announced that PPB (omitting the 'S' for 'Systems') would be introduced. The main intention was to improve the linkages between financial provision and performance. Technical assistance, mainly American, was provided to assist the reform process. Peace Corps Volunteers were recruited. The initial approach was to extend PPB throughout the government system. By 1972 all federal agencies (i.e. central government bodies) had adopted the new methods of budgeting. However, this early experience was not considered successful for a whole range of reasons:[6] over-emphasis on technical aspects of the system; neglect of the human factor; failure to develop adequate capacity to use the data provided for analysis; lack of commitment on the part of senior administrators; lack of training; and lack of treasury support (despite that body having introduced the system). There was thus a change only as far as outward appearances were concerned, but

65

this was not in any way the transformation that was intended. If anything, the new approach only succeeded in creating confusion. Following an evaluation it was decided to continue with PPB on an 'in-depth' basis. This involved concentrating on a small number of 'pilot' agencies before extension throughout the whole system. Accompanying this change was the establishment of a steering committee to oversee implementation. A start was made with the Ministry of Health, followed by six other agencies. Interestingly, one of these was the Ministry of Finance where PPB never really took off.

The PPB method of budgeting has still not proved a success. The problems identified in 1972 still seem to exist. However, it should not be regarded as a complete failure. As Dean argues:

> it would be wrong to assume that programming has been entirely meaningless. It has led ministries to question and modify their structures. Besides, on some occasions it has helped focus attention on related items, which before the programming exercise would have been considered in isolation.[7]

He cites the case of the Ministry of Education where a 'Student Welfare and Teacher Training Programme' apparently was assisted by using PPB. On the whole, however, the lack of strong administrative support has been a crucial weakness. It is likely that the difficulty with PPB also stems from the way it was introduced — as a foreign technique which was assumed to be suitable to Malaysia without perhaps detailed analysis of what was really suitable for the country's conditions. As in many states in the Third World, Malaysia seems to have a conservative senior bureaucracy which cannot easily adjust to the importation of new techniques. Top-level apathy towards PPB is well illustrated by the fact that the steering committee failed to meet between 1980 and 1983.[8]

● *2 Auditing*
Whilst budgeting is essentially a pre-expenditure activity, auditing enters the picture once money has been used. It is a control device aimed at ensuring that funds are spent in the correct manner. It can assist in budget preparation as well, by drawing attention to lessons to be learnt from experience. For example, if auditing reveals that the funds allocated to a particular project were wastefully used the officials preparing the next budget may find that information useful. Auditing has been a weak link in many financial management systems, but it is a vital component if used effectively. Perhaps of most importance, it is capable of serving as a valuable check against corruption, a malaise found in many countries.

Auditing in Lesotho

The Lesotho case, which will be reviewed here, provides an excellent illustration of both the strengths and weaknesses of auditing. The Report of the Auditor-General for the three years ending 31 March 1978 was only submitted on 11 May 1982, in itself a significant fact about financial management in Lesotho.[9] One of the central purposes of auditing is to enable the legislature to review how public expenditure is being used, but there is not a great deal of point to the exercise if information about 1975 only becomes available seven years later. Another purpose is to enable the budget office to make its preparations in the light of experience; a function which is largely irrelevant if a long period elapses before detailed review of accounts is complete.

The reasons for this somewhat remarkable delay may be briefly stated. Only part of the problem concerned weaknesses within the Auditor-General's office (staffing problems etc.). Of more importance was the failure of the treasury to prepare accounts in time. Without these accounts for analysis there is little that the auditors can do, except wait and perhaps do some prompting. By early 1981, however, the accounts for 1975/76 were still incomplete. Following various explanations from the Accountant-General the Auditor-General had hoped to prepare his report by April of that year. However, further delays were encountered for the following reasons, as given by the Accountant-General:

a) absence of relevant accounting records;
b) many crucial documents missing;
c) 'Compilation of financial statements from recurrent records of the three years was a time consuming exercise.'[10]

Eventually, following considerable correspondence between the two officers, the relevant financial statements only became available *in toto* in March 1982. Thus, the legislature, cabinet, press, and other interested parties were only able to see the audit report on 1975's experience seven years later. It is little wonder that the Auditor-General saw fit to refer in his report to 'the extremely critical backlog of accountability facing the Government.'[11]

The report goes on to make clear that delay in the preparation of accounts was not the only problem being confronted by Lesotho's financial management. The Auditor-General's view was:

> The last decade has witnessed a progressive decline and laxity in the management of the financial affairs of the Government and these have in turn resulted in considerable accounting delays. Widescale financial indiscipline has led to disregard of financial regulations and instruction and has culminated in the breakdown of accounting controls that has reached catastrophic dimensions in recent years.

67

Inbuilt safeguards against financial irregularities have been vitiated, and this has presented opportunities for the perpetuation of peculation and fraud which have escaped early detection. Moreover, the default and delays in the supervision and processing of public accounts have provided an ideal climate and an excellent cover for the criminally intent who are only too aware that the detection of their misdeeds is made all the more difficult and protracted in such circumstances. This knowledge, in itself, is an added incentive to misappropriation of public funds.[12]

There are, thus, several interrelated elements at work. First, laxity causes delay; secondly, control of public funds becomes very loose and almost non-existent in several cases; thirdly, opportunities arise for fraud and other criminal actions because those so inclined are reasonably sure that they will not be detected. Failure to manage finance effectively constitutes a large part of the problem of corruption. Some examples of laxity can be given.

(1) There was a tendency to disregard tender board procedures. 'Tendering' is a process whereby government contracts (usually for construction of roads, buildings, etc.) are awarded to the companies (or contractors) who can offer the best terms (price, quality of performance, completion date and so on). A 'tender board' (or similar body) is established to ensure procedures are followed properly. However, it appears that many contracts in Lesotho bypassed these procedures without the approval of the Minister of Finance. There are obviously negative consequences which arise from such negligence. For example, by avoiding the correct procedures an officer in the Ministry of Transport and Communications was able to award himself various contracts for which he had inflated the prices by about £5,000.[13]

(2) Failure to act promptly on staff movements (such as retirement, study leave, occupation and vacation of houses) can also result in financial errors. Thus, a retired officer may continue to reside in a government house (provided for use by civil servants) long after he has ceased to be employed, without even paying rent. Worse still, failure to keep adequate records of the transfer of schoolteachers resulted in double payments being made.[14]

(3) The Auditor-General also draws attention to problems arising from excessive motor-mileage claims. Sometimes there was very obviously no connection between the mileages claimed and the known distances between places. Thus, if the distance between X and Y is 50 miles, yet a mileage claim for a return journey quotes 250 miles, there is clearly a discrepancy. Yet apparently such claims were frequently paid so that some officers gained £200−£300 in the course of a month or so.[15]

(4) This example concerns a particular unit within government, the Lesotho National Tourist Office (LNTO). Numerous examples of laxity were brought to light, among them being:

a) absence of records on saleable items (thus inaccurate records of sales);

b) no accounts kept of participation in international shows and fairs;

c) absence of receipts;

d) personal loans paid out of petty cash;

e) payments made in the absence of official purchase orders;

f) payments to a local hotel by the general manager for liquor etc., but unsupported by official orders;

g) weak control over the use of vehicles.[16]

(5) A serious general problem has been indifference to audit correspondence. The raising of points through correspondence from the Auditor-General were frequently ignored by the officers to whom they were addressed. Particularly serious was the case of the Ministry of Finance — the key ministry. To quote the eloquent words of the Auditor-General for the last time:

> I wrote a series of memoranda/letters to the Permanent Secretary for Finance on extremely important issues affecting the disbursements of public funds, but I regret to report that one hundred and twenty of these memoranda, issued between July 1978 and June 1981, remain completely unanswered to date, a classic illustration of the apathy, indifference, lethargy and inertia prevailing in the Public Service.[17]

What is significant about this particular case is the fact that the report reviewed here was published at all. Tax-payers were thus able to know quite a lot about where their money was going, even if belatedly. Given the high levels of secrecy that often surround government in many countries this fact is of some importance in itself. The report also paved the way for improvement in that it at least contributed to a growing public awareness of the need for reform. Some prosecutions did ensue, even if in only a small minority of cases, and these perhaps provided a deterrent for the future.

The Lesotho case was not chosen for its intrinsic interest, but rather because it illustrates common problems. Some countries, no doubt, have more adequate means of control while others — notably in much of West Africa — suffer from rather more severe problems of corruption. The case presented illustrates well the importance of auditing, the difficulties involved in doing it, and the various types of financial mismanagement which conscientious auditing can bring to light. Administrative reform strategies are likely to prove inadequate if there is no effective auditing function.

• 3 Development plans and financial management

There is a well established theme in the literature on development planning, namely that there should be close links between these two government functions. Studies written some time ago by writers such as Waterston, and Caiden and Wildasky concern themselves a good deal with this issue, whilst World Bank reports in the 1980s make very similar points,[18] and criticise governments for failing to practise the theory adequately. This is thus another discrepancy between what should and what does happen. The theory is one matter — the practice is quite another. Caiden and Wildasky give several examples of the ways in which this discrepancy occurs. For instance, access to information from other public sector bodies is crucial for both financial and planning purposes, but:

> The occasional man who has worked in both planning and finance notices immediately that power differentials are reflected in the ability to gain information. 'When I worked in the planning organisation, we met no success when we asked for information. But when I ask for this type of information from my place in finance, we get the information we want'.[19]

The English proverb 'he who pays the piper calls the tune' sums up the dilemma for planners aptly. Since the ministry of finance is responsible for the financial resources of government it has power over other ministries which the planners can envy, but are scarcely in a position to emulate. Yet it is obvious enough that successful planning is impossible without the provision of appropriate finance. This means the right sums of money have to be available at the right time for specific programmes, projects, etc. Many would, however, echo the complaint made by Nepalese planners, 'We make the plan and somebody else holds the purse',[20] with the result that the financial managers in effect have an informal veto over plan proposals. In this way, the treasury officials contribute significantly to the meaninglessness of much planning activity in less developed countries.

Part of the problem, however, lies with the planners themselves. There has been a tendency to select highly ambitious projects which go way beyond the financial capacity of the government concerned. Under such circumstances, it should not be considered odd that financial administrators feel that they have to play a controlling role, even if this means being accused of conservatism and of holding back development. The problem here is thus not one-sided. Rather it centres on the nature of the relationships between finance and planning. Making those relationships work in the most effective way remains a major requirement of administrative reform.

Planning and financing in Botswana

According to a recent World Bank report, Botswana is one country which has achieved a satisfactory integration of planning and financial processes.[21] One ingredient which seems to have helped is that finance and planning are contained within the same ministry (the Ministry of Finance and Development Planning — MFDP). This alone would have not been enough, however, because financial considerations could still have outweighed planning ones. A second ingredient appears to have been crucial — the determination of the political leaders to see that planning is adequately supported. When Botswana first embarked on planning, its president eloquently expressed what was needed:

> Botswana's need for sound economic planning is great. Our country is beyond doubt one of the poorest nations in Africa. There are unique problems: the lack of independent access to the sea, the presence of powerful neighbours whose racial policies differ greatly from those of Botswana, the lack of a national currency, the inability to impose customs tariffs, and so on. In these circumstances direction and impetus must be given to the economy ... My Government is aware, too, that planning by itself is not enough, that efficient implementation of the Plan is even more important and pledges itself to this task ... the energies of the nation must now be devoted to the economic and social development of the country.[22]

Similar quotations could be given for other heads of government. What is distinctive about Botswana, however, is that these statements of intent do seem to have resulted in concrete measures which have been successful, some of which are worth brief review.

First of all, there is the crucial question of the organisational structure of the MFDP itself. The Vice-President heads the ministry, assisted by a Permanent Secretary. This high-level co-ordination seems to have helped to ensure that planning and budgeting are closely linked. Thus, no expenditure can be incurred on a project which has not been included in the plan. At the same time in preparing projects for plan submission it is stressed that ministries should ensure that the costs involved should be realistic within the government's general financial framework. Thus, a reasonably effective two-way relationship seems to exist. It is one in which financial managers have to ensure that expenditure is linked to activities provided for by the plan, and in which planners have to ensure that plan proposals are financially realistic or feasible (in conjunction with planning units of the various sectoral ministries). This has apparently been achieved by the creation of channels through which the planning and budgetary processes interact. For example, Botswana's system of 'Rolling Plans' helps to ensure that plans are revised in the light of changed financial circumstances. Instead of having a plan for a fixed period (say five years), Botswana's arrangement is one whereby periodic change can be made within the plan period (hence the expression 'rolling').

However, there is some danger of over-estimating how far Botswana's adoption of innovative procedures has contributed to the creation of a relatively successful system. After all, the legal framework of financial management is not very different from that which was inherited by most ex-British territories in Africa. What makes Botswana distinctive is that this system has been put into practice more effectively than elsewhere. The influence of British expatriates for some time after independence may have been of importance here. Planning in Botswana was grafted on to an adopted British colonial model. Thus she has avoided some of the pitfalls which have occurred elsewhere, where two extremes have been observed. On the one hand, rigidity or conservatism tends to inhibit change, and thus discourages effective planning. On the other hand, laxity of financial management creates too great an opportunity for corrupt practice and the unwise use of scarce financial resources.

The lessons of Botswana seem to be: a) the importance of political leaders taking finance and planning seriously; b) the need for integration between the two; and c) the value of building creatively and flexibly upon inherited models rather then dispensing with them entirely, as though their colonial origins made them unworthy of serious attention in the 1980s. From this it should not be inferred that Botswana has solved all the problems experienced elsewhere. A further caveat should perhaps be entered — it is a small country with, therefore, relatively simple issues to resolve. These two points aside, however, there is no doubt that much has been achieved which is instructive for politicians, planners and administrators in other less developed countries.

• 4 Donor finance

In a review of recent African experience, the World Bank states:

> foreign assistance poses a critical challenge for the management of public investment; in some countries, the public investment programme has become little more than the aggregate of projects that donors wish to finance. These projects have not always been consistent with the priorities necessary for achieving national development objectives.[23]

This passage implies criticisms both of donors and of the countries which receive aid — the recipients. There are few countries which have avoided the dilemma being described here. Aid is needed because of the overall shortage of finance in less developed countries. This may be described as supplementation of domestic funding. Over-dependence on aid may mean that the donors determine the priorities, the recipient countries becoming largely passive observers of the aid process. This has been the case, for example, with much recent donor activity in Southern Africa. It is sometimes argued that aid is little more than a mechanism of dominance. The capitalist countries and their various aid agencies are described as being motivated by self-interest and use aid as a means of promoting their objectives (profits for their companies, political support, etc.), in the process undermining development rather than promoting it.[24]

Radical critics of aid clearly have a case. It is a form of 'leverage' or influence exerted by donor countries. Unfortunately, it is less easy to see an alternative to some sort of donor-recipient relationship. A realistic objective would be the discovery of ways to ensure that aid is in the real interests of the recipients. In turn, this means improving the capacity of governments to formulate policy in an effective way, which genuinely reflects the interests of their people. Thus, part of the aid question centres on the concept of absorptive capacity mentioned in Chapter 1. For this concept to be meaningful it must include the policy-making element, not just implementation. The weakness of policy-making clearly has a lot to do with the phenomenon of projects being virtually imposed by donors, rather than originating from a reasonably authentic dialogue between representatives of aid bodies (e.g. Britain's Overseas Development Administration, the USA's US Agency for International Development, the World Bank, United Nations Development Programme) and recipient negotiating teams.

Related to this is the need for donors to be flexible when dealing with various national programmes. A fair criticism of much that has been done through donor channels is that a 'blueprint' approach has been followed which tends to assume single solutions applicable to a multitude of circumstances, without adequate consideration of the uniqueness of particular countries (and indeed regions within them). Over recent years there has been a call for greater flexibility. There are signs, for example, of World Bank thinking undergoing a slight shift of direction, although many would argue that it has not gone far enough. For example, it still has a bias towards the private sector which may well inhibit it from supporting projects which do not give much scope for entrepreneurial development (whether by foreign companies or by national). This sets limits to its flexibility.

Indebtedness: the African case

There are, of course, various forms of donor assistance and some are clearly much more favourable than others. Grants which are given 'without strings attached' as a general rule are more favourable than loans, whatever the rates of interest involved. Loans have constituted a major problem for many countries for some time as Table 1 shows.

Table 1   *External Public Debt — Sub-Saharan Africa (excluding South Africa) (in US $ million)*

	Official Sources		Private Sources		Total	
	1970	*1982*	*1970*	*1982*	*1970*	*1982*
Low income economies	1,950.1	15,408.4	827.8	4,763.6	2777.9	20172.0
Middle income oil importers	909.9	10,285.1	894.9	6,810.3	1804.8	17095.4
Middle income oil exporters	683.2	3,474.6	153.0	7,321.4	836.2	10796.0
Totals	3,543.1	29,168.0	1,875.7	18,895.4	5418.8	48,063.4
Sub-Saharan Africa as a percentage of all developing countries	9.7	15.3	9.6	7.9	10.0	11.3

Derived from World Bank (1984) p. 70.

NB These figures do not consistently add up to the totals given by the Bank, apparently because the totals are derived from figures which go to more than one decimal place. The Bank notes that these figures should in any case be treated 'with caution'.

The World Bank's classification of Africa's economies is:

Low income economies: Chad, Mali, Burkina-Faso, Somalia, Niger, Gambia, Ethiopia, Guinea-Bissau, Zaire, Malawi, Uganda, Rwanda, Burundi, Tanzania, Benin, Central African Republic, Guinea, Madagascar, Togo, Ghana, Kenya, Sierra Leone, Mozambique.

Middle income oil importers: Sudan, Mauritana, Liberia, Senegal, Lesotho, Zambia, Zimbabwe, Botswana, Swaziland, Ivory Coast, Mauritius.

Middle income oil exporters: Nigeria, Cameroon, Congo People's Republic, Gabon, Angola.

Several comments can be made about these statistics.

i)   Africa's debt burden has been growing alarmingly, even though it remains relatively modest within the world as a whole (only 11.3 per cent of the total debt of developing countries). This implies that it is very important to ensure that future investment based on loans is not of the 'white elephant' type (e.g. international airports with little or no international air traffic for which to cater).

ii) African states now have to face the task of renegotiating these debts as far as possible. Much financial management expertise will now have to be focused on discussion with the various donors about how fast these debts can be eliminated, or at least reduced.

iii) Donors see these figures as suggesting the need for greater caution in future dealings with less developed countries. They will wish to be much more certain that a particular loan will be serving a worthwhile purpose. This shift of emphasis will also make significantly increased demands on the management capacity of African states in order to convince donors that proposed projects are worth taking the risk that the money may be misused.

iv) Finally, the debt problem is likely to increase the dependence of African states on the donor community. The latter is all the more inclined to impose tight conditions on the uses to which its funds are put, thus increasing the levels of influence it has on the policy-making processes in recipient countries.

Is aid dispensable?

In the late 1970s Guy Arnold drew this conclusion from his detailed study of aid in Africa:

> No African country appears to be able to dispense with aid. Some are better off and because of oil or other resources have good collateral for loans, although requiring technical assistance. Some need grant aid and technical assistance and may have a sound resource base awaiting development or may have no obvious resource base at all. Some try the socialist path: others the capitalist path. Most African politicians speak the rhetoric of development and self-reliance but it is for the future. In the present they need aid to survive and this situation fits neatly with the policies of the wealthy west, which is prepared to help, largely to retain a political hold and access to Africa's massive natural resources, but not to help change towards development and some measure of self-reliance.[25]

This comment could equally be made today, although less optimism about the oil exporters would have to be expressed in view of the generally uncertain future of that industry; the 'oil boom' may well be over. In broad terms, however, Arnold's conclusion presents well the general difficulties with which Africa's governments now have to deal. His study, like others which are critical of the aid business, does not contain a hopeful message. The alternative to economic dependence, he argues, can only be through violent revolution, but he adds, 'that fails more often than it succeeds'.[26] Within the limitations posed by the framework of the donor community, the implied need is to soldier on, but in a more creative fashion than hitherto, identifying more precisely one's own development needs and negotiating with donors in a more skilled and forthright manner. This is no easy remedy or panacea but it is some sort of way forward even if a difficult and often frustrating one.

Conclusions

Finance is a resource of critical importance for any country. This chapter has presented a broad picture of some of the issues involved in managing it effectively, using illustrations from countries which have performed well and from others whose performance has been indifferent. The evidence presented indicates that there are numerous possibilities for reform. However, there are no clear-cut routes to success and every country needs to look very carefully at its own circumstances after obtaining as precise a body of financial information as possible. Finally, however excellent and innovative new financial systems may look on paper or in 'blueprint' form, all is probably in vain if politically disturbed conditions prevent them from being put into practice adequately.

Discussion questions

1 Why is it important to ensure that there are closer linkages between financial management and development planning?
2 Prepare an action plan aimed at rectifying the weaknesses illustrated by the case-study of auditing presented in this chapter.
3 From the case-studies of Botswana and Malaysia, what seem to be the main *strengths* of financial management in the two countries?
4 Suggest ways in which governments in the Third World might try to improve their capacity in negotiating with donor agencies.

5 Bureaucracy and Rural Development

Introduction

Over recent years it has become almost routine to observe that rural development is vital for the less developed countries. Given the distribution of population between rural and urban areas, there are clearly strong arguments in favour of emphasising development activity in the villages and farms, rather than in the towns. Governments have thus taken the view that a wide range of measures should be adopted to improve the quality of life of people residing in the countryside. These measures obviously include agriculture as a significant element. However, there are various other issues embraced by rural development — these include health, water, the provision of communication facilities, education and small-scale industry. Some of these issues will be discussed in this chapter but priority will be given to what is the most important element for nearly all countries — agriculture.

Behind the concern of governments, there are a number of supporting arguments.

(1) Most less developed countries are overwhelmingly rural. Zambia has about 60 per cent of its people living in the rural areas. This statistic is significant because it is a relatively *low* figure, 80 to 90 per cent being more typical elsewhere in sub-Saharan Africa; Zambia can be regarded as being highly urbanised in comparative terms.

(2) Governments and observers of the development scene have for many years been concerned about the drift of population from the countryside to the towns and cities. Even countries where this drift is slow have shown apprehension. There are a few exceptions to this general picture (Sri Lanka being one), but in general rural development is seen as a way of reversing or at least slowing down this movement of people. Thus, in part, the solution to the 'exploding cities' problem is seen to lie in the rural areas. The assumption is that if people have an adequate livelihood in the countryside they will not need to move to the urban areas, where their presence creates many problems.

77

(3) Interest in programmes aimed at benefiting the poorer members of society is increasingly expressed by governments. This concern with equity implies a stronger emphasis on rural development since the rural poor are such a significant group in virtually all less developed countries. In particular, countries such as Sudan and Ethiopia — which have recently experienced the ravages of famine — attach priority to ways of serving the interests of the rural poor, for whom starvation and malnutrition are everyday conditions of life.

(4) Economists now tend to play down their earlier belief in industrialisation as the key to prosperity. For the past twenty years or so, it has come to be recognized that the rural areas offer considerable potential for the production of food for domestic consumption and cash crops for export.

The question is: where does bureaucracy fit into this picture? This is by no means a simple question to answer, partly because the experiences of different countries vary quite widely, but for other reasons too. Rural development should not be seen as depending entirely on strong administration. Rural people have to work for their own welfare. How far they succeed in doing so may only have an indirect connection with how well the bureaucracy is performing its various roles. Colonial Kenya illustrates this point well. Africans were not permitted to grow such crops as coffee and tea for most of the colonial period because the white farmers, who were highly influential in politics, objected to the idea. They nevertheless wanted to do so and in many cases they successfully demonstrated that they could be effective producers without government assistance.[1] There is thus a danger that people who write, talk and study public administration will over-emphasise the importance of their particular object of study and make it seem that rural people are passive, devoid of initiative, and manipulable by government. This danger should be avoided.

The bureaucratic role

Bureaucracy has an important role primarily because it is the arm of government intervention in the rural areas. There are numerous ways in which it is expected to assist in rural development. For example, agriculture, co-operatives, nutrition, health, and family planning may all be government-led activities which employ bureaucratic resources. One way in which governments have tried to foster rural development is through area-based programmes which aim at providing a variety of forms of assistance to specific rural areas. The former Special Rural Development Programme (SRDP) in Kenya is an example of this.[2] One feature of these programmes and projects is that they tend to

78

be most demanding administratively. Sometimes they have separate administrations from the rest of the government machinery; sometimes they are closely linked to the existing ministries and departments. Whichever is the case, however, the demands made upon bureaucrats are considerable, especially because large sums of money (generally derived from donor sources) are involved.

In addition, various types of sectoral programme have been initiated by central government. Again, donor support may be involved in a substantial way. An example would be co-operative development programmes aimed at supporting various types of development activity undertaken by co-operative societies. This support can be of various forms. Loans, technical advice, training and marketing may all be included. Administration is important in ensuring both that such programmes are realistically and comprehensively prepared and that they are properly implemented by the bodies concerned. The demands on bureaucratic resources are liable to be high for such programmes; failure has often been blamed on weak administration.

Another feature to look at is governmental arrangements for what may be termed 'area administration'. All countries of any size at all are divided into administrative areas (variously called provinces, divisions, districts, locations and so on). Each of these areas contain hierarchies of officials (sometimes mixed with politicians) who are supposed to co-ordinate the work of government (Kenya has District Commissioners, Zimbabwe District Administrators, Zambia District Governors and District Secretaries, and so on). This task is of a complex nature and many countries have found some difficulty in carrying it out successfully. It is particularly demanding since it is normally combined with the performance of duties concerned with law and order (e.g. dealing with political unrest).

The involvement of bureaucracy has been supplemented by the work of non-government organisations (NGOs), such as Oxfam and Development Associations. Indeed, it can be argued that a greater role should be played by such bodies because their relatively unbureaucratic structures provide them with more freedom of action than bureaucrats normally possess. This point of view has received a sympathetic hearing in many countries but has yet to result in a major diminution of government's role.[3] Thus the bureaucrats (the primary objects of our study) remain conclusively in the front line, where they confront numerous problems in the development field.

● *The problems*
Observers of bureaucratic intervention in rural development have observed various shortcomings. To start with, the political context of

rural development can create difficulties; when politicians become involved in matters of rural administration their contributions have often been regarded as harmful.

Additionally, criticisms have focused on the performance of bureaucracy itself.[4] Shortages of suitably qualified manpower have been frequently noted as a major constraint. Although this point is made less frequently now that a large amount of training has been done, it is still worth some discussion here. Rural development administration has to compete with other sectors of the economy for personnel. This involves competition with the other organisations within government plus the private and para-statal sectors. Posts in rural development often do not attract the best qualified people, especially if residence in a remote area is required (e.g. the mountains of Lesotho, the North East of Kenya).

Rural development tends to require highly specialised people such as foresters and veterinary surgeons who are still scarce in most less developed countries. Manpower (or human resource) planning has often been weak with the result that the resources available for certain job categories may be over-supplied (e.g. general administration requiring a social science degree) whilst an under-supply may be experienced for crucial rural development jobs (e.g. water supply technicians, public health nurses, tractor mechanics).

Apart from staff shortages, some comment has also been made about the morale of staff in the field. Staff posted to rural areas are often described as being poorly motivated, lacking in initiative, lazy, irresponsible and all too liable to indulge in private matters during working hours, e.g. drinking alcohol or running businesses. These indicators of poor morale are obviously difficult to quantify and do not apply equally everywhere. Nevertheless, there is a problem to be confronted here. Weak management has certainly been a contributory factor.

Examples of this weak management are:

a) the poor selection of personnel for rural development work;

b) unsympathetic attitudes by top management towards the conditions under which field officers work;

c) weak communication channels between headquarters and the field (this refers not just to physical communication, but also to the flow of ideas, complaints and so on);

d) conflicting directives from different parts of the headquarters machinery causing confusion in the field (and possibly paralysis — it may be wiser to do nothing than make the wrong decision);

e) over-frequent transfers of personnel (in many countries it is normal to spend less than one year in a particular post);

f) poor conditions of service (salaries, allowances, etc.).

The third problem area is more a matter of how administrative structures are managed. It is often argued that there is a lack of co-ordination in the management of rural development. In a number of activities a variety of organisations may be involved. As well as the government ministries and departments, there may be local government bodies, para-statals and a host of non-government organisations with a part to play in, for example, nutrition programmes. Co-ordination is essential if confusion and duplication are to be avoided. Achieving this is difficult, but it has to be attempted. A note of caution here: there is a danger of 'committee-itis' setting in, i.e. the creation of numerous co-ordinating committees which absorb vast amounts of valuable staff time. This is a danger which reformers should consider when proposing remedies. Considerable discussion has taken place about the desirability of adopting an 'integrated' approach to overcome this problem. More detailed discussion follows later in this chapter.

Diagnoses of rural development problems have often focused on the need to reorganise the government machinery (e.g. the creation of 'umbrella' rural development ministries or of new para-statal bodies). Sometimes these ideas may be justified. However, it should also be borne in mind that the creation of new organisations may cause as many problems as it solves. Discontinuity, confusion and misuse of resources may result, in turn leading to the poor provision of services to rural people. There are thus substantial costs to be considered; it follows that structural change needs solid justification and should not be undertaken thoughtlessly.

Another problem to be acknowledged at the outset is that rural development is not a field where there are clear formulas for success. Agriculture, for example, has a number of technologies which have been successful in specific settings. However, this does not mean that the senior civil servant advising the Minister of Agriculture in a particular country has a great deal of proven knowledge to offer with any real feeling of confidence. The applicability of technologies is partly dependent on suitable physical environments, but adding to the complexity of the issue is the fact that social, economic and political factors have to be considered too. This makes it particularly difficult to offer effective advice on policy and the issues arising are often so complex that highly qualified agriculturists may be no better placed than generalist administrators; indeed, the latter may even be able to advise more usefully if they have a good understanding of the nature of rural society. Well designed research programmes, which have recently been accorded higher priority, can make an important contribution towards finding solutions to this problem.

Finally, increasingly it is being said that some tasks hitherto undertaken by government could be handed over to the private sector.

Marketing boards, for example, have come under fire for their excessively bureaucratic nature and their tendency to absorb resources rather than promote the welfare of rural people. Privatisation of their activities has been proposed as an alternative.[5] This approach is worth serious consideration, although it also has dangers. Discussion of privatisation in general (for industry, as well as for rural development) will be found in the next chapter.

The administration of agriculture

Not many countries have been successful in the promotion of agriculture. India's 'green revolution' is a significant exception to the generally low levels of performance achieved elsewhere, especially in most of sub-Saharan Africa where levels of agricultural production have been declining. There may be much to learn from countries like India which have been relatively successful. It is not easy, however, to specify at what point the administrative contribution to India's success ends and where more technical and external factors within the environment of the administration enter the picture. A particular set of 'technical packages' suited to India's needs was prepared, and this must have had a great deal to do with her success. How far this case represents a model which can be replicated elsewhere is an open question.

Numerous factors are relevant to agricultural development. In a useful article, Elder mentions several which are amenable to intervening action by bureaucracies.[6]

(1) The first is the *accessibility of markets*. This covers a number of points, such as roads, railways, availability of port facilities (for export crops), as well as the existence of people able to buy the produce. Many countries face significant problems because commodities cannot be brought to market sufficiently easily because road networks are poorly developed or because adequate port facilities are not conveniently located (as in the case of landlocked countries in Southern Africa, such as Malawi, Zimbabwe, Zambia, Botswana, Swaziland and Lesotho). Matters such as these do not perhaps directly concern ministries of agriculture; but they are important policy matters which affect agriculture greatly.

(2) *Irrigation* is also an important factor in many cases. Irrigation schemes are costly, both in capital terms and the management capacities required. In many countries, irrigation has been treated as an approach best suited to the para-statal type of organisation, thus falling outside the structure of ministries and departments.

82

However, the primary objective of irrigation is agricultural; hence the agricultural ministries have generally close links with schemes of this type.

(3) Also worth mentioning is the *provision of power or energy*. Few countries are in a position to depend entirely on labour and animal power sources (an example of the latter would be the ox-drawn plough). These sources of energy have to be supplemented by others of a more costly type (electricity, diesel power, wind, water etc.). Again, this requires a measure of government intervention. Some of this work may be carried out by an agricultural ministry as such, as in assistance with the provision of fuel to run tractors and other forms of agricultural machinery. Other forms of energy (e.g. electricity) may be the responsibility of para-statal bodies, which might be expected at least to take into account the needs of agriculture in preparing their plans, determining their costs and so on.

(4) Governments are also normally involved in the *distribution of agricultural 'inputs'*, e.g. fertiliser, seed, farm implements. Farmers' requirements have to be met at a price which they can afford. This issue has presented governments with a great deal of difficulty because the inflationary trends of the past twenty years have greatly increased the financial burdens involved, both for farmers and for governments. It has also been argued of late that government's bureaucratic structures are a poor way of providing these inputs efficiently, and that there is a strong case for privatisation. Even if the private sector were to play a bigger role (as is likely), the agricultural ministry would still have a part to play in monitoring the process to identify problems and weaknesses which can be rectified by government intervention.

(5) Numerous factors are involved in the highly complex issue of *land*, of which some will be mentioned here. The distribution of land may be a problem because a few landowners may own a very large part of the land whilst many families have little or no land at all. This issue has been a marked feature of the debate on development in Latin America, for example. The system of land tenure may also be a concern of governments where, for example, occupants of a piece of land have no security of tenure, hence no real incentive to invest. Traditional authorities (such as chiefs) may still control land resources but fail to do so in ways appropriate to agricultural development. In some countries (e.g. Kenya, Zimbabwe) settlement schemes have been organised to enable families to move on to land previously occupied by settlers from overseas countries. All of these aspects of land raise issues for government to confront. They are often of great political and social sensitivity. The government bodies involved in agricultural policy will obviously have both a direct and indirect interest in them because improved agriculture requires a land system which contributes as much as possible

to the achievement of that goal. This brings in questions of law, politics and economics as well as administration.

(6) Agricultural credit arrangements are an essential part of any agricultural improvement scheme. In most countries, farmers have difficulty in improving their levels of productivity because they lack funds for farm investment. The ordinary commercial banks may not be prepared to lend money to most of them because of the risks involved (especially where there is no security of land tenure to serve as some sort of guarantee). Because of this deficiency governments have intervened by creating banks which can assist the farming community. Again, these bodies tend to be of the para-statal type. However, close liaison with the Ministry of Agriculture or equivalent will quite clearly be needed.

(7) Another factor is *village leadership.* The chiefs of a traditional type, where they still exist (as in Swaziland) can play an important role, sometimes positively, sometimes not. There are, however, other forms of leadership found at the village level which may also be vital — elected members of local committees, for example. The activities of both modern and traditional leaders can have profound effects upon agricultural administration by, for example, encouraging change toward more productive farming practices. In many countries there is much debate and controversy about such leaders, particularly where the question has been raised as to the extent to which traditional leadership is suitable for a developmental role.

• *Agricultural extension*
The seven factors so far mentioned are all relevant to agricultural administration but on the whole tend to be indirectly linked to ministries of agriculture. Land reform, for example, may well have a ministry of its own, albeit closely linked to whichever ministry is directly concerned with agricultural matters. However, most countries have ministries of agriculture with large staffs posted throughout the countryside who are involved in what is commonly termed 'agricultural extension'. Precise terminology naturally varies from one country to another but the general title 'agricultural extension worker' will be used here to depict such job positions as 'Extension Assistant', 'Agricultural Assistant', 'Junior Agricultural Assistant', 'Livestock Assistant', 'Horticultural Assistant', and so on — all of which names are to be found in different countries.

Generally, such workers operate within a ministry of agriculture or its equivalent. However, this is not necessarily the case; semi-autonomous agencies (para-statals) may also employ them, often on secondment (loan) from their parent ministry. Whether extension workers perform effectively or not depends to some extent on the overall organisation and efficiency of such bodies. If the ministry is badly run (through lack of finance, for example), then it follows that the quality of extension services is likely to suffer too.

There has been much criticism of agricultural extension workers. It has been said that they can be blamed for the failure of many agricultural development programmes. For example, it has been argued that they do not visit enough farmers and that even when they do so they contribute little that is helpful. There is perhaps some truth in such criticisms. However, it is unfair to assume that the problem always rests with agricultural extension workers, given the circumstances facing agriculture in many countries (e.g. under-investment, unsuitable land tenure arrangements) which agricultural extension cannot change.

Apart from the problems of morale already mentioned — which tend to affect rural development field staff generally, including those concerned with agriculture — some specific problems associated with agricultural extension workers are:

i) They are too few and far between. Because they are also poorly provided with transport, they cannot really develop good contacts with the farmers.

ii) They tend not to know as much about agriculture as they should. To some extent this implies criticism of the training they receive. Improvements in this sphere seem to be needed so that there is a closer link between the knowledge workers possess and the requirements of farmers. At the moment it is probably true that many farmers have a better knowledge of agriculture than many agricultural extension workers. This is a clear example of the wastage of scarce resources, requiring urgent reform.

iii) Too often their attitude towards farmers is ill-suited to the tasks they are supposed to perform. If they are to be successful, it is clear that they have to be effective communicators with the farmers. But aloof, 'elitist', attitudes may render smooth communication unlikely. Thus, even if there is a worthwhile message to put across it may fail to achieve any significant improvement in agriculture. Allied to this is the criticism that extension workers tend to ignore poor farmers, concentrating on the better-off ones who are closer to their social status.[7]

However, sometimes the difficulty is compounded by the lack of a worthwhile message (or 'technical package') to convey to the farmers. Experimental research, for example, has often not produced results convertible into the appropriate combination of fertiliser, seeds and other inputs to be of service to a particular farming community. Thus, the research and development function in agriculture also needs greater attention, a point emphasised in much recent technical assistance (e.g. the 'farming systems' approach pursued by USAID).

A significant factor in agricultural extension is farmer participation. Without this element, programmes are likely to fail and resources will be wasted. As a general principle, it can be argued that farm communities will increase their commitment to agricultural programmes if they are involved in the various planning processes of formulation, implementation, monitoring and so on. Further, such involvement can provide a useful channel for obtaining information (e.g. about possible technical problems) from the farmers to the government agencies concerned. This approach has been frequently adopted in less developed countries with, however, varying degrees of success.

The case-study which follows below gives one of the more successful examples.

Case-study: Kenyan Tea Development Authority
Kenya's Tea Development Authority is a semi-autonomous body closely linked to the Ministry of Agriculture.[8] This agency has made significant progress in promoting smallholder tea-growing. A number of factors explain this achievement, but the enlistment of local participation through the growers' committees has been a major one. In general these 'grass roots' bodies have gone a long way toward legitimising the strict regulations required for tea growing as laid down and enforced by the KTDA.[9]

These committees have been observed to perform various functions.
i)   They provide a useful opportunity for farmers to express their grievances, such as complaints about extension workers. A noteworthy feature of KTDA administration has been its willingness to look into grievances and handle justified ones sympathetically, thus giving committee members a reasonable degree of confidence in the responsiveness of the system.
ii) This system provides a valuable channel of information to KTDA staff at various levels (from top management to extension worker). This information has considerably assisted in long- and short-term planning.
iii) The committees have helped by persuading farmers to adopt certain improvements in their tea-growing. The elected farmers' representatives reinforce the work of extension agents by acting as educators themselves, aiming to persuade the farmers to adopt new or improved practices (e.g. better picking).

Thus, the KTDA seems to have successfully integrated local participation into its system of agricultural extension, a success which has not always been achieved elsewhere. One important factor seems to be the degree of commitment of the agency concerned to the principles of effective participation and responsive administration.

The need for improved management procedures

Improved management procedures may also assist the quest for better extension performance. Mainly discussing East African cases, Chambers has argued that a measure of joint work planning between extension workers and their supervising officers (e.g. District Agricultural Officers) may make a worthwhile difference.[10] Various management systems have been evolved in different countries for this purpose. What is really involved is a type of 'management by objectives' approach in which clearly identifiable objectives are jointly agreed on, and towards which extension workers can direct their efforts. This approach can introduce a more purposeful mode of working, thus contributing to improved morale so long as the objectives are not imposed from above in an authoritarian manner. Adoption of such an approach may also significantly contribute to better use of the scarce resources available for agricultural development. Management by objectives will be discussed in more detail in a later chapter.

Primary health care

Health is clearly an important dimension of rural development, not just because the idea of good health for all is a desirable one in itself, but also because it is closely related to other policy issues. For example, a productive agricultural labour force depends on good general levels of health, whilst opportunities for education may not be fully exploited if the school-age population is subject to frequent illness. Numerous rural development programmes — for reasons such as these — have included a major health element. Also, rural communities often feel quite strongly that improved health care is a major priority for them (e.g. the building of 'harambee' (self-help) clinics in Kenya).

The focus here will be on what is termed 'primary health care' (PHC) rather than health in general. The PHC concept aims at improving the health and well-being of all the people in a country, not just those in a position to afford the more expensive facilities available in advanced hospitals and clinics. PHC emphasises various factors:[11]

i) It is primarily concerned with rural populations, inaccessible areas and the poor in particular.

ii) Because the mass of the population cannot afford sophisticated services, the emphasis is on basic health services — there is a notion of a basic minimum standard of health care which should be accessible to all.

iii) Emphasis is placed upon prevention and promotion rather than cure. This does not mean neglect of the latter, but it is certainly an attempt to operationalise the motto 'prevention is better than cure'. It is also somewhat broader than the conventional approach because it includes health education in schools, nutrition, agricultural programmes, and so on. The notion here is that many common illnesses can be prevented, thus avoiding the considerable expenditure of curative treatment.

Although there is controversy about the degree to which principles of PHC can be specified, there are a few points which analysts agree should be taken into account by the policy makers — in the Ministry of Health and connected bodies (e.g. in central planning agencies). For example, PHC strategies should attempt to take into account the dominant life patterns of the communities concerned. This obviously does not mean condoning unhealthy behaviour but does suggest avoidance of 'going against the grain' in order to minimise resistance. Thus, involvement of the community becomes rather an important component. Related to this idea is the need to maximise use of the community's resources, but not a utopian hope of absolute self-reliance. Another principle is that of integration of all activities in health — so that the different parts of the system work together as a team rather than independently. This does not mean the rejection of the specialist approach but a downplaying of it in the interests of one better geared to general needs. Also involved is the provision of care ('health care delivery' in the jargon) to remote areas, which need to receive higher priority than central areas that have the benefit of clinics, doctors, hospitals and so forth. It therefore becomes vital to identify the needs of those who live far from the better served areas. There is also a need to ensure that linkages are developed and maintained with outside bodies, whether private or public, which have an interest in various health matters (e.g. the Red Cross, Oxfam, Nutrition/Home Economics organisations in other ministries, mission-run hospitals and clinics).

During the 1970s many Third World countries adopted PHC as a national policy. The World Health Organisation (WHO) played a significant role here, as did many donor-countries interested in health projects and programmes. This new emphasis reflected a growing criticism of conventional policies which were accused of being too costly for the needs of less developed countries. Some experts have adopted the derogatory expression 'disease palaces' to describe conventional hospitals.[12] However, PHC has not been an easy policy to implement even where there appears to be firm government commitment because it requires a substantial change from existing arrangements. Under these arrangements, the priority has been high costs and curative medicine; this militates against the improvement of services in an equitable way. Of course, this is not only a matter of economics but also concerns political influences on health policy.[13] Budgets, passed by elected legislatures, which give 95 per cent of health expenditure to the already relatively well provided urban sector, clearly do not reflect a profound commitment to the PHC approach. Instead, the need is to improve rural facilities such as clinics, train village health workers, provide transport and other support to rural services, transfer suitably trained health professionals (doctors, nurses, technicians, administrators, etc.) to centres where rural people can have access to them, and so on. On the other hand, there is an understandable desire on the part of the health profession to aspire to the sophisticated services their training (often in the West) has encouraged them to believe to be of importance. This results in a resistance to PHC which has to be overcome.

Another implementation problem is that PHC implies decentralisation, a change which governments tend to resist because of its possible political consequences. PHC implies a close knowledge of the conditions under which communities actually live, which certainly means more than knowing about the cases which find their way to the centrally located hospitals.[14] For example, to draw up district health plans without considerable knowledge of the needs of communities in the districts can only be a highly superficial exercise. This implies at least two changes in most countries. One is a shift in the location of expertise, the other is a greater effort to provide for community participation in the planning of health services.

Decentralisation of finance also seems to be needed. Administrators in the capital city do not have the detailed knowledge to enable them to make correct decisions about the districts. Providing that suitably qualified personnel (in both the medical and administrative senses) can be posted away from the centre, it is certainly advantageous for some financial decisions to be made in the districts. Decentralisation may also ease the frustration associated with slowness in release of funds by the centre because decisions would be possible 'on the spot' instead.

Because PHC highlights the use of village-level workers, a good deal of attention has to be paid to supervision and training. Adequate supervision by, say, a district medical officer should both motivate and control local health personnel. This is difficult if he or she lacks discretion to do so.

The various measures discussed here depend on numerous factors if they are to succeed. Not all have been mentioned, and much in any case depends on the circumstances of individual countries. However, for our present purposes it is important to note that efficient administration is only part of the issue. What is also required is a genuine political commitment, which entails a willingness to take firm decisions to change the allocation of resources. The literature referred to in this section suggests that political leaders are not always able (or willing) to translate a stated commitment to PHC into a genuine one. China has often been cited as an exception to this,[15] whilst a detailed study of Tanzania, whilst critical, is optimistic in tone.[16] These cases are, however, somewhat exceptional. For the most part, there is a great deal to be done to transform existing systems into ones which provide a satisfactory service to the rural areas, but what is required by individual countries varies greatly.[17] There are numerous variables to consider, some directly medical (e.g. disease patterns affecting rural society), some not (e.g. government financial resource management). A quite centralised, non-tropical country such as Lesotho is obviously faced with different problems from a quite decentralised one in a tropical setting, such as Nigeria.

Case-study: primary health care in Uganda

This study illustrates well the potential contribution of a PHC strategy where financial and material resources are extremely scarce. The 1970s saw the Amin government in power in Uganda. Its policies resulted in a substantial running-down of the country's health services. Efforts undertaken in post-Amin Uganda in the early 1980s illustrate both how PHC can assist in reconstruction and the nature of some of the difficulties involved.[18]

The particular programme under review began at the Ngora Mission hospital in Teso District in the late 1970s. Thus, like much PHC work, it was initiated by a non-government organisation. The first two or three years were not successful ones. The eight appointed village health workers (all male) were making little impact. They were paid by the hospital to carry out work focusing on nutrition, hygiene and health education but soon ceased to perform adequately. Apparently their activities were confined to collecting their salaries each month and − in some cases − selling for private gain the small quantity of medicines supplied to them for use in the community.

It was therefore decided to make a fresh start by involving more closely the communities in the eight parishes served by the hospital. Local chiefs were brought into the process and committees were elected after public meetings had been organised by them. This generated some enthusiasm but of a short-lived kind. Several committees did not function at all and the new village health workers proved to be little improvement on the former ones.

It was then realised that the programme still had too much of a 'top-down' emphasis. To involve communities fully it was decided only to work with those whose commitment extended to making a very small financial contribution (a 'down payment' of U.sh. 10,000 − less than £10) towards the payment of workers, thus giving them a definite stake in the programme. The results in some areas were thereafter more impressive. In such fields as midwifery, nutrition and immunisation a substantial improvement was reported, much of it attributable to the redesigned PHC strategy. A crucial ingredient here seems to have been the involvement of more women, both as workers and as committee members. Thus, the shift from a top-down and male-dominated approach to a locally based one in which females were enabled to play a large part proved to be a positive one. The danger to such a programme is likely to come from conventionally trained hospital staff (whether governmental or non-governmental) who are liable to treat the committees with contempt or indifference. Also, 'big' programmes involving a large 'free' contribution element represent another danger as they may discourage local initiatives of this sort.

Village water supplies

The case for the provision of potable (drinkable) water in the rural areas requires only a brief statement. Saunders and Warford summarise it thus:

> It is universally accepted that an adequate supply of water for drinking, personal hygiene and other domestic purposes, and an adequate means of waste disposal are essential to public health and well-being.[19]

There is, thus, a clear relationship between village water supplies and primary health care. However, this quotation neglects a significant benefit which may be derived from the provision of improved supplies — the convenience factor. Many rural families in less developed countries face long journeys on foot to collect water. Journeys of 15 km are not unknown in many countries. So long as a convenient site is chosen, the provision of village supplies can considerably reduce this problem. The idea is not to provide services equivalent to those found in the towns and cities because the costs of doing so would be too great to bear. However, there are still possibilities of closing the gap even if not entirely.

Governments thus have a number of decisions to make, in the light of the various constraints to be faced in terms of finance, human resources and so on. Clearly, governments are expected to intervene, but a number of possibilities have to be considered. What sort of role should the private sector play (e.g. feasibility studies, design, construction)? Should maintenance be left in the hands of the villages, and if so to what extent is government help required? How far should government insist that villages raise funds themselves before making a contribution itself? Should donors be approached, and if so which? What sort of training is needed? Where should supplies be located?

What sort of technology should be used (simple wells and springs, highly advanced pumps, etc.)? These questions, like many in rural development, are not just technical ones because they involve governments which have a political complexion. Thus, it can again be seen that political questions are vital to rural communities; the bureaucrats concerned with village water supplies can hardly expect to conduct their work on the basis of purely technical considerations.

The 'Community Development' Approach

The idea of rural communities playing a part in development, rather than being mere passive receivers of services provided by government, has been a recurring theme of this chapter. Agriculture, health and village water supplies are all policy issues which affect the welfare of rural people; it is thus not difficult to draw the conclusion that they should play a major role.

Out of such considerations the 'Community Development' (CD) idea developed after the Second World War. It was initially promoted by the British colonial administration but was subsequently adopted by other governments concerned with development (both donors and less developed countries). A standard definition of CD given during this early period was:

> A movement designed to promote better living for the whole community with the active participation, and if possible on the initiative of the community, but if this initiative is not forthcoming spontaneously, by the use of techniques for arousing and stimulating it in order to secure its active and enthusiastic response to the movement.[20]

This definition was formulated at a conference of colonial administrators. However, the basic ideas it contains were inherited by the new governments which were emerging at that time.

There are several elements to the CD approach. The first is the emphasis upon 'felt needs'. The principle is that CD officials have to identify what a given community actually feels its needs to be, and not force ideas upon it from above. However, it is not always easy to do this as these needs may not always be clearly expressed in communities.

The roles of the CD workers or officials are crucial. Sometimes they are employed by central government, sometimes by local authorities. Whichever is the case, they are expected to stimulate initiative and interest within communities, using various techniques of persuasion. Thus, CD has very close links with adult education, which is why both these functions are often found within the same ministry. In theory, this educational emphasis should not be authoritarian, but should be centred on the exchange of ideas in a reasonably open way.

The idea of 'community' is a key one. A community may number one hundred or a thousand people, but they live in the same quite small area or locality, toward which they feel a sense of belonging. Such communities exist in the towns as well, but they are mostly in the rural areas. The CD approach aims to make use of community loyalties and sentiments to bring about change with consent and participation.

Thus, CD bureaucracies may encourage communities to carry out a variety of projects, such as building their own schools (very popular in Kenya, for example), building health centres, water supplies, cattle dips (or 'dip tanks'), irrigation ditches, dams, roads and soil conservation terraces. Thus, through working with communities the idea of CD is to create rural capital at a relatively low cost to the central government (because the community itself is expected to contribute a large proportion of the labour, money and materials involved).

• The role of field workers

Clearly, the activities carried out by CD workers are of some importance. Most of them are employed by a department or ministry (perhaps a general rural development one) but other agencies may also have CD staff (e.g. district or local councils, non-government organisations). These organisations depend heavily on what are often termed their 'frontline' workers (i.e. the people who work in the field and who are in regular contact with rural communities). Ideally, they should operate at village level. This is a difficult ideal to realize in practice and therefore a number of villages may have to be covered by one worker. This can be a major problem because some villages may then be neglected.

It is essential that CD workers communicate effectively with people in rural society. Normally, this means working with groups interested in some particular type of project (e.g. providing more classrooms for a school). Prior to this, however, groups have to be formed; the CD worker may be able to help in this process by, for example, addressing public meetings.

The Women's groups (or 'clubs') that have been formed in many countries provide examples of the group approach. As their name implies they aim to be of assistance to women, and in so doing may contribute substantially to rural development. Most groups are multi-functional. They may carry out a number of different activities such as agriculture, house-building, sewing and nutrition. It is considered preferable to have female CD workers to work with such groups, although it is not essential: some men workers have been quite successful too. A difficulty which has often occurred is that the dividing line between helping such groups and *interfering* with them may become blurred in practice. Because of this, the relationship may become tense, not the co-operative one suggested by the theory. Women's groups — like other types — tend simultaneously to desire autonomy from government and hope to obtain help from it. CD in general suffers from this contradiction and, as a result, it sometimes takes on a more authoritarian form than the conventional text books would imply. Thus, CD workers find themselves caught in a dilemma: on the one hand, they are trained to help communities help themselves, whilst on the other they work for a government which is likely to have an altogether more authoritarian perspective.

A few other problems regarding CD workers need to be mentioned.[21] It is not easy to find people with the right qualifications. A minimum level of education is necessary (3—4 years of secondary school roughly) but people who have attained this may not be attracted to a job in CD which might well entail being posted to an isolated area. Also, education in itself is not enough as personality factors should really be taken into account, especially the likelihood of recruits adjusting to a rural environment. For this reason, ideally such workers should themselves have rural backgrounds. It is also difficult to attract suitable people because pay scales tend to be low. Additional allowances, where provided for, do not make a great deal of difference.

There are also problems with training such workers once they have been recruited because the trainers tend to be out of touch with the situation in the field. In principle, trainers should spend a lot of time in the rural areas so that they become acquainted with the various problems being faced. It would also be helpful if they were able to follow up on their training, but this is often not done except in a rather superficial way. Training tends to be of short duration (perhaps only a matter of six months). Thus, trainees may not benefit much. They may finish knowing very little more than they did when they began. The big problem here is finance. At one time, bodies such as UNICEF were keen to help (e.g. in Kenya) but are less enthusiastic now. Many governments find it difficult to allocate sufficient funds from domestic resources, so training is likely to be abandoned or too marginal to meet the real needs. To these difficulties facing CD workers, can be added those already noted for various other types of field staff — poor work planning, management neglect, low morale, lack of transport, etc.

● *Community Development Committees*
CD also depends heavily on a network of community committees, which have a great deal of responsibility for running projects. In the

Kenya case, 'Harambee' projects are usually run by a committee of six or seven, consisting of a Chairman, a Vice-Chairman, Secretary, Treasurer, and two or three ordinary members. Usually, elections are held at public meetings to select these members, voting normally being conducted by a show of hands.

The tasks of these committees are various. Meetings have to be held with all who are involved in projects — government officials, donors, representatives of non-governmental organisations, researchers, and the local people who are expected to contribute (whether in terms of labour, cash or materials). These meetings will discuss various matters but fund-raising is likely to be high on the agenda. The committees are also likely to communicate with government in other ways, for example by sending delegations, or by correspondence. This can be very important where fund raising is involved, but can also be necessary in order to obtain government approval for a proposed project (in cases where prior approval has to be obtained). Moreover, the committees will probably have to submit progress reports on their projects (usually this is to the government but it may also be to non-governmental organisations). The committees are expected, among other things, to raise funds and organise labour for projects. This may, for example, involve visits to individual households.

On top of all this the committees have to be accountable for the funds obtained. They may even be prosecuted for misuse of funds, as has happened from time to time in Kenya, for example. They also need to deal with contractors in cases where building work is involved. The complication here is that only very large projects are likely to be in a position to use professionals to check up on the work of contractors. Therefore an important responsibility in small projects has to be borne by the local committee — to check on delays, overcharging and other problems. Scope for corruption also arises, where, for instance, a committee member may also be the contractor for projects in the same area.

●*The problems of community development*
Numerous problems have been experienced in CD. Thus, although substantial achievements have been recorded,[22] alternatives to this approach are now being pursued. Because CD exists in a political setting, it is not surprising that it is affected by factionalism — by opposing groups competing for power within a CD framework. At its most extreme, this politicisation of CD can result in the disintegration of committees and the abandonment of projects. Also, CD committees may lack a clear understanding of their functions, for example how to go about planning projects. Training can be a partial remedy to this

but — as in other fields — it is beset with difficulties, such as the use of poorly qualified trainers, or inadequate facilities. Corruption can also be problematic. It is exacerbated by inadequate financial management (especially auditing). It can thus be quite easy for leaders to misappropriate funds. Some may actually become participants in CD projects with this as their sole objective. There has also been a tendency for government to act coercively — to force people to contribute, in violation of the voluntary principle dear to CD's advocates. Confiscation of property, livestock and other possessions may take place, making CD little more than an unofficial taxation system.[23] Finally, a problem observed with CD in a number of countries has been its weak links with the planners. Since field workers and other locally based officials usually lack planning skills, many projects are poorly planned and little attempt is made to consider long-term costs or the real needs of the community. Projects are sometimes started because they make political sense for some influential persons, to the neglect of other factors. This often results in failure to complete projects or to run them properly (e.g. non-maintenance of village water supplies, clinics with no supply of drugs, schools with no furniture). Another result is that evaluation or monitoring is inadequate, thus making it impossible to plan in the light of analysed experience. This is another matter requiring the attention of the policy-makers.[24]

Integrated rural development

Whilst not discarding the participatory elements of CD, integrated rural development (IRD) attempts to move beyond it. Like CD it aims to intervene in the lives of rural people in ways which cut across the departmental divisions in government. The idea is, however, not just to pay attention to avenues for participation but rather to plan so that the various interrelated elements which make up the total rural development scene are fully taken into account. Thus, agriculture, health, education and so on are all supposed to be part of the same planning process rather than each of them being planned separately.

The basis of IRD lies in the assumed interrelatedness of the various aspects of human life. This assumption and its consequences for administration are explained clearly by Mullen who argues that 'the different aspects of human life constitute sub-systems related to one another and to the system as a whole.'[25] This central assumption then leads on to various propositions regarding patterns of administration. IRD is expected to 'activate' the various sub-systems (health, agriculture, etc.) by designing specific projects. This involves providing services through bureaucratic structures which are well co-ordinated 'as each department is responsible for a functional activity which is irreplaceable in the overall development pattern, like a link in a chain.'[26] Finding organisational forms for doing this is likely to be difficult, because most governments normally operate with an emphasis upon departmentalism and centralised hierarchies of authority. These two factors, in combination, make it difficult for district-level officers of different departments to co-operate together for fear of incurring disapproval from their central ministries or departments. By way of example, district agricultural, co-operative and community development officers may all be interested in the possibilities for promoting horticulture in their district but it will be difficult for them to do so if their respective central authorities do not allow adequate discretion.

Inter-departmental co-ordination thus is of critical importance if IRD is to make any great progress. Various attempts have been made to solve this problem. To generalise, two basic approaches can be discussed. The first is to set up special programmes, usually confined to specific areas, and to manage them through a relatively self-contained authority. Plenty of examples of this can be given.[27] Two of the best known took place in Kenya and Bangladesh.

- ● *Case-study: The Special Rural Development Programme (Kenya)*
SRDP's origins can be traced to a conference held at Kericho, a town in Kenya's Rift Valley Province, in 1966.[28] This conference was concerned with the three connected issues of education, employment and rural development. The participants, consisting of a mixture of administrators, political leaders and academics, drew attention to a number of problems being encountered in these fields and made suggestions for their solution. It was concluded that rural development had a number of 'fundamental requirements' to be fulfilled, one of these being to stress the interrelated nature of rural development.

The outcome of this was the SRDP which was launched in six administrative divisions (sub-units of a district) in 1971. Like most of these programmes, it depended heavily on donor funding. The literature on SRDP (which is plentiful) is rather critical of the outcome of the programme.[29] One factor that is often mentioned is that the principle of integration was not adequately reflected in the administrative structures which were devised. The reasons for this are complex because the donor involvement, for one thing, may not have helped much by confusing lines of authority. However, another aspect of the problem was that SRDP existed alongside the conventional structures of administration which had an uneasy relationship with SRDP. The lesson of the programme, as far as administration is concerned, is that a

97

compatible relationship with the rest of the government machinery is essential. SRDP, as an early experience of the integrated approach, was however a valuable learning experience for Kenya's policy-makers; attempts in recent years to introduce district planning have clearly benefited as a result.[30]

● Case-study: Comilla (Bangladesh)

The 'Comilla Model' has had a considerable influence on rural development policy-analysis in a number of countries, including Kenya. In this instance the problem of co-ordination was to a large extent resolved by decentralisation so that local co-operative bodies, in liaison with government co-ordinators, initiated the planning process. The latter, in turn, filtered upward to the government's departmental structure.

The basis of the programme was the realisation that a multi-sectoral approach was required. Its inspiration came from the Pakistan (now Bangladesh) Academy for Rural Development at Comilla, led by Dr A. H. Khan, whose thinking on rural development has been a very important influence, not confined to Bangladesh.[31] Initially, an integrated model was tested in one 'thana' (a sub-unit of a district) and was gradually expanded by replication in a number of other thanas, a process which gathered momentum after the secession of Bangladesh from Pakistan in 1971.

The Comilla approach is now thoroughly accepted as part of the country's development planning process. Detailed methods of local planning have been evolved, based upon a high measure of decentralisation through farmers' co-operatives (KSS) organised into co-operative federations (TCCAs). These bodies, managed by the people themselves, are assisted by 'Thana Project Officers', the secretaries of TCCAs, who liaise with the various departments. So strong have these participatory structures become that 'many of the agencies find it more convenient to administer their programme through the TCCA/KSS structure'.[32]

The crucial lesson of Bangladesh seems to be that integration is best achieved by decentralisation, both by means of local representative bodies and through decentralised administration, the Thana Project officers being the vital administrative link. In addition, the Bangladesh case suggests a higher level of compatibility between the programme and the general machinery of government than was the case in SRDP.

● Rural development and district co-ordination

The other approach which has been followed will not be discussed in detail here but is covered in the chapter on decentralisation. Most countries have tried to solve the problem of integration by trying to improve the co-ordination of existing government bodies at district level. Three main elements have been included in these efforts:

a) a committee system linked to various administrative levels (district, province, etc.);

b) a senior official given responsibility for local co-ordination, with varying degrees of authority to fulfil this role;

c) an attempt to link with members of the community as a whole through a variety of processes, depending mostly on the political climate (selection, nomination, election, etc.).

Conclusions

Effective administration is clearly a vital ingredient in rural development. What this means in practice raises a number of questions which we have considered in this chapter. The danger of overloading bureaucracies by giving them tasks which cannot be fulfilled has become acute; many failures occur because this danger has not been adequately addressed. To make this point does not necessarily imply advocacy of sweeping reform, but it does mean that a review of the role of government is in order to see if alternatives cannot be found. Greater involvement by non-governmental organisations may be possible, for example. However, the use of public sector bureaucracy is bound to continue to be important. Several elements of its performance have been discussed in this chapter.

i) *Decentralisation* (both administratively and by creating institutions for community participation) would seem vital and examples have been given of how this has been achieved with a measure of success in some countries.

ii) Linked closely is the factor of *co-ordination*, which is needed to overcome the adverse consequences of the departmental approach.

iii) *Resource allocation* is a crucial dimension. Three types of resource have been mentioned: human, financial and technical. With regard to human resources, a key need is to allocate suitable personnel to rural development tasks in more effective ways than at present, whilst financial policies in many countries do not reflect rural development needs (e.g. under-funding of primary health care whilst spending large sums on city hospitals). The pursuit of technical policies to meet rural needs is also important (e.g. village water supply).

iv) Effective communication between the rural communities and the various agencies involved is important. Cases like Kenya's KTDA illustrate the possibilities here as does the CD approach — which has substantial benefits to offer despite the criticisms of recent years.

v)   It is necessary to improve the linkages between rural development and national planning. This was a weakness of CD which the IRD alternative was intended to overcome, but with only limited success. The Bangladesh case, however, offers positive lessons.

vi) Finally, strong political support for the various requirements mentioned here is vital if real progress is to be made. Rural people are invariably in the majority in less developed countries; that does not mean that they have real powers to decide how government resources are used.

At the political level, as well as in the administrative sphere, greater urgency is needed. This does not mean, however, that new projects should be rushed into without proper planning. Under conditions of scarcity (as they are present), policy-making for rural development needs to be undertaken with more thoroughness than ever before.

Discussion questions

1   Extract from this chapter examples of successful rural development administration. Suggest any lessons which can be derived from these examples.

2   In what ways has resource management been less than successful in its contribution to rural development programmes?

3   How far has the poor quality of extension workers caused the difficulties faced by agricultural development programmes?

4   Select a rural area with which you are familiar and prepare a plan for a project there, using community development principles as guidelines.
    The project may be of any type — a school, a road, a clinic etc. If you do not know the rural areas in your country well, try to do the same exercise for an urban area.
    What problems would you anticipate in implementing the plan you have drawn up?

5   Answer the following questions based on the case-study of primary health care in Uganda:
    a) What advantages did the programme in Teso possess because it was run by a non-governmental organisation?
    b) What lessons from this study can you obtain for the application of the PHC strategy in your country?
    c) Investigate a small-scale PHC programme in an area with which you are familiar, and write a short (one- or two-page) report covering the sorts of issues discussed in this case-study.

6 Public Enterprises

Introduction

All Third World countries have pursued development policies which have involved a substantial measure of state intervention and ownership of economic institutions. The precise policies vary greatly from country to country, but even states which favour private enterprise (or capitalism) have found it desirable for the State to own a variety of commercial, industrial, financial and agricultural concerns. Kenya may be quoted as an example of a state which, although inclined to a capitalist strategy, has a large publicly owned sector. A government review, using the term 'para-statals' for these publicly owned concerns, described the situation as follows:

> At independence, Kenya inherited an elaborate framework of para-statals especially in the agricultural sector. In its efforts to promote development, decolonise the country, increase citizen participation in the economy and ensure more public control of the economy, the Government established more para-statals. As a result, para-statals are now to be found in all sectors of the economy — in agriculture, commerce, industry, tourism, housing, construction, insurance, banking, basic services etc.[1]

Pakistan is another example. Again, the government looks favourably upon the private enterpreneur, but:

> Public Enterprises in Pakistan play a very important role in the vital sectors of the economy, including railways, transport and communication, water, power, fuel and minerals, banking, insurance and basic industries. Their efficiency is, therefore of crucial importance to the economy of Pakistan.[2]

However, the significance of the publicly owned sectors of the economy is even greater in countries which have been influenced by socialist approaches. Tanzania and Zambia both adopted such policies in the late 1960s and early 1970s.[3] The Zambian take-over of the foreign-owned copper industry was an important shift in policy which greatly increased state ownership in that country and markedly diminished the scope of the private sector. Other aspects of the economy also came under state ownership at around the same time. In Tanzania President Nyerere's policies tended to emphasise the need for state ownership and control, following the famous 'Arusha Declaration' of 1967.

What are the key reasons for adopting such policies? Clearly, ideology is only part of the answer. Zambia and Tanzania both adopted policies which were influenced by socialist ideas, the principle being that social justice and equality would be furthered by removal of much economic activity from private hands and the transfer of it to public ownership. Private enterprise was seen as exploitative in various ways and therefore had to be reduced in scope by what has often been called 'nationalisation'.

At the same time, however, ideological considerations cannot completely explain why regimes favouring private enterprise have also established large public sectors. The quotations given earlier for Kenya and Pakistan provide part of the answer. Kenya's inheritance from colonialism, especially in agriculture, included many 'para-statals' which could not easily be dismantled. They had been found necessary under colonial rule and the incoming government saw no alternative to them. Continuity was thus an important factor. In addition, the government pursued policies which were aimed at reducing the foreign-owned share of the 'national cake'; to promote 'citizen participation' it had to adopt state ownership policies. Although looking favourably on capitalism, it was not possible for the government to hand over to the private sector because that would largely have meant making transfers to foreign business interests, there being few financially strong Kenyan entrepreneurs available soon after independence.

The new Kenyan government also expressed a commitment to development planning; state ownership of certain activities was seen as a necessary pre-condition for achieving a strong planning system. Another consideration — which has been important in both Kenya and Pakistan — has been the assumption that public ownership is desirable to achieve objectives which could not be attained through private enterprises which solely emphasise the profit motive. To quote the Pakistan case, it has been observed that:

It is well known that many of them (public enterprises involved in manufacturing) are set up and operated for purely socio-economic or political objectives. A textile mill in Baluchistan and a sugar mill in a predominantly rice-growing area in Sind are typical examples.[4]

The motives for establishing public enterprises can accordingly be seen to be complex and varied. Nevertheless, broad trends are discernible, the key one being the assumption that their establishment is a fundamental component of development strategy. This assumption has been viewed more critically in some circles recently but has by no means been discarded.

Types of public enterprise organisation

In his classic study of public enterprises and development, Hanson identified four types of public enterprise organisation.[5] His typology, which has been generally accepted, is as follows:

● Departmental enterprise

In this instance, the enterprise is run as a normal department of government with direct responsibility for its affairs being vested in a minister (e.g. for agricultural enterprises the Minister of Agriculture). A lot of the services provided by colonial administrations (e.g. postal services) were organised thus, and this pattern has often continued after independence. An important feature of them is that they are managed by civil servants who have very little autonomy from government. This has meant that management tends to be excessively bureaucratic and lacking in flexibility and creativity, qualities which are needed if such enterprises are to achieve a reasonable measure of economic success. Departmental enterprises, although they have faded from the scene somewhat, are by no means things of the past.

● Public corporations

This important type of public enterprise has several characteristics of interest. Among them are:-

i) Normally, there is 100 per cent state ownership (there may also be some non-government capital stock).

ii) There is usually a special law which sets out its objectives, structure, and so forth. This is why the term 'statutory board' is often used — as, for example, in Kenya. The law (e.g. an Electricity Act, establishing an electricity board or corporation) gives such bodies a legal status. Technically, they are *bodies corporate*, able to enter into contracts, sue and be sued, and so on.

iii) Although the central government may provide finance for capital or to cover losses, the public corporation is expected to have a substantial amount of financial independence.

iv) Financial regulations tend to be different from those applicable to the government department. Thus, budgeting, accounting and auditing procedures are generally not the same as those which civil servants have to apply to their departments.

v) The employees in public corporations are normally not civil servants. Their terms of service, salaries paid and systems of personnel management are likely to differ in various ways from arrangements applicable to the civil service.

The public corporation model has been influential in many Third World countries largely because of the British influence. It was in Britain that this approach became accepted practice after the Second World War. Countries such as India, followed by many others (both before and after independence), followed suit from the later 1940s onwards. The appeal of the model is that it combines a measure of political control (through ministers answerable to parliament on major policy issues) with the freedom and flexibility managers need to operate in a businesslike way.

● *State companies*

These tend to have a larger measure of autonomy than the public corporation. In particular, this form of organisation is used to undertake joint ventures with private concerns — which may have a substantial share in the enterprise. Sometimes such companies are established by special laws, but normally it has been found convenient to use the existing legislation pertaining to companies in general. This type of public enterprise is of particular interest to governments which wish to operate in partnership with private companies and investors. For example, in many countries factories, hotels, garages and breweries have been established in this way. Often, such companies are subsidiaries of an 'umbrella' development corporation.

● *Operating contracts*

Hanson's fourth type of public enterprise has recently become popular again, after a period of being little used. This is an arrangement whereby the government enters into a contract with a private company to run businesses on its behalf. In the past ten years or so, the hotel industry in various countries has been influenced by this type of organisation. This trend seems likely to continue; for example, the collection of customs duties in Indonesia is now supervised by a Swiss company.

For our purposes, the most interesting type is the public corporation (PC) as at the policy level it is definitely more significant than the others, particularly since many state companies are subsidiaries of PCs, whilst operating contracts are often signed between PCs, on behalf of the government, and private companies. This PC form has been put to various uses, some being charged with a wide diversity of development functions, whilst others may be narrower in scope — e.g. river valley corporations such as USA's Tennessee Valley Authority or India's Damodar Valley Corporation,[6] or industrial development corporations.[7]

Public enterprise in practice

In public administration, it is frequently found that formal theory and practical reality are quite different matters. As far as public enterprises are concerned, this gap is quite pronounced — the law provides merely a rough guide to what is happening in the real world. Thus, there is a danger that legal forms of public enterprise will be taken too seriously so that other aspects of their nature are ignored.

To avoid this danger, it is necessary to review how public enterprises have operated in practice. By and large, observers of these organisations have not arrived at very positive conclusions. A wide range of criticisms have been made. The case of Pakistan may again be cited. Although the record of public enterprises in that country is not entirely negative in that they have made useful contributions to development, it has nevertheless been observed that:

> At present there is a general feeling in Pakistan that public sector enterprises are inefficient. It is undoubtedly true that there are quite a few public sector undertakings that are running at a loss and others whose performance cannot be regarded as satisfactory even though they may be working at a profit.[8]

In virtually all countries similar observations have been made. Whilst public enterprises originated as ways of bringing about development they have often proved in practice to be a major headache, a burden to governments rather than a valuable instrument of policy. So great has the concern been that some observers have even begun to argue for the abolition of many of these organisations, advocating, for example, 'privatisation'. This attitude is similar to that of many governments in the developed world as well (e.g. Britain where the public corporation model is currently on the retreat).

The dimensions of the public enterprise problem are complex and, again, the scope for generalisation is limited by the different characteristics of individual countries. Nevertheless, certain key issues are common to the debate, regardless of national context. It has to be recognized that the PC model, which was so widely adopted, tried to combine two distinct requirements. Combining political control and management freedom in practice has proved extremely difficult. Where the model originated, in the developed countries of Europe and North America, it has scarcely escaped criticism. When, in addition, the model is transferred to quite a different context, it is hardly surprising that it has turned out to be a mixed blessing, to use a phrase which many would regard as over-optimistic. Because of the general dissatisfaction that has existed a 'pendulum' effect may be observed. Many countries have swung uneasily from an emphasis on political control on the one hand to an assertion of management freedom on the other. When political control is strong, it may be argued that managers of enterprises lack the freedom to act in a sufficiently business-like fashion. When managers do have freedom, politicians tend to worry about losing control, especially when that freedom does not produce the desired results — whether measured in terms of profitability, quality of service or whatever. This pendulum tendency can be expressed diagramatically thus:

Political Control	————————————	Management Autonomy

In principle, every country needs to find a point on the pendulum which suits its various enterprises; in practice, finding that has proved to be very difficult.

The difficulty in finding organisational stability has been often compounded by the various weaknesses of political institutions and by the inadequacies of management. Strategies for reform need to address both of these issues.

● *Political control issues*

Autonomy may result in public enterprises (funded through taxation) embarking upon activities which are not under the control of those who funded them and legislated them into existence. Thus, whilst autonomy is to some degree necessary for effective management it is also vital that mechanisms for *accountability* and *control* also exist. Accountability may be defined as *the obligation to give a reckoning or explanation for an organisation's actions*. The laws establishing public enterprises (and especially public corporations) normally specify the following:

i) *Who* has the obligation to give a reckoning or explanation for an organisation's actions? In many political systems this would normally mean the minister responsible for a particular area of policy — for example, for an agricultural marketing board this obligation would fall on the Minister of Agriculture; for a publicly owned manufacturing industry it would be the Minister for Commerce and Industry.

ii) *The form* that accountability should take. For example, annual reports may have to be submitted, perhaps including the audited accounts of the enterprise.

iii) *The institution* to which an account is to be given. In parliamentary systems this will normally mean that the minister is required to give an account to parliament on major policy matters. However, there are many countries where parliaments do not exist and where accountability may instead be to military councils or other non-parliamentary institutions. In some parliamentary systems, there may also be parliamentary committees (as in the United Kingdom) which have specific terms of reference concerning the public enterprise sector. Thus, parliamentary control is facilitated where the minister is required by law to be accountable for the activities of a particular enterprise. Where no parliament exists some other institution (e.g. President or Military Council) may be expected to exercise control by requiring accountability from the minister (or the equivalent) whose portfolio includes the enterprise in question.

In practice, numerous problems have arisen over accountability and control. Some of the more significant ones are mentioned here.

(1) Public enterprises have actually not been very accountable at all. Some observers of the African scene have argued that in many countries this has been the result of the inherited British legal system which has required accountability in only the very broadest terms and has thus tied the hands of parliament excessively.[9] In such a context public enterprises may operate with a high degree of freedom which they may be only too ready to abuse by nepotism and political patronage.

(2) Closely connected to this has been the uncertain status of public enterprises. The 'pendulum' effect has already been mentioned. Policy has tended to swing between two extremes without ever achieving a real measure of stability. This lack of equilibrium can be viewed as in itself harmful to the accountability of public enterprises as it tends to paralyse decision making, and frustrate those institutions which are expected to be able to exercise a measure of control.

(3) Furthermore, the institutions which theoretically have the capability to exercise control may be weak or non-existent. For instance, where parliaments exist they may lack vitality, partly because of constitutional-legal constraints but also because the political realities

may make genuine review and control impossible. Many parliaments in practice have only a 'rubber stamp' function which means that very little by way of independent opinion can be expressed within them. This, in turn, will weaken the control function unless government and parliament have a shared objective in controlling the management of a particular enterprise. Zambia represented the latter approach in the early 1970s when some expatriate-dominated managements of public enterprises came under criticism from government and parliament in a more or less unified fashion.[10]

(4) The sheer proliferation of public enterprises in the less developed countries renders accountability and control difficult. Most countries by the early 1980s had a public enterprise sector which was very much larger than had been the case twenty or thirty years before. From the point of view of parliamentary control, this meant that in a relatively short time (in most countries about a ten-year period from the early 1960s to the early 1970s) the number of organisations had grown enormously within the public sector, the financial issues had grown both in scale and complexity, there had been an enormous growth in the number of people employed by the sector, and the sheer amount of legislation for parliamentarians to oversee had also increased greatly. Even strong parliaments would have found all this difficult to handle. In the Third World, the problem has been compounded by the fact that parliamentary representatives have often not possessed the knowledge (commercial, technological or whatever) to discuss public enterprise performance in an informed fashion.

Given the political circumstances facing many countries, it is difficult to see how effective arrangements for accountability and control can be established. Several countries are faced with a measure of political upheaval which makes the maintenance of stable, effective and accountable management virtually impossible (although it is surprising how much managerial continuity can sometimes be obtained as, for example, in Uganda). In these conditions, it can even be argued that it is best if politicians involve themselves with public enterprise as little as possible. There is a thin dividing line between 'control' and 'interference'. The latter may be directed at political gain or self-interest rather than the achievement of the formal goals of the enterprise. Thus the power to control can become subject to abuse and may only make mismanagement worse. The pessimism of this conclusion is justified by the evidence which exists. It is thus extremely important to look at ways of reforming systems, always bearing in mind the particular features of individual countries and the likely direction that political change will take.

108

• Management issues

A very important area of concern has been personnel management, although there are other weaknesses to consider — such as financial management and the functioning of management boards. Personnel management covers a number of matters — examples being recruitment, training, conditions of service, discipline and industrial relations.

Recruitment of personnel

On this question it will be recalled that one way in which public corporations and state companies differ from departmental enterprises is that the latter are staffed by civil servants whilst the other two types of organisation are not. Thus, the recruitment process for departmental enterprises differs in a fundamental way from that which obtains in other types of public enterprises. Public corporations and state companies have a substantial degree of autonomy from standard public service procedures. This difference is based on the assumption that the selection of staff should be carried out by the managements of enterprises themselves, with the minimum of interference from outside bodies or individuals. Only in this way, so the argument goes, can people and jobs be matched in the most efficient way possible.

There has, however, been controversy over this issue. For example, in India in the 1950s it was the subject of study by the Estimates Committee.[11] Various conclusions were reached, and some are of general interest:

i) Companies which are owned by the State should be run on business lines as far as possible. Overall management rests in the hands of the boards, which should be trusted to exercise their authority wisely and impartially in respect of staff recruitment, as in other management matters.

ii) Standardisation of procedures should be attempted in order to remove doubts in the public mind about the fairness of those procedures. There should, however, be sufficient flexibility to meet the requirements of individual enterprises.

iii) The idea of recruiting personnel directly through the Public Service Commission channel should be rejected, because it would infringe the autonomy of the companies and probably cause considerable delays in recruitment.

iv) Greater standardisation of pay scales should be attempted to prevent undue competition for recruits among various undertakings. Thus, within the public enterprise sector there should be equal pay for equal work.

Similar conclusions to these were arrived at in Kenya in the late 1970s.[12] Again the problem arises — how can the need for autonomy co-exist with the desire for political control?

A further difficulty is that it is difficult for the recruitment process to operate on the merit principle in the way that Weber intended. Departures from legal-rational criteria have been widespread in that education, experience and potential have often been set aside or given little attention; other factors, such as family connection, ethnic origin and political affiliation, have been given greater weight. Several points arise here.

i) A motive for the expansion of public enterprises was undoubtedly to create jobs which could be available for purposes of political patronage.

ii) It would be wrong to assume that enterprise managements are completely divorced from politics. Generally speaking they are not; as a result political factors are likely to be considered in the process of selecting staff.

iii) Where the environment is highly political, in the sense that political factors affect decision-making in a wide range of settings, the recruitment of public enterprise staff is unlikely to escape.

iv) In many societies there is a low level of acceptance of bureaucratic principles (such as merit recruitment); under such conditions, public enterprise will be affected in much the same way as other organisations.

Thus the conclusion may be drawn that recruitment is often not carried out in a rational or in an autonomous way. Greater or lesser autonomy would not necessarily lead to a more rational process. Again, a crucial dimension is politics which can, in practice, often stand in the way of the adoption of more rational ways of recruiting staff.

In theory the autonomy most public enterprises possess means that they can carry out *training* programmes geared to their own specific requirements. They may, of course, supplement their own efforts by recourse to central government bodies such as institutes of public administration. Some examples of public enterprises' individual training arrangements may be given:[13]

a) Indian Telephone Industries Ltd's Staff College in Bangalore for training its managers;

b) Indian Airlines' management training centre for training senior managers; also its centres for commercial, flying operations, engineering and cabin crew training;

c) The Jamaican Industrial Development Corporation's Training/ Human Resource Development Department which offers a wide range of training programmes relevant to the Corporation's work, e.g. work-study, production management;

d) Bangladesh's Institute of Bank Management which carries out training, consultancy, and research functions for the nationalised

110

commercial banks of the country as well as for the Bangladesh Bank (the monetary authority).

Another possible arrangement is to create training organisations which cater for public enterprises in a country as a whole. Sri Lanka is an example. The Public Enterprise Division of the Ministry of Finance/General Treasury runs a training programme as well as assisting public enterprises in various other ways (notably through consultancy).

Many of the problems of training for public enterprises are very similar to those obtaining generally in the Third World, for example lack of co-ordination between institutions, low level of output of people with scientific/technological knowledge and skills; a tendency to use conventional and rather inadequate techniques of training; a frequent lack of financial provision; and inadequate planning of training programmes. Detailed review of general training issues will not be attempted here but can be found in Chapter 8 (on human resources management).

Conditions of service

Here the question of uniformity again arises. The problem takes differing forms and can be posed in different ways. For example, how far should there be uniformity between different state-owned companies within the same industry? To what extent should there be uniformity between different regions of a country? To what extent should there be comparability with conditions of service in similar jobs within private enterprise? Perhaps the most important question of all is: what sort of uniformity should exist between public enterprises and the civil services?

By and large, the approach adopted has been to try to introduce a large element of uniformity in respect of salaries, fringe benefits and the like, but obviously it is not possible to achieve complete compatibility with private enterprise salaries where these are vastly superior to those pertaining in the civil service. There is often a big gap (some would say chasm) here, which tends to result in public enterprise salaries falling somewhere in between the two extremes. A particular difficulty arises where there is stiff competition to obtain the services of highly qualified people, engineers and architects being good examples. There is, then, an argument in favour of flexibility in addition to the need for uniformity. However, most countries are cautious about flexibility because of what they see as the dangers inherent in allowing public enterprise salaries to move far beyond those in the civil service, which would have the effect of draining qualified personnel from the latter. A related notion, which arises particularly in states which have attempted a socialist approach, is that public enterprises should not be allowed to form breeding grounds for a class of highly privileged technocrats and managers whose sympathies may be elitist and out of line with the official ideology. This issue has been a bone of contention in Tanzania.

Human resource planning

The implication of these various questions is that *human resource planning* becomes a very awkward task indeed. On the one hand, the various organisations need to be able to maximise their opportunities to obtain the personnel they need. On the other hand, this can only be done by striving to find some sort of compromise between the principles of flexibility and uniformity, which are potentially in conflict with one another. At the same time, a completely free market approach would not be acceptable because it may mean that the private sector dominates the process of obtaining personnel and thus may deprive both public enterprises and the civil service of their requirements.

Industrial relations

In many countries the pattern of industrial relations was originally derived from the British model, based on conflict and bargaining between trade unions on one hand and management on the other. However, a significant post-independence change has taken place in that trade unionism has to a large extent been incorporated into the State, thus considerably reducing the scope for independent action on the part of workers. The right to strike, for example, has been considerably restricted. These tendencies have, of course, affected the private sector as well but public enterprises, being closer to the centres of power, have been under particular pressure to toe the line. This has, however, sometimes resulted in quite severe tension between workers and the State. Zambia during the 1970s offers a good example of this phenomenon. The mineworkers on the copper belt, employed by companies which had recently been taken into state ownership, resisted strongly the efforts made by the Zambian government to control trade union activities.[14]

Worker participation

A related issue of some interest is the role played by public enterprises in promoting the ideas of worker participation in management. In India, for example, these ideas were introduced in the 1950s whilst both Zambia and Tanzania were strongly influenced by such thinking in the 1970s. The Indian Second Five Year Plan cogently expresses some of the typical arguments in favour of greater participation by workers:

> For the successful implementation of the Plan, increased association of labour with management is necessary. Such a measure would help in:

112

a) promoting increased productivity for the general benefit of the enterprise, the employees and the community;

b) giving employees a better understanding of their role in the working of industry and of the process of production, and

c) satisfying the worker's urge for self-expression, thus leading to industrial peace, better relations and increased co-operation.[15]

Typically, councils are set up in which managers and workers have representation. A difficulty which has arisen concerns the scope of the activities of such councils. The Zambian case is again a useful one to cite. In that country councils created in the early 1970s were not permitted to discuss matters of investment policy, financial control and economic planning; in these important spheres management's powers to run the enterprise without significant worker involvement remained unchanged.[16]

Generally speaking, these experiments have not proved a major success. Confusion and inefficiency have often resulted, leading to abandonment of worker participation and reversion to conventional styles of management. Part of the problem has been that workers have mistrusted management's motives, seeing the hidden hand of managerial control behind the rhetoric of participation. These setbacks, however, have not resulted in a complete rejection of what the principles of workers' participation may have to offer. There remains, for example, an active interest in various European experiments which have taken place (e.g. in Yugoslavia and Sweden). The International Labour Organisation (ILO) has also had some influence upon industrial relations in less developed countries, and advocates the adoption of a more participatory approach. Thus, the issue of the involvement of workers in the management of public enterprises is likely to surface again.

Planning and public enterprise

Apart from these (and other) questions of personnel management, there are other management issues to be considered. Management planning in public enterprises inevitably differs somewhat from that which is generally possible with private enterprise. The main difference concerns the diversity of objectives which public corporations, state companies and the like have been set up to achieve. Whereas private enterprises may be largely concerned with the objective of profitability, the situation facing many public enterprises is a very different one, especially public corporations responsible for running public utilities. Much of this explanation lies in politics, as Hanson has noted in his discussion of the limited value of an 'economic rationality' approach in analysing and evaluating the activities of the public sector in less developed countries.[17]

Management planning for such enterprises has to combine two broad perspectives which it should try to reconcile as far as possible. On the one hand, it will normally have to look outwards in the direction of development planning at the national level because it is within that framework that its objectives will largely be determined, in theory at least. At the same time, planning is a fundamental function which has to be performed for the efficient internal management of the enterprise. Obviously, these two perspectives can be conflicting where the objectives set nationally might turn out to be impossible of attainment, given levels of efficiency existing within the enterprise. It should also be borne in mind that development planning in general has not been a great success, as noted in Chapter 3. Public enterprises have been affected by these general problems more than most organisations because they have often been regarded as crucial tools of state intervention, particularly where they were expected to control the 'commanding heights' of the economy.

• *Public enterprises and national plans*
Beyond these general considerations, however, there have been other serious difficulties which have applied with particular force as far as public enterprises are concerned. Some of the more important ones are mentioned here.

(1) The relationship between individual enterprises and the planning process has often been a very blurred one. In Lesotho, for example, few enterprises undertook any planning which reflected national planning concerns.[18] Thus, in many cases public enterprises have often operated with a substantial measure of autonomy. However, this was largely an unintentional consequence of a failure to assess clearly what kind of relationship should exist. From the point of view of the advocates of a closely planned economy such a degree of autonomy is clearly not desirable as it may result in the enterprises pursuing policies at variance with what is contained in the national plan. A useful example here (and one which has been a matter of controversy in a number of states) is the relationship between technology and employment, where the national plan may stress the need for labour-intensive methods of production (employing a lot of people) whilst the individual enterprise may opt for imported capital-intensive technologies which do little to create additional jobs.

(2) Weak integration between public enterprises and national planning may occur because enterprise managers may find it strategic to avoid

communication with the central planners in order to maintain autonomy. This may result in flows of information from enterprises to the planners being quite inadequate for purposes of detailed and analytical planning. Thus, planning has been limited in its effectiveness because reliable information is lacking. 'Planning without facts' is a phrase which describes this phenomenon quite well.

(3) As noted earlier, the whole question of enterprise objectives has been problematic, especially in countries pursuing socialist ideologies where planning authorities have felt obliged to adopt strategies which emphasise not just market forces but also the need to take into account objectives such as redistribution of wealth, geographical coverage of service provision, and employment creation. But even in non-socialist states such as Papua New Guinea this has been an important issue. Enterprise managements, however, may have quite a different approach because they will wish either to make a profit or at least to achieve self-sufficiency. Indeed, government policy may require them not to make a loss because subsidy funding may not be available. In these circumstances, there is likely to be a considerable measure of conflict between planners and public enterprise managers. This may, of course, not be entirely harmful if the outcome is a better understanding between the two sides resulting perhaps in a more realistic approach to strategic questions. What has, however, happened quite frequently has been that the public enterprise has attempted to achieve a multiplicity of objectives, many of them unconnected with profitability, to the point where heavy subsidies have been needed merely for survival. This is one of the reasons why critics have recently argued that the profit motive has been treated too dismissively. Whilst this argument may have been somewhat overstated, a more appropriate balance does appear to be needed between the need for profitability or at least self-sufficiency at the enterprise level (in many enterprises, if not all) and the need to achieve other objectives which governments may regard as vital. This is of greater importance now because the development crisis currently being experienced has greatly narrowed the financial choices available to many governments. For example, shortage of foreign exchange has been a major constraint for some considerable time now.

(4) The sheer rapidity of the growth of the public sector has also raised severe problems for planners. It was often felt desirable to co-ordinate the activities of all these new creations but the planning agencies were themselves new and lacked the capacity to cope with the numerous pressures. For example, in the Tanzanian case, President Nyerere noted in a 1969 circular that the rapid spread of public corporations had not been linked closely with comprehensive planning, a failure which he saw as leading to innumerable problems such as unclear lines of responsibility, undue complexity of structure and over-

115

lapping jurisdictions.[19] Thus, the ideal arrangement by which planners monitor public enterprise performance and either suggest or require modification, as appropriate, was often either not possible at all or else carried out in such a rudimentary way as to be almost devoid of meaning.

● *Planning within public enterprises*
There has been growing concern that 'internal' planning has been neglected. The function of project appraisal, for example, is a vital aspect of planning which has often been neglected or else carried out in very superficial fashion. The result has been a plethora of projects which should probably not have been undertaken. Several contributory factors can be mentioned, but one important one has been the shortage of indigenous expertise in many countries. This has led to the use of foreign consultants who may, however, not be able to do much better and may even make all manner of false assumptions about environments with which they lack familiarity. Some of the literature about public sector management in Tanzania, for instance, is critical of the role of foreign consultants.[20]

Project appraisal is only part of the problem. For example, high-powered appraisal is irrelevant where decisions are made on the basis of political expediency or because of 'kick backs' paid to leading political figures. The latter is especially liable to occur where private enterprise enters into partnership with the public sector. Thus, political considerations may force managers to look upon planning in any real sense as an impossibility or at least as an irrelevant activity which will only waste scarce resources of time, staff and money.

Case-study: Tanzania
A useful case-study of enterprise planning is provided by the Tanzanian National Development Corporation (NDC).[21] This body was obliged to formulate its investment planning proposals within a framework provided by the national plan and various statements of policy by the Minister of Commerce and Industries. Thus, eight criteria for project selection were identified; these had to be taken into account by the NDC's Project Appraisal Committee when considering the viability of projects. Two categories of criteria were specified:-

Primary criteria, which had to be satisfied by *all* projects because of their importance to the economy as a whole:
● profitability
● national cost/benefit
● foreign exchange effects

Secondary criteria also had to be considered in the following order of importance:

- employment
- location
- industrial linkages
- budgetary impact
- investable surplus

Thus, the NDC management had to consider a whole host of factors which extended beyond those normally taken into account by privately owned companies. Bearing in mind the newness of the NDC — it was a post-independence creation — and its inexperienced management, it is not surprising that difficulties presented themselves, especially where politicians took a strong interest and tried to interfere in the planning process.

How far is the Tanzanian case typical? Clearly the ideological factor has often been less pronounced elsewhere. Nevertheless, in many instances managers were faced with a mixture of factors which their private sector counterparts would have found decidedly unfamiliar. Thus, the normal uncertainties of planning in unpredictable business environments (a growing problem in all countries today) have been compounded by the expectation that individual enterprises, sometimes with little relevant expertise, can plan their future activities within a framework of highly diverse and sometimes controversial criteria. Because of this, it has been argued that a more business-related way of planning should be adopted. In the public enterprise case, however, it is inevitable that additional criteria will have to enter the picture (e.g. where an Electricity Board may have to provide energy to certain areas at a loss because of certain urgent needs facing particular communities).

The call for change

One of the main themes of the 1980s has been what many writers and consultants have referred to as 'privatisation' of the activities of the public sector. Confusion over terminology may occur, so clarification is needed. Goran Hyden, in his book on Africa, prefers the term 'denationalisation' whilst the World Bank currently seems to have opted for the broad term 'liberalisation' which connotes a general opening up of economies to market forces. In this section, the term 'privatisation' will be used, bearing in mind that in the literature a variety of terms are employed.

A starting point for most of these advocates of change is the generally disappointing record of public enterprise which has already been noted.

117

For example, they attack the widespread use of subsidies for public enterprises which are unable to achieve self-sufficiency (i.e. make enough money to keep themselves in business without outside help). This general disquiet has led to a search for solutions. In this connection, the possibility of reducing the scope of the public sector by handing over certain activities to private enterprise is being considered and advocated by a number of analysts, a view which many Third World governments and aid agencies have also adopted. This seems to be part of a world-wide trend. It was recently reported that 'seventeen of the world's twenty most populous nations are initiating measures to privatise state owned industry' and that market economies have a better record then those carefully planned, citing Africa and Latin America in particular.[22] Paul Cook has recently reported on a USAID survey which obtained the views of 65 governments in less developed countries. Of these, 61 responded that they were interested in privatisation as a policy option which could be a means of improving performance.[23]

• The advocates of privatisation

Goran Hyden

Hyden's advocacy of what he prefers to call 'denationalisation' is particularly interesting because of his long record as an observer of the development scene in Africa. His views can hardly be discounted as those of a 'fly by night' consultant since his academic and research career has included over twenty years in East Africa. Having been relatively optimistic about the role of the State during the 1960s and 1970s, a change of perspective later occurred, as illustrated by a book he published in 1983, known as *No Shortcuts to Progress*. His argument in this book runs as follows.[24]

As far as Africa is concerned, there are few grounds for optimism about public enterprise performance. Policies involving a high measure of state intervention are misplaced because where society is still characterised by peasant modes of production the environment is not conducive to the business-like running of enterprises. He uses the term 'economy of affection' to depict this sort of environment, which he sees as one in which, for example, it is relatively easy for individual employees to divert public resources for their own private purposes, a further example of deviation from the Weberian model, in which there is a sharp distinction between public and private property.

From this standpoint, he concludes that it is necessary to find 'alternative institutional approaches' to public enterprise. Part of the answer he sees as lying in a significant running down of the public sector and a transfer of all sorts of activities into private hands. He

118

links this with a greater general emphasis on market forces, thus helping to build up effective institutions by encouraging people to think in a more business-like way. The market, he argues, also has the advantage of being administratively simpler and more flexible than the orthodox government machinery. To sum up, he suggests that such measures will produce greater efficiency and thus help Africa move towards greater self-reliance.

The World Bank

Hyden's argument is in some ways a rather complex theoretical one, involving the somewhat tricky concept of the 'economy of affection'. However, the Bank's approach does not carry with it the same theoretical trappings even though its prescriptions have tended to be quite similar to Hyden's. Recent years have seen a major rethinking of the Bank's policies, privatisation being viewed as a reform to which high priority should be attached in many countries. The so called 'Berg Report' on Africa is an example.[25] It argues that many functions currently being run by various forms of public enterprise could be usefully transferred to private hands. Key examples given are agricultural marketing, transport, civil works and drug distribution. The encouragement of the private sector would be possible through a scaling down of the public sector activities in these fields.

This type of thinking was quite well illustrated by this comment on civil works:

> No better training exists for construction industry entrepreneurs than the use of small contractors, and it is highly likely that greater efficiency will come from contracting out such activities as road maintenance and building repair. There are, of course, problems — in particular, the development of simple contract letting procedures and controls. But these problems are easier to solve than are those involved in government maintenance.[26]

One of the principal mechanisms the Bank uses to persuade governments to adopt such policies is *Structural Adjustment Lending* (SAL). This involves linking the provision of finance with a commitment by governments receiving aid to undertake reforms of a kind the Bank wishes to see take place. This does not always mean privatisation, but in many cases that is part of the package. To this end, the Bank's headquarters in Washington has units which ensure that a private sector perspective is brought into the scrutiny of projects.[27]

Recent examples of Bank projects with direct links to privatisation include a Malawian wood production project, whilst in the same country assistance is being given to 'help reorient future housing development in the country toward a market based system.'[28] Projects with a similar emphasis on privatisation are being implemented in Turkey, Brazil, Malaysia and Nepal. In the case of Turkey, for example, one of the key activities is 'to explore the potential for selective privatisation of State Economic Enterprises.'[29] Privatisation is currently even on the agenda for countries which are often thought of as inclining towards socialism, Tanzania and Zimbabwe being examples. In most cases, Bank influence has been a major factor in prompting changes of policy.

● *Arguments against privatisation*

It is, however, worth raising the question of whether privatisation might not be a case of the prescription being worse than the disease. In other words, it may turn out to be not so much a solution as a cause of further problems of a different kind.

Some of the counter-arguments are really quite similar to those employed previously in support of public enterprise's role in the economy. They include:

i) Privatisation will make it harder to plan adequately. In theory, the close linkages of public enterprises to the planning machinery facilitate effective planning, a benefit which would be removed by privatisation.

ii) Public enterprises are often needed to pursue objectives besides purely commercial ones. Privatisation, by emphasising profitability, is likely to mean the subordination of these wider objectives. This may well be regarded as too expensive a price to pay in many instances.

iii) In the absence of an indigenous entrepreneurial class, privatisation may give economic opportunities to foreigners, multi-national corporations, etc. This may be politically unacceptable to many governments.

These arguments have not entirely disappeared with the emergence of arguments favourable to privatisation. At a recent conference on 'The Southern African Economy After Apartheid' a number of contributions argued for an approach which would necessitate a high level of state intervention and ownership. Seidman, for example, concluded that there would be a 'need for an alternative strategy which calls for more, not less, government planning and intervention.'[30] The various arguments are of some complexity, much depending on the situation facing individual countries. To be fair to the Bank, too, its approach seems now to be less strident and dogmatic than it was in the early 1980s, partly in response to the reluctance many governments show in adopting policies which they see as being contrary to the interest of their people.

120

Conclusions

There are undoubtedly cases where privatisation could be a genuine alternative policy worth pursuing, but the multiplicity of public enterprise objectives means that it is far from being always a suitable solution. There are numerous activities where a switch from public ownership could be shown to be undesirable (e.g. the provision of most essential services). What seems to be needed is a highly selective approach to privatisation, combined with greater attention to the improvement of public enterprise management. At the moment, it is not entirely clear how and why management has gone wrong and, therefore, there is a lack of clarity about what should be done. Further investigation of these questions is clearly needed, along the lines suggested throughout this chapter. As part of the inquiry, it is desirable that account should be taken of the minority of success stories to see what the key ingredients have been. For example, Kenya's Tea Development Authority has a largely favourable record from which valuable lessons could be derived[31], whilst the World Bank cites the Senegalese case as a possible example to follow[32]. In these, and other successful cases, a vital factor has been the striking of a stable balance between accountability and management autonomy.

Discussion questions

1   Identify six public enterprises with which you are familiar and list as many objectives of each one as you can.

2   What are the main arguments for and against privatisation of public enterprises? Find out if there is a policy on privatisation in your country and, if so, outline its main features.

3   What are the main problems which have arisen in planning the activities of public enterprises?

4   Imagine that you are a consultant asked to explore what can be done to improve the performance of public enterprise management in a country. Prepare a list of *at least ten* issues you would wish to examine in carrying out such an assignment.

121

7 Local Government and Field Administration

Introduction

Public administration is primarily concerned with the activities undertaken by central governments, and the content of this book reflects that fact. However, our concern is not solely with administrative work performed by officials in capital cities. It is also important to review the structures which are not found at the heart of the system of government, but which function elsewhere. This means discussing a variety of institutions operating in a diversity of environments, ranging from the hot, dry, thinly populated deserts which make up such a large part of the total land areas of many countries (e.g. Botswana, Burkina-Faso) to highly urbanised centres which have large populations and provide significant services for an economically important region (e.g. Karachi which, whilst not the political capital of Pakistan, has massive economic significance). It has been universally found that even in the smallest countries where there is a strong central government, adequate control of the 'periphery' requires a system of administration which is effective in the various districts, provinces, and so on.

The term 'decentralisation' is commonly used to describe the various arrangements which in this chapter will be looked at in detail. There is some dispute amongst scholars about the use of this term.[1] Some (e.g. Maddick, Smith) are of the view that it should be used to describe two distinct sets of arrangements. First, there is 'local government' which involves some sort of locally established assembly (normally termed a 'council') with, usually, elected members. This, crucially, has a substantial element of autonomy from central government, even though it is linked to it in different ways. Secondly, there is 'field administration' which consists of officials appointed by the centre but posted to the 'field' (district, province, etc.) to act as central government's representatives. These officials vary in the extent to which they can freely exercise discretion in the performance of their duties. In this view of decentralisation, then, there are two elements: a) *devolution* —

local government, a form of political decentralisation: and b) *decon-centration* — field administration, or administrative decentralisation.

This way of seeing matters has been challenged by Mawhood who believes that 'decentralisation' can only be meaningfully used when looking at local government. To him, deconcentration is of quite a different nature involving as it does the use of centrally appointed civil servants (in the main) who are posted to the field to represent the central government and defend its interests (supporting development policies, providing intelligence reports on dissident politicians, etc.) He therefore uses decentralisation in a narrower way than do Maddick and Smith. In this chapter, the terms devolution and deconcentration will both be used, bearing in mind, however, that in reality deconcentration may turn out to be more about the exercise of central control than the granting of autonomy to local institutions or administrators.

Local government

The experience of local government in less developed countries closely parallels that of public enterprises, as reviewed in chapter 6. It will be recalled that the conflicting aims of autonomy and control have made it important to find an appropriate balance between them, and that it has been difficult to achieve this goal. Much the same can be said of local government. Like public enterprises, there has been a continuing instability of organisational life which has, in itself, been a problem of no little significance. Recently interest in local government autonomy has revived in some countries. But the question of how long this will last, before central control re-emerges on the scene, has to be raised. We will explore some of the underlying features of these problems.

The issue of local-level participation in public affairs has emerged as a major theme in development studies over the past fifteen years or so.[2] In this connection, local government may be regarded as one of the crucial channels through which people may participate in decision making within their areas. Whilst it is probably true that 'village government' may be impossible to establish in a meaningful sense in the modern state, it is normally considered feasible to set up a system of councils which have a sufficiently local basis for people to identify with them as significant elements in their lives. In numerous countries the district has been seen as an appropriate geographical level at which to establish local government (or local authorities). Typically, this would mean a single council serving about 500,000 people within an area of perhaps 2,000 sq km — although obviously conditions vary a great deal from one country to another.

• Arguments in favour of local government

Numerous arguments have been given in support of local government of a reasonably strong kind (i.e. with substantial autonomy from central government). There has been a mixture of pragmatic and ethical perspectives. On the pragmatic side it is often argued that development projects and programmes often fail because the people most affected, those living within the local area, are not allowed to play a part in deciding how the various activities should be carried out. This seems to be particularly true in cases where changes in people's behaviour may be required, for example in attempts to change agricultural practices. This argument has often employed terms like 'bottom up' and 'top down' to refer to two different approaches. On the one hand, proposals for development which are 'bottom up' tend to take into account the views of local people, for instance in the siting of a school or health centre, whilst the term 'top down' suggests a more hierarchical and somewhat authoritarian style in which most decisions are made at central government level in a fashion quite unacceptable to the people directly affected. In some ways this type of argument is similar to that employed in support of community development, as reviewed in chapter 5. However, it can also be used as a justification for local government, and often has been.

Added to this, there is the argument that was used by many colonial administrations in the 1940s and 1950s. Local government was justified then as a means of political education, so that people could first learn the rudiments of political activity at the district (or equivalent) level prior to embarking on national political activities (the latter was often envisaged only as a very long-term possibility). This argument has similarities with those which were used in Western countries in the nineteenth century; Smith quotes de Tocqueville and John Stuart Mill as examples.[3] Maddick is perhaps the best known exponent of this view as applied to development. His book on decentralisation, published in the early 1960s, has acquired the status of a classical statement of how local government can promote a better understanding of the meaning of political life in developing countries because it offers a training in citizenship.[4]

The argument for local government, however, has an ethical element as well, and is linked to questions of human rights and democracy. There is a widely accepted notion that people should have the opportunity to participate in public affairs, especially where they are directly affected by whatever decisions are made and implemented. Thus, the stifling of local participation can be condemned from an ethical, as well as a pragmatic, standpoint. Arguments of this sort can be traced back to political philosophers such as Mill and Locke. However, not all democratic theorists can be cited in support of local government.

124

Rousseau argued that attention to local concerns may be interpreted as divisive, a diversion from the exercise of democratic rights at the national level. Most of these arguments have been open to controversy. The educational argument, for example, has been rejected as paternalistic.[5] However, they have been mentioned here, not because of their validity or otherwise, but because of their influence. Apart from these rather theoretical viewpoints, similar arguments have also been employed by those closer to the practical reality of the development scene. For many years now, development plans, if only by convention, have pointed to the importance of local government within the overall planning process.[6] Political leaders, too, often acknowledge the role local government can play when addressing public meetings, rallies and so on. One of the reasons for this is, of course, that national leaders often rely on local leaders for support and the latter's political 'arena' is often the district council rather than parliament.

There is, however, a substantial gap between rhetoric and reality to be examined here. What planners and politicians say about local participation may have very little connection with conditions actually prevailing at the 'grassroots' level. There is a distinction to be made between what it may be convenient for leaders to say in public and what may be happening in reality. A regime may, for example, wish to convince donors that it strongly believes in local government in order to improve its chances of receiving aid but it may well avoid converting such beliefs into practical policies of institutional development at the local level. Donors such as the World Bank and USAID have experienced this sort of discrepancy between rhetoric and reality in several countries.

● *The practical issues of local government*
In reviewing the experience of the less developed countries, much of our attention will be on the rural areas as that is, after all, where most people in these countries live. This will not, however, mean completely neglecting the urban scene because there are close connections between urban and rural centres. Towns, for example, are important providers of services to rural areas in many cases whilst council areas often contain both rural and urban areas. Urban local government also requires consideration because local institutions have frequently been more fully developed in the towns and cities than they have in the countryside. This is true, for example, of most countries in Eastern and Southern Africa.

A further consideration to note at the outset of our discussion is the general tendency towards centralisation (the opposite of decentralisation) which has been experienced in most countries during the last

25 years or so. There are a variety of reasons why this happened. However, in many cases political factors have played a major part. In Africa, for example, several regimes have felt their positions to be highly insecure, particularly where they faced strong opposition movements based in certain geographical regions. Nigeria, Ghana, Uganda and Kenya have all been relevant examples at various points in their history. The low level of legitimacy of these regimes, in other words, led them to believe that a policy of decentralisation was too risky because of the possibility of losing power as a result. In these circumstances, such governments tended to concentrate power at the centre, with a minimum of autonomy for local government; which became more and more incapacitated as a result. The tightening of central control in this way has certainly been a significant trend. However, it is also an avoidable and reversible one, as can be seen in cases such as Botswana and Tanzania.

• Ideological factors

A factor worth consideration here is that of ideology. Clearly, ideologies can have implications for the kinds of institutions a regime decides to create to facilitate local participation. This has certainly been true in some parts of Africa: for example in Zambia and Tanzania ideas of 'Zambian Humanism' and 'Ujamaa Socialism' have at various times influenced the approach adopted, whilst the People's Republic of China (especially during the Mao era) is an important Asian case. The dilemma often posed in such cases is that such governments want strong local participation which is supportive of their particular ideological standpoints, but may become uneasy if these grassroots institutions become focal points for dispute and confrontation with the centre. This appears to be a particularly serious problem in many socialist-inclined countries, leading to an emphasis on *de facto* central control — as in the Zambian case. Thus, such regimes experience particular pressures towards centralisation, which can be regarded as additional to those experienced in most regimes regardless of their ideological stance.

A further point is that ideologies are important, but not usually overwhelmingly so; other factors more directly of a politically self-interested kind are probably of rather more significance in most cases. To put it bluntly, the Zambian government's policy-making process clearly involves ideological issues, but the desires of leading politicians to maintain and, if possible, improve their political and economic standing, are likely to carry more weight. At the same time, such ideologies cannot simply be ignored; they are part of the policy-making equation out of which strategies for local participation have emerged in various countries.

126

• *Historical factors*

Most Third World states came to independence with some kind of local government structure inherited from colonial rule. In the case of the British colonial possessions, India stands out as an example of early development, at least in urban settings (Bombay, Calcutta and others had a form of local government in the nineteenth century[7]), whereas in much of Africa little of significance happened before the Second World War. In 1947, however, a notable breakthrough took place when the Colonial Office decided to introduce what it described as an 'efficient and democratic system of local government' in each of its imperial possessions.[8] This dual emphasis on efficiency and democracy was explained by the Colonial Secretary, Arthur Creech Jones, thus:

> I use these words because they seem to me to contain the kernel of the whole matter: *local* because the system of government must be capable of managing the local services in a way which will help raise the standard of living; and *democratic* because it must not only find a place for the growing class of educated men, but at the same time command the respect and support of the mass of the people.[9]

A major concern of the British was to proceed gradually, with a strongly felt belief that local government could provide a political education whilst at the same time allowing Africans to learn something about administrative activity through working with and for the new bodies. A further consideration, related to this, was that central control and guidance were important elements; at the district level, the District Commissioners (in most territories) had to play the roles of both tutor or guide and inspector to local government. This was partly in order to avoid mismanagement as far as possible (preventing wastage of funds etc.) but also to try to promote the gradual institutional development which the British government at that time wished to see. Without this form of development it was thought unlikely that other goals, such as democratic participation and economic development, could be pursued effectively.

Following on from this policy announcement (often known as the 1947 dispatch), various local government structures were created in most parts of British-ruled Africa (there were some exceptions, Botswana being one). In several cases, existing structures were given a more powerful status (e.g. Kenya) whilst in others it was a question of starting from virtually nothing (e.g. Lesotho). This implied that a delicate balancing act had to be undertaken. Greater power for district councils (or whatever they might be called — precise titles varied) was considered desirable but was seen as risky, both politically and financially, unless arrangements for central control were also made. Added to this, there was the problem that financial resources were limited almost everywhere, thus making it difficult for highly visible achievements to register in the public mind and give the new bodies a much needed aura of legitimacy. Finally, of course, the political climate was undergoing rapid change simultaneously with the implementation of the new policy. This had the inevitable consequence that local government became part of a wider political arena in which the various nationalist parties were pursuing independence as soon as possible, an objective which was in conflict with the gradualism implicit in the colonial policies.

In much of Asia the pattern was quite similar, except that rather more had happened before the Second World War in such important countries as India, which became independent in the same year as the Creech Jones dispatch saw the light of day. However, the Malaysian case, as presented by Norris, indicates close parallels with the African experience. A programme was set in motion soon after the restoration of British rule in 1945 (the then Malaya had been under enemy occupation during the war). Norris sees the parallels with the African policy as follows:

> It was in some respects idealistic, being seen as a constructive step towards gradual self government, and in others pragmatic, hopefully reducing and redirecting political pressure at the local level. In these respects the experience of Malaya reflected that of other British colonies, notably in East and Central Africa and in the Eastern and Western Regions of Nigeria.[10]

Further, as in most of Africa, in Malaysia the nurturing of local government took place in a difficult climate of rapid political mobilisation and growing conflicts exacerbated by ethnic rivalries.

The British inevitably tried to introduce the type of local government with which they were familiar at home. There was, however, one important difference which arose from their desire to ensure that central government control was adequately preserved. The district administration, usually headed by the District Commissioner, was never part of the British local government scene but was of some importance in most parts of the empire.

The French case can be briefly summarised. As with the British, significant change only took place during the late 1940s and 1950s. Another parallel was that the home model influenced the thinking of policy-makers in the colonies. Mawhood, writing of French-speaking Cameroon, observes that:

> Commune administration, as imported from France in the 1950s, came as something almost completely new. Very little local representation had been built into the earlier system, which was essentially

one of direct administration by European officials with African 'chiefs' used as their subordinate agents.[11]

As pressures for change developed (coming from the nationalist parties and from various international sources such as the United Nations) attempts were made to introduce a more representative form. The results naturally varied but the general tendency was for them to be modest in scale whilst central administrative control (through the equivalent of District Commissioners, often termed 'Chefs de Commune') was perhaps even more emphatically brought to bear than in the British possessions.[12]

Post-independence experiences

Although some recent work is optimistic in tone, the pattern which has emerged in most countries since independence inclines one towards pessimism. Various general tendencies can be discerned, although the precise picture naturally varies from one country to another. As already noted, there have been tricky political questions associated with local government. In some cases, such as Lesotho and Uganda, the party governing at the centre had less representation within local government than it wanted and decided to assert central government power in response.

The Lesotho case serves well as an illustration. In 1965, one year before independence, the Basotho National Party (BNP) under the leadership of Chief Leabua Jonathan, won a General Election, defeating the opposition Basutoland Congress Party. The latter party, however, held control in all nine of the country's district councils. The stage could hardly have been better set for a bitter tussle between central and local government, in which arguments about mismanagement, financial irregularities and political sabotage featured prominently. The conflict, however, did not become a protracted one because the BNP-controlled parliament proceeded to abolish local government in 1968. It is only now in the process of being revived.[13] This somewhat extreme case illustrates a common problem: so often political conflict at national level had profound, and often negative, consequences for local government. Whilst few countries went as far as actually abolishing it, in a number of cases local government emerged after the first decade of independence in a less healthy condition than that in which it had started.

• Financial factors

Political considerations have undoubtedly been paramount, but other factors need attention. A second set of issues concerns local government finance. Various problems can be readily observed.[14] The weak revenue base of local government is one factor to which attention has often been drawn. Rondinelli and Cheema base the following comment on analysis of a number of Third World states, 'Local governments and subnational administrative units in most developing countries lack both the resources and the authorities to raise sufficient revenues to carry out the tasks transferred from the centre'.[15] Thus, inadequacy of revenue can be seen as a major constraint hindering effective local government in many countries. Often, sources of revenue directly available to councils are of a relatively insignificant sort: cesses (taxes on crops marketed), market fees and the like. Further, some important sources of revenue have been transferred from the local to central government since independence, an example being Kenya's Graduated Personal Tax which until its transfer had been the main type of revenue collected for local authorities within the districts.[16] Allied to this removal of key revenue sources, weakness has also stemmed from the ineffective collection of taxes and other forms of revenue from members of the public, especially in remote rural areas and where support for government is weak or virtually non-existent.

Of course, whether or not revenue is adequate can only be understood within the context of what local government spends its money on, and how it manages its finances. Often the financial resources available make it impossible for local government to provide the services expected of it (e.g. primary education, public health, markets, minor roads). This problem has been exacerbated in two main ways. First, political pressures have often resulted in councils embarking upon a number of schemes which were over-ambitious, given the existing (and foreseeable) revenue base. Secondly, there has certainly been a tendency for financial mismanagement to occur, which has made it easier for corruption to flourish. This has weakened the financial health of local government, whilst simultaneously reducing public confidence in its developmental value. Arguments such as these have often been given by central government to justify tighter control.

In a number of cases, local government has virtually reached the bankruptcy stage, becoming heavily dependent on central government support to survive. Where central government's financial condition is itself poor, the prospects for local government become doubly grim. Faced with this dilemma, it is not surprising that central government has tried to exercise a greater measure of control, thus further reducing local government autonomy. This point is obvious enough in relatively wealthy states such as Britain (where similar problems have arisen), but is much more so in poor states where central budgetary authorities are facing severe pressures under conditions of economic recession. It remains to be seen whether recently revived interest in decentralisation can reverse these tendencies in a concrete way. There are some positive signs on the horizon but little evidence yet of definite results being achieved; on the one hand governments may express an interest in reform, but it is quite another matter for them to take appropriate measures.

- • *Issues of personnel*
Local government has also experienced problems in the field of personnel. The way any organisation is staffed is obviously vital. What makes the case of local government a special one is that central-local relations play a major part. Central government is likely to want staff who are satisfactory from its particular point of view, whilst the council members (especially of the elected variety) are very likely to want to be involved as well. Again, there have been a variety of approaches adopted in dealing with this problem, but certain broad trends stand out. The colonial experience is again relevant because the introduction of British and French systems has often been an important influence. In some countries, however, substantial departures have taken place. Where the latter has happened the motives have generally been associated with the desire to assert central government control. Personnel issues also closely parallel those of financial management; again, the political environment is an important ingredient to be discussed.

Local government personnel administration is usefully considered in terms of a three-fold typology: separate, integrated and unified. Not all countries can be fitted precisely into each of these three types as many operate with a mixture of two or even all three of them. Nevertheless it is helpful to look at the issues in this way in order to illustrate the range of possible variations between systems, and to indicate the problems which can arise.

i) The *separate* system is one in which each local authority is able to appoint and dismiss its own personnel, which cannot be transferred elsewhere by any central body. In principle, this system is one which is characterised by a high level of local government autonomy.

ii) On the other hand, an *integrated* system is one in which personnel working in local government are simply doing so within the framework of the national public service. They are civil servants and can be transferred, both to other local authorities and to other government departments, by the bodies responsible for the civil service as a whole (e.g. public service commission, directorate of personnel).

iii) Finally, the *unified* system is one where local authority personnel are part of a special career service for all local authorities in the country. Personnel are thus transferable from one authority to another, but are not part of the national civil service. In this system, there may be a commission established to regulate the appointment of personnel to local authorities.

Within each of these systems there are, of course, variations and in several countries a mixture can be found as, for example, in Kenya where senior appointments are a central government matter but junior staff may still be appointed by individual local authorities, as in the separate system.

Certain advantages and disadvantages are observable for all three systems. The separate enhances the autonomy of local government but is open to abuse in the forms of nepotism, patronage and the like, whilst the poverty of many local authorities can make it difficult for them to offer competitive salaries.

The integrated system has the advantage that employment conditions, pay and so on, will be in line with those of other civil servants. The disadvantages boil down to questions of loyalty: a centrally appointed civil servant is likely to feel unable to commit himself fully to the performance and objectives of the local authority to which he has been posted especially where there is considerable central-local conflict. Thus, autonomy can be undermined, and the problems associated with over-centralisation may be incurred.

There is quite a lot to be said in favour of the unified system. After all, it goes a long way towards providing adequate conditions of service whilst largely avoiding difficulties in regard to loyalties. The dangers of nepotism and patronage may also be avoided, or at least reduced. The difficulties which have so far arisen seem to have been mainly ones of implementation. Some local authorities have resented not being directly involved in the recruitment process, whilst it may prove difficult to establish a reasonably impartial recruiting body to satisfy all parties (trade unions, political parties, local authorities, etc.) However, given the nature of the problems facing most countries the unified system seems to offer the best prospects. The Botswana case may yet demonstrate this point, notwithstanding the early implementation problems faced when it adopted this system in 1973.[17]

There are, of course, a wide range of other considerations which concern local authority personnel. Morale, for example, is often low, especially where working conditions are poor, disciplinary practices are often in need of reform, and so on. Yet these issues also face central government, albeit in a slightly different form. As such, it is appropriate to leave discussion of them to the next chapter.

● *The autonomy debate*

Looking again at local government as a whole, it can be seen that there is widespread dissatisfaction with existing levels of performance. There have been various views adopted about what action should be taken. A good deal of the debate centres on the issue of autonomy. On the one hand, there are those who advocate the adoption of what has been termed the 'classical model' of local government. Mawhood, following a strong British tradition of thought, breaks this model down into five components.[18]

> A local body should exist which was constitutionally separate from government, and was responsible for a significant range of local services.
> — It should have its own treasury, a separate budget and accounts, and its own taxes to produce a substantial part of its revenue.
> — It should have its own qualified staff, with hire-and-fire powers over them, though there could be secondments of government officers to fill some of the top posts at first.
> — Decision making on policy and internal procedure should be in the hands of a majority elected council.
> — Finally, the central government administrators should be external advisors and inspectors, having no role within the local authority.

The model, whilst accepting that there can be a role for central government to play, places a strong emphasis on autonomy. Advocates of it have rarely been naive enough to assume that it can be introduced overnight, and have generally argued for a gradualist or incrementalist approach to its adoption. Some, such as Mawhood, have seen its applicability as being dependent upon cultural or traditional factors. He argues, for example, that such factors mean that the classical model has less chance of widespread adoption in Asia than in Africa because traditions of hierarchy and centralisation are stronger in the former than in the latter, where in many places (e.g. Kenya, Uganda) strong traditions of local self-help can be traced back to pre-colonial times.[19] Thus, the arguments for the classical model should not be viewed as simplistic because its advocates often duly acknowledge the complexities involved.

These arguments are, however, quite distinct from a different type of reasoning which tends to see more to be gained by accepting the importance of central government's role and working towards an adequate form of partnership between the centre and the locality. In this view, the classical model is regarded as an unattainable ideal which is therefore not worth pursuing in less developed countries. For instance, Harry J. Friedman argues that it is possible to achieve a 'successful balancing act' in which the dual requirements of 'limited participation' at the local level and 'central control', which he sees as often essential for good implementation, can be reconciled.

He argues this case by reference to research conducted by Hadden in India.[20] The term *controlled decentralisation* was adopted by this researcher to describe the nature of this 'balancing act'. In the case she describes, a rural electrification programme in north India, an attempt was made to decentralise decision making partially to a local committee — the District Agricultural Production Committee (DAPC), which consisted of local politicians, administrators and technicians. Its composition indicated that it could be termed a 'mixed authority' because it included representatives from both the 'political' and 'administrative' sides, an arrangement of which the autonomy school of thought tends to be critical. In this case, however, she demonstrates that success was achieved in that the two criteria of efficiency and political acceptability were met.

Friedman takes the view that the notion of controlled decentralisation can be a useful one for reformers to adopt elsewhere in Asia, referring in this context to the cases of Malaysia and the Philippines. In the latter example, he points to the success which has been achieved in using participatory irrigation associations as channels through which existing social organisations can be involved in the decision-making process.[21] What is, however, noticeable about much of the evidence he presents is that it refers to the performance of bodies with specific local functions (e.g. electrification, irrigation, health) whilst local government is normally multi-functional (minor roads, public health, markets, education, etc.). It may be, therefore, that the scope for this approach is confined to the more functionally specific bodies. Why this should be so, however, is not so clearly indicated except that manageability may be a factor to be included in the analysis. Where only one function is being considered it generally makes for a greater ease of management whilst at the same time perhaps limiting the possibilities for political conflict.

The evidence produced by either side is by no means conclusive but two points stand out clearly. On the one hand, substantial autonomy looks very much an unattainable ideal in view of the political and economic considerations prevailing in most countries. On the other, there is a trend now in favour of some form of decentralisation (which looks likely, however, to stop short of a real commitment to local government autonomy). Scope for a limited form of the 'bottom up' approach probably exists in a number of countries where hitherto highly centralised approaches have prevailed. Precisely what will happen in practice will obviously be the outcome of a complex range of forces, political, economic and otherwise. There is a great deal to be observed with interest.

Field administration

Not all public servants work in the capital city. In practice, many of them are dispersed to a variety of areas. These officers are often very important within the total system of government, partly because they provide a good deal of the 'face to face' contact which individual citizens have with the different ministries, departments and public enterprises. Thus, policies which depend on this sort of contact are bound to concern such administrators, and indeed are likely to rely on them for successful implementation. Given growing trends in the direction of more decentralised ways of working, these administrators are becoming of increased significance in many less developed countries.

• Questions of terminology

Before a detailed discussion of Third World experience, a couple of points need to be made about terminology. First, the expression 'field administration' simply refers to administrative activity outside of the capital city itself, and which is based in a specific geographical area (province, district, location, region, city etc.). Thus, field administrators work for the central government but their responsibilities are for a *part* of the territory of the state, *not the whole of it*. This, in essence, is the meaning of deconcentration, as explained at the beginning of this chapter. Secondly, field administration is often described as a form of bureaucratic decentralisation. Whilst this may often be a helpful way of putting matters, in reality much field administration is not bureaucratic, because other forms of administration (e.g. customary types) may also be important.

Within Southern Africa, the examples of Botswana and Lesotho may be given; in both cases, important local administrative roles (e.g. concerning land) are played by chiefs who occupy their positions because of hereditary factors, not because of decisions made by the Public Service Commission. The significance of this point varies as one goes from one country to another: Kenya, for example, is much more bureaucratic than Swaziland as far as local administration is concerned because there is no traditional chieftainship in the former, whilst in the latter its role is very prominent indeed.

• Reasons for field administration

A number of reasons can explain why governments make considerable use of field administrators.

(1) Public services can often only be provided by some sort of 'on the spot' administrator, i.e. one who is present in the area concerned. This applies not only to the provision of services (e.g. the Post Office) but also to agencies involved in enforcing laws (e.g. tax officials, health inspectors) and those who are required to assist in development activities (e.g. agricultural officers, community development officers).

(2) To concentrate all administration at the centre is to create enormous pressures on officials there, resulting in a form of congestion or administrative paralysis often termed 'over-centralisation'. The use of field administrators can go some way towards easing these pressures.

(3) Without field administration, officials would frequently have to go to the field anyway on special assignments, a 'to-ing and fro-ing' which would be very wasteful in terms of both time and money.

(4) Field officers are in a good position to obtain accurate information about their areas. Such information may pertain to any one of a number of activities being carried out by governments, whether it be in the field of development (e.g. the local unpopularity of a particular agricultural innovation) or of law and order (e.g. the likelihood of subversive organisations mounting campaigns to undermine the government). Thus, this role is important not only because it enables governments to be better informed about how well development strategies are working but also because it can assist in the maintenance of the political system. There is, however, a danger to note here. Field administrators can become over-involved in local interests to the point where their sympathies may run counter to those of central government.[22] For example, there is the story (perhaps not entirely true) of the British District Commissioner in colonial Kenya who led a delegation of Masai warriors to see the Governor about various grievances and began his speech with the words '*We* the Masai'! Such extreme cases are rare, but over-identification on a more modest scale frequently occurs.

(5) Field administrators can be innovators in the sense that they are well-placed to present new ideas to the communities with which they work. There are three reasons why much is often expected of them as far as introducing innovation is concerned. First, the more senior ones (e.g. The Collectors in India, District Governors in Zambia) may represent the full authority of the State. Hence, the ideas they present are more likely to be heard by large gatherings of people (the 'barazas' of East Africa are good examples). Secondly, field administrators are usually knowledgeable people who have received training with a high developmental content. They therefore can expect to have worthwhile ideas and information to impart in a competent manner. Thirdly, where they have local contacts they can be expected to transmit messages about development with enhanced effectiveness, bearing in mind that

136

communication is normally most effective when the communicator knows his audience well.

(6) Field administration may also be used as a way of demonstrating a government's belief in decentralisation. This has happened in a number of states especially in Africa where some policies of decentralisation do not involve any real element of devolution at all but simply mean a strengthening of field administrators such as District Co-ordinators (as in Lesotho pre-1986) and District Commissioners (as in Kenya currently). Such governments may thus use field administration to foster a decentralising image, even though the reality may prove to be quite the opposite, as was certainly true of the Lesotho case just mentioned.

To these six main points we can add several subsidiary ones. Work in the field can be a good testing ground for new recruits. In the British colonial service this philosophy was followed: young graduates started out in the countryside, subsequently taking more senior positions at the centre once they had proved their abilities. Where local government exists (as in most states) field administrators can play very important supervisory and supportive roles, as for example in Zimbabwe where District Administrators have been both co-ordinators of government in the field and chief executives of district councils. These roles can be especially important when local government is in its infancy. Field officers can also provide protection for the public by commenting on proposals which may have adverse effects locally or by ensuring that genuine local grievances are effectively communicated to the appropriate authorities. Finally, the presence of senior officials in the field may in itself be developmental because it may result in facilities being provided which otherwise would not have been (e.g. good quality schooling for their offspring which also benefits other local families, or improved urban sanitation systems which may benefit most of the urban public).

- *Inter-organisational relations in the field*

Field administration obviously involves a number of different departments and agencies. Arising from this, there is the question of how the officers representing these diverse bodies relate to one another. Smith's typology is a helpful way of presenting how these relationships can be structured.[23] He sees three different models applying in different countries.

1 Functional system

According to this model, 'the senior representatives of the state bureaucracy in the province are in charge of functionally specific state services, such as education, health, industrial development or agricultural extension work'.[24] There is considerable emphasis placed on specialisation and the structures of government are arranged accordingly. The various specialist senior officers are not expected to play an important political role, even though they may find themselves occasionally obliged to do so. In such systems there is hardly any co-ordination of activity within the field as all the separate hierarchies concentrate their energies and resources on providing their various specific services. It is likely that co-ordination will be effected at national or central level instead. Even administrative area boundaries may largely be determined on the basis of technical or specialist criteria. Thus, the boundaries operating for health services may not be the same as those operated by the agricultural extension department. What such a system rather conspicuously lacks is a strong co-ordinating area-based generalist officer, such as a District Commissioner, Government Agent or Collector.

Several developed countries operate with the functional system, the main examples being USA and UK, where the strength of it is the emphasis on specialisation. It is, however, unlikely to be appropriate in fully fledged form in most Third World settings because it tends to result in fragmented government activity in the field. This can be appropriate where government activities do not need much co-ordination with the work of other field agencies (e.g. postal services, registration of births) but usually there is a need for the work of different bodies to be linked, for example where there is a policy of integrated rural development. In such circumstances, some sort of co-ordination needs to be undertaken so that the work of the specialists can be harmonised.

2 Integrated prefectoral system

This system places the main focus upon the status and role of the 'Prefect', a term derived from France which refers to an officer who represents the State (or the 'National Interest') and who has powers which make his position superior to that of the other government officials within the area (district, provinces, etc.). Often, such officials also play important roles in relation to local government. They may, for example, be the chief executives of such bodies as councils within their areas and have substantial powers enabling them to control the activities undertaken by local government. In this model, the political dimension receives much greater attention, primarily because the prefect is expected to represent the government's interests. Thus, his role may be both a public relations one (addressing public meetings etc.) and an intelligence one (the 'eyes and ears' of government as it is sometimes termed). In this system, the distinction between politics and administration becomes a very blurred one. On the other hand, technical or specialist interests may be markedly de-emphasised, resulting sometimes in clashes between the two types of officer. The system does have significant disadvantages because of this and because it tends to prevent local government from exercising real autonomy. However, it is strong on co-ordination and political authority, which is probably why it has been adopted in many countries especially those which inherited the French administrative tradition after independence. It can be seen as vital by insecure governments which need strong political control throughout the countryside.

3 Unintegrated prefectoral system

This differs from the integrated model because the prefect, although he may be a prominent and respected figure, only has very limited formal control over other agencies within the geographical area for which he has responsibility. Typically, such an officer is expected to co-ordinate the work of the various technical departments but does not have any formal authority which enables him to do so. He will also have no direct control over local government, which may instead be answerable to the Ministry of Local Government (or equivalent) at the centre. It can easily be seen that this system blends the two other systems with the technical or specialist officers operating in styles reminiscent of their functional system counterparts whilst there is also a senior generalist who may well be expected to perform a substantial leadership role, not unlike that which is performed by the prefect in the integrated model. This system is found in many countries in Africa and Asia which were formerly under British rule (e.g. Kenya, Malaysia). Although the prefect may find himself in a weak position it should not be concluded that he has no value at all. His influence may be strong, deriving both from his personal qualities and his status within the government hierarchy; and his role in the realm of politics may be one of great significance. Thus, his importance must not be underestimated.

• Criticisms of field administration

Much of the literature to which reference has already been made paints a somewhat gloomy picture of the performance of field administration in many states. There are various dimensions to be considered, bearing in mind that the precise details vary considerably from one state to another. In general, however, four criticisms are commonly observed.

(1) The calibre or quality of field administrators may be unsatisfactory. It is not always easy to ensure that capable officers are posted to the field, especially when hardships may be involved for which adequate compensation is not provided. This problem is only partly one which

can be remedied by training because it also involves the attitudes and preferences of civil servants. It is sometimes said that life in the cities should be made less comfortable for them, thus making postings to remote rural areas a little more acceptable!

(2) The unintegrated prefectoral system, which is probably the most common in Africa and Asia, has not always been very successful in fostering close co-ordination in the field. Much depends on informal methods and personalities; under these circumstances, it is too easy to allow administration to become stagnant and leadership effectively non-existent.

(3) Field administration is not in itself decentralisation. A great deal of confusion is generated by assuming that it is. Mere strengthening of field officers may contribute to a tightening of central control in areas where political dissent is strong but to call that decentralisation is surely a misuse of language. Under some circumstances, however, a policy of deconcentration may form a desirable element within an overall policy of decentralisation. This, for example, may be said of the Botswana case where decentralised planning has involved both administrators and councillors.

(4) In many countries the image of much field administration still reflects colonial history. Taking both the British and French cases as examples, the colonial powers used field administration for purposes of control (what is often called the law and order orientation). Many administrators still see their role in that way, especially the prefects who often see law and order as the priority, development being of only indirect concern to them. In fairness, it should be said that law and order is often very problematic in many countries; hence it is understandable that such a perspective should be adopted.

Conclusions

Clearly many governments are very concerned with the issues discussed in this chapter. There is a widespread recognition that the high levels of centralisation found in many countries are unacceptable because they appear to work counter to the requirements of development. Partly, this belief has been fostered by the donor community (e.g. the World Bank) but that is by no means a complete explanation for the fact that decentralisation occupies an increasingly important place on the development agenda in a number of countries throughout the world, notably in Africa and Asia.

Whilst the need for decentralisation may be clearly seen, a great deal of confusion still prevails. This is not merely an academic debate about what decentralisation really means, how it should be defined, and so on. Much of the confusion about the subject stems from the mixed motives governments have when they claim to support such policies. It is worth stressing that decentralisation involves some transfer of power from the centre to the localities. Following from this, it can be seen that a political risk is involved; from the point of view of central government, to decentralise may mean offering opportunities to one's opponents. But the risks are not only political. There are financial questions to deal with as well. Governments which cannot manage their central finances very efficiently may fear decentralisation because it may add to their already existing problems. Thus, there are advantages and disadvantages to be considered. Finding the right balance between all the factors arising, risks included, has proved a most trying problem in a number of states. This point can be put in another way. There is a tendency for governments to wish to maximise the control they have over society as a whole. At the same time, there may be a strongly held view that participation should be open to all at the local level. Again, questions of balance and risk have to be analysed. These uncertainties and confusions aside, however, many countries are still seeking effective ways of decentralising and see local government as a vital part of the development scene. Efforts such as Kenya's District Focus for Rural Development Programme or Sri Lanka's emphasis on village councils still show that there is optimism in the air and these should continue to be observed with interest.

Discussion questions

1 Which of three systems of field administration described in this chapter most closely resembles your own country's? What do you consider to be its main strengths and weaknesses?

2 Why in practice has local government autonomy been restricted to such a considerable extent? What are the possibilities for introducing reforms to introduce greater autonomy?

3 In what ways has local government suffered from a failure to manage adequately its human and financial resources? Answer with reference to countries with which you are familiar.

4 What continuing role do you see for the generalist field administrator in the regional and district structures of government?

5 Outline the main features of both local government and field administration in your own country. Suggest measures which might be taken to strengthen the contributions made by both to the development of the areas for which they are responsible.

8 The Management of Human Resources

Introduction

It is hard to imagine any organisation which does not require human resources. Any department of government, for example, is based on relationships between people. A key task of management is to harness the resources these people represent in order to achieve the purposes or goals of the organisation. Thus, a Department of Agriculture will probably have numerous staff whose jobs require them to carry out tasks relating to the development of the farming sector of the economy. Some are involved in looking after money (the financial management dimension), others are concerned with providing transport services for farmers, still others carry out work of an advisory or extension kind. Clearly, a large number of staff may be involved, at considerable expense to the government. It is obviously of considerable importance to ensure that these various individual workers give as much value for money as possible. This argument, which is a vital one even in the more developed countries, takes on a particular significance in an environment where financial resources are scarce — as in most of the less developed countries.

The importance of human resource management

The example above has been given in order to indicate some of the dimensions we will be considering in this chapter. It also illustrates *why human resources management is of major concern in less developed countries*. However, the question of technology should also be mentioned at the outset. In the more developed countries, the age of the computer arrived some time ago.[1] This factor is less important in less developed countries, but is nevertheless a growing influence. Whilst the computer is a form of technology which clearly has the effect of replacing jobs otherwise carried out by people, it should not be assumed that human resource management is in danger of becoming irrelevant in the process.

142

This argument applies particularly strongly to less developed countries where computerisation has so far not had a significant effect on jobs, but even if computers were to become more important than they now are they would not altogether eliminate the human factor because staff would still be needed for programming, operating and, perhaps most fundamentally, interpreting the data produced by the new technologies.

Another reason why human resource management is particularly important for less developed countries is a political one. Jobs are a vital resource for political leaders to use in order to further or maintain their levels of support. On the whole, these politicians have limited scope as far as the allocation of jobs in the private sector is concerned, even though the vulnerable foreign entrepreneur may occasionally be persuaded to carry more staff than he really needs. Far more important as a source of political support is the public sector, within which the public or civil service contains a number of jobs which can be allocated in order to promote political self-interest. Many governments operate thus, not only in less developed countries, but often the structure of politics in these states is such that job allocation becomes central to the survival of regimes. This point also goes some way towards explaining why public sector bureaucracies often have very high levels of staffing, giving rise to the criticism that they have a surplus of human resources. This in turn, results in unnecessary claims on scarce finance.[2]

Politics aside, there is another reason why jobs and hence human resource management are so important in less developed countries. Because unemployment is such an immense problem almost everywhere, a high priority tends to be attached to job creation. As population grows and more school leavers and university graduates become job seekers in the cities so the need for governments to take effective action to create jobs becomes more and more pressing. Public sector employment, which usually accounts for a high proportion of the total number of jobs in less developed countries, represents one way of creating more jobs by expanding the size of the public sector to ease these pressures. Such policies imply the need for effective management of human resources because financially weak countries can ill afford expenditure on public sector employment if ineffective performance of the jobs created is allowed to continue for very long.

The scope of human resource management

The management of human resources covers a *wide range of activity*. It is often referred to as 'personnel management' or 'personnel admin-istration'. However, these terms are less used nowadays because they tended to imply that concern was only with the activities of personnel managers or officers. Whilst part of our concern is with these very important public servants, we are interested in all administrators who have substantial dealings with the human resources of an organisation — which means that we are discussing virtually everybody who does administrative work in the public sector. Thus, we are concerned *both* with specialist personnel functions (as performed by personnel officers, for example) *and* with the more general human resource management work done by, for example, heads of department or district agricultural officers.

In this chapter we will be looking at a number of areas of human resources management:

1 Recruitment covers the selection of staff and the placing of them in jobs within the organisation.

2 Training involves a review of how individuals are prepared for their jobs and given the opportunity to develop their skills and capacities.

3 Planning: like the other resources, the human element requires forecasting and the preparation of plans to meet objectives in the most effective way possible.

4 Staff appraisal and management by objectives are both ways of assisting individuals to contribute better to organisational objectives, and assessing the progress staff are making.

5 Morale and motivation: here we will be concerned primarily with people's attitudes to their jobs and towards their organisation. Mention of discipline will be made under this heading.

6 Participation and communication: here the concern is with how individuals are enabled to take part in deciding how the organisation carries out its tasks, and how members of the organisation communicate with one another.

This, however, means that certain aspects of human resources management will only be lightly touched upon. For example, *transfers of staff* are important ways by which governments can allocate their human resources to perform certain jobs. Criticism is often heard that transfers take place too frequently, thus creating serious problems of administrative discontinuity. Nor will we be making more than passing mention of *salary administration*, although the significance of this area is obvious enough. *Promotion* and *probation* are other aspects of human resource management which cannot be discussed in much detail here. Another one which can only be mentioned in passing is that of

144

labour relations, a matter of particular concern where trade unions are strong. However some selection has to be made, in view of the wide range of matters coming under the human resource management heading. In this chapter we therefore focus on just a few of the main issues facing less developed countries.

• *Recruitment*

The bureaucratic model of administration, as outlined by Weber, has already been discussed. One of the features of the model is the idea that recruitment to the civil service should be strictly on merit. Thus, the allocation of jobs to those who seek them is supposed to take place on the basis of various qualifications, including levels of education, combined with consideration of relevant experience. Many countries have adopted institutional arrangements aimed at achieving this goal, although with marked variations in terms of effectiveness. In some instances, there is no doubt that the Weberian model is closely approximated to in practice but there are other instances where what seems to be merit recruitment turns out to be an illusion, the reality being a complex mixture of other factors. The qualifications of candidates may thus be of less direct importance than political, ethnic or kinship affiliations.

Public Service Commissions

Many countries adopted some variant of the British system before or just after independence. In Britain, the idea of a Civil Service Commission was proposed in the 1850s, and was adopted about twenty years afterwards. The argument used was that the previous system had been too open to abuse, particularly as it had been used to reward political supporters rather than ensure that 'the best man for the job' was actually appointed. The situation was, if anything, even worse in the USA where the political doctrine of 'To the winner, the spoils' was used to justify what came to be known as the 'spoils system' in which most administrative posts were filled by those best able to satisfy the government of the time that they deserved jobs because of their political contributions, without any real attempt to assess their potential or ability as administrators. The Civil Service Commission idea was also eventually adopted in the USA, but at a substantially later date than in Britain.

The central idea was to maximise protection for the merit principle.[3] There was felt to be a need for an independent commission, unaffected by political considerations, to judge the suitability of candidates for civil service jobs. As a result of British rule, such bodies came to be established in many parts of Africa and Asia during the twentieth century, mostly towards the latter part of the colonial period. Initially, these bodies were only advisory to the colonial Governors, who actually had to make the final decisions. Subsequently, however, the Public Service Commissions or PSCs (as they became known in most countries such as Malaysia and Kenya) changed their status to an executive one, meaning that they were supposed to make fully binding decisions, usually not just on recruitment but also on promotions and disciplinary matters as well. Often they were advised by a central personnel agency or office. By and large this change in the status of PSCs occurred as part of the transfer-of-power constitutional package negotiated between the outgoing British and the incoming national leaders. This point is of some significance because it means that the idea of PSCs did not acquire a great deal of acceptance before the new governments came to power and helps to explain some of the difficulties which have arisen in practice as far as a number of states are concerned.

The idea of a politically neutral commission required the meeting of a number of conditions. First of all, the legal framework had to be established. Normally this was done by making provision for it within the independence constitution. Associated with this, the powers held by the commission required reasonably precise statement in order to avoid the possibility of political conflict. However, there was an important consideration which went beyond mere legal provision. Wamalwa has rightly commented:

> It has been said that legal instruments, even international treaties, are in essence no more than pieces of paper. This perhaps, is even more so in the new states in Africa. For, one aspect of the history of independent Africa, is the story of a trail strewn with the debris of broken promises and constitutions trampled into the dust. Therefore, another requisite for the success of a commission is the total and unequivocal acceptance of, and support for, the principles of the commission by the government.[4]

Thus, a vital factor is the extent to which governments support the idea of an independent and neutral commission. Wamalwa's comments on the Africa scene can equally be applied to many other less developed countries.

Next, it is necessary to consider questions of membership. The Head of State normally has the power to appoint the members. How he performs this important function is of some interest because he can appoint people who lack any of the qualities which members should ideally possess. In principle they should be of above average honesty and integrity, and be uninvolved in politics. They must have a thorough understanding of civil service needs but at the same time be capable of resisting pressures which are bound to come from all directions (including

146

from within the civil service itself). Obviously, membership of a PSC is a great honour but it is at the same time a burdensome responsibility, the stresses and strains of which can be excessive.

Little detailed study of PSCs in practice has been done, largely because processes of civil service recruitment are usually confidential. However, it seems clear from some of the accounts available that theory and practice are often a great distance apart. Wamalwa, who was in a position to observe the Kenyan experience at close quarters having formerly been chairman of that country's PSC, notes the tribal or ethnic difficulties which a number of these states confront. These factors are clearly felt by members of the PSC, although he argues that it is possible to resist such pressures. He does, however, admit that PSCs may sometimes have to act on biased information:

> In its operations, the commission relies very heavily on information supplied by heads of departments. One of the most likely effects of tribal sentiments is that a recommending officer might be inclined to give an unrealistically favourable assessment of an officer of his own group. Thus kinship sentiments tend to diminish objectivity in assessment of officers. Where this happens, the commission would be operating on false or distorted information and it is likely to make decisions which are not based on merit.[5]

These observations are clearly relevant to a number of countries with which we are concerned, both in Africa and Asia. If anything, the situation has worsened since Wamelwa wrote these words in the 1970s. Institutional collapse and decay has affected PSCs as well as parliament, civil services and other public bodies. It cannot be denied either that the growth of corruption in many parts of the world has affected civil service recruitment, whether it can be in theory controlled by a PSC or not. A recent survey of developing countries argues that 'patronage and nepotism tend to fill the ranks of the civil service with inept and incompetent individuals, thereby lowering the productivity of public bureaucracies'.[6] The difficulty of applying merit principles in a situation where clan or ethnic affiliations tend to be paramount is stressed by the authors of this survey:

> Bureaucrats in developing countries frequently seem to be faced by two sets of values: having been trained in the norms of modern organisations, they publicly adhere to these standards of recruitment and selection; but privately, and to a significant degree, they subscribe to traditional norms. Thus bureaucrats in developing countries are said to be torn between two sets of ethics, which, because they are dissimilar, create an identity crisis for civil servants. The weight of tradition is such that, even when the bureaucrat himself does not

profess a belief in traditional values, he is nevertheless subjected to constant pressure to give in to those values.[7]

This point can be made for many countries, even if it somewhat overstates the relevance of traditional factors. In several states, the problem seems to be that tradition has broken down but has yet to be replaced by firmly held alternative norms.

Improving recruitment methods

It may seem almost redundant to mention ways in which recruitment can be made more systematic. However, an attempt should nevertheless be made: corruption is by no means the dominant factor in all countries and reform may turn out to be possible in several countries despite the real problems which are involved. Thus, it is worth considering ways in which a sharpening of the tools of recruitment may be usefully undertaken.

The application of the merit principle is not as simple as it may seem. Choosing the best possible candidate for a particular vacancy within the organisation is an exercise which ideally requires a systematic approach. The maintenance of political neutrality and the avoidance of favouritism represents only a small portion of what is involved.

Beyond this, it is desirable that the job which has become vacant is adequately described. Job analysis, or the preparation of a job description, has to be carried out. Typically, the following information will be included in this exercise: the job title; to whom the holder of the job is accountable; the number of supporting staff, for whom the holder of the job will be responsible; the routes to promotion (prospects, etc.); the main purpose of the job; the various tasks or activities involved — this section of the description is likely to be the most detailed; the conditions under which the work is to be carried out — including any special difficulties (e.g. an isolated rural location); and the special responsibilities which may be involved.

It is also desirable that job specifications be drawn up quite thoroughly. These give information about the sort of person required, not about the job itself. Educational attainment is obviously important here but other matters which require attention are the amount of experience required; the extent to which the job requires physical (or manual) skills; the level of intelligence (admittedly not easy to establish); temperament (personality or character factors) — this is important because jobs differ greatly in the psychological demands they make on people; and personal circumstances (because, for example, some jobs may require a person to spend a lot of time away from home and thus be unsuitable for someone with pressing family concerns).

Normally, the job will be advertised in some way (through newspapers and other forms of media) and application forms drawn up to ensure that all relevant information is supplied. Other possible elements of a recruiting system include selection tests (e.g. typing speed tests) and an interview. Both of these methods of selection require serious thought: bad interviewing, for example, may result in the wrong decisions.

In many less developed countries, attempts have been made to approach recruitment more systematically. Within the public sector more progress has probably been made by public enterprises (or parastatals) than by public services because the former have greater autonomy, enabling them to introduce systems that meet their needs, whereas the public services are often required to follow inflexible procedures. In sum, however, it is clear that most countries could do a great deal to improve the quality of their recruitment systems in the public sector.

• *Training*

In many less developed countries formal arrangements for the training of public administrators have only existed since independence.[8] There are three main reasons for this. First, as shown in an earlier chapter, the idea of localisation was introduced very late in the day in many cases especially in Africa. An effect of this lateness was that very little attention was given to the notion of training indigenous personnel to take over from staff from the colonial power itself. Secondly, as far as the British example is concerned, there existed a tradition that training for public administration was unnecessary because the leadership qualities required could be derived adequately from attendance at the right sort of school and university. The public schools (which actually were expensive and private) followed by undergraduate study (often in Latin or Greek) at Oxford or Cambridge Universities were considered to make men into versatile and resourceful amateurs who could exercise the kind of leadership qualities required. Thus, even the British administrators posted to the colonies had received very little training. Thirdly, such training as was done for higher level staff took place in the colonial power itself rather than in the colonies. For example, French-speaking Africans attended the École Nationale d'Administration in Paris rather than receiving formal training at home. Ironically, the colonial powers did provide formal training for lower-level staff (e.g. Post Office and Railway Training Schools); thus, it was at the higher levels that most neglect was to be found.

'Crash localisation'

In several instances policies of 'crash localisation' were adopted as the pace of the transfer-of-power process became more and more rapid. As part of these policies, there was a demand for training so that the jobs being done by the departing expatriates could be adequately taken over by local officers. As Wood writes of Zambia, for example:

> Although administrative training was originally designed to provide a small trickle of African civil servants into administrative posts within the colonial regime, it very quickly became the sole device with which to localise administrative posts while at the same time attempting to retain standards and integrity within the service.[9]

So, in the Zambian case, the idea of training quickly shifted from being marginal, irrelevant even, to being a very high priority indeed (note Wood's phrase 'sole device').

Zoe Allen depicts the case of British West Africa thus:

> Crash localisation training as it finally emerged was largely an attempt to make good, or to make up for, the deficiencies in conventional qualifications which constituted the lowered standards. Most of the formal training courses were devoted to producing District Officers, the field administrators who were the backbone of colonial administration.[10]

As this quote implies, the approach was in a sense aimed at continuity. This was, for example, the reason for emphasising such generalist field administrators as District Officers. Even in India, where training was established long before most African countries, this central objective seems to have been much the same.[11]

However, localisation of many crucial administrative positions was generally achieved with rapidity, albeit also with some disruption as young and inexperienced officers suddenly found themselves occupying such positions as Permanent Secretary. Subsequently, the role of administrative training institutions changed. From the late 1960s onwards the trend almost everywhere was to emphasise administrative development or improvement. Localisation ceased to be an issue almost completely whilst the perceived importance of continuity became considerably less observable in many instances. Institutions such as the Kenya Institute of Administration, and Zambia and Pakistan's National Institutes of Public Administration were now expected to improve the performance of public administrators so that they could really assist in the development process rather than merely contribute to stable government. Their efforts were generally supplemented by national universities. Their role, however, will not be discussed at length here because they have not generally been involved directly in training. In this process, foreign aid came to play a significant role, as the USA, the UN and other donors took a growing interest.

150

Difficulties experienced in training

In reality, the achievements of training have not entirely justified the hopes and expectations which were expressed twenty or so years ago. Training has not failed; to take such a view would be to oversimplify considerably. Equally, however, the difficulties have been many and they should not be ignored in any attempt to analyse what the experience has been. Our discussion will focus on training programmes of an 'in country' kind, thus largely excluding programmes run in developed countries which are attended by administrators from less developed countries.

Part of the problem has been quite simply that the expectations themselves were unrealistic. Training was too often seen as a 'panacea' (or 'sole device') which would provide the dramatic breakthrough which was so desperately needed. On reflection, however, this can be seen as a naive view because the environment of public administration is often hostile to effective performance. Political and economic conditions, for example, may be very negative in the way they have been for large parts of Uganda's or Sudan's post-independence history. In such conditions, it is clearly wrong to see training as providing a transformation which can put the country back on course.

Foreign aid has also been problematic. The history of donor involvement in training goes back at least as far as the early 1950s when the American agency USAID became heavily involved in the Indian subcontinent and in other parts of Asia (e.g. Thailand, the Philippines). Indeed, the growth of development administration as a field of study in the USA may be directly related to this assistance policy, which developed somewhat uncertainly during its early years.[12]

Reviews of how these policies were carried out indicate that several problems arose, particularly during the 1950s and 1960s. This discussion will focus on the American case but much of what is said can be applied to other countries as well. The main difficulty seems to have been that Western management perspectives and methods turned out to be inappropriate when applied to non-Western environments. Faced with this dilemma, American public administration trainers often felt that they did not have the tools with which to make the necessary adjustments. Hence, training was often felt to be unhelpful because it did not offer practical solutions to the problems being encountered in less developed countries.

In addition aid for public administration is bound to be of greater political sensitivity than, say, aid for the development of physical infrastructure. Senior administrators are very close to the top political leaderships in their countries. Attempts to influence their thinking and behaviour are not only bound to be part and parcel of administrative training but can also arouse political suspicion. Thus, the use of foreign

151

assistance for this type of work has meant that the accusation of political interference has from time to time been made. In extreme cases, the charge has arisen — perhaps not always unreasonably — that American administrative trainers have doubled as officers of the Central Intelligence Agency (CIA). Finally, and related to the previous two points, aid policy has not been consistent. There have been times when such assistance has been highly fashionable, others when disillusionment has meant withdrawal. At the present time, for example, there seems to be a bit of an upswing; ten years ago there was rather less interest.

There are several other dimensions which relate to how training has been managed and implemented by the governments of less developed countries themselves. A few of them will be discussed here.

Reilly is critical of the frequent failure to give adequate attention to the relationships between overall national policies — as expressed in development plans and other documents — and training policies and programmes. He offers two useful examples of what should happen, but regrettably too often does not:

> For example, a national policy to strengthen the role of women should be reflected in a policy to select more women to attend training programmes. A policy to decentralise government to the districts should stimulate a policy to mount courses in field administration and local government.[13]

Training institutions, then, often operate in a way which rather isolates them from the real world of policy making. Efforts, however, are increasingly being made to see that this does not happen. Kenya's Institute of Administration (KIA), for example, is now running programmes which provide valuable and essential support to the government's 'District Focus' approach to rural development.[14] Such linkages, nevertheless, are not as commonly made between training and national policy as they could be.

Another deficiency has been in the sphere of training materials. Clearly the textbooks, lecture handouts, exercises, and so on, which are used in training need to be of practical relevance to the day-to-day working lives of the trainees. This implies a measure of flexibility as, ideally, the materials used in training should be undergoing review and adaptation as changes take place in the broader administrative system. None of this is easy, as trainers know, because of the time factor. Setting aside a sufficient part of one's working life for revising teaching materials is not possible if one is in constant demand to undertake numerous other tasks (e.g. administering a department within the training institute). Yet the importance of undertaking this kind of work in less developed countries is great, particularly in view of the still existing tendency to make excessive use of materials based on the experience of Western countries, the USA in particular. For many countries, a high priority in training is to ensure that relevant and well prepared materials are available to be used in courses, workshops, etc.

This point is really part of a broader concern with course design, an issue which also involves the use of effective methods of teaching.[15] It is now considered 'old hat' to speak of the limited value of the conventional lecture and the need for using other methods to facilitate learning (e.g. role playing, management games, field studies, syndicates). However, because so many administrative trainers still seem to be attached to conservative methods, it is nevertheless worth comment. The primary weakness of the lecture is that it is based upon a relatively passive role for the trainee, whereas a more participative or active style is more likely to produce effective learning. The use of group work, field studies, individual assignments (not necessarily of the academic essay type) can all help provide a more stimulating climate in which trainees are more likely to benefit. What is needed is often a very 'non-directive' role for the trainer, in which it is largely left to the trainees themselves to explore the nature of problems, seek solutions and thus push back the frontiers of their own understanding.

More effective training requires more effective trainers. Twenty years ago a large number of the trainers working in less developed countries were expatriates, in most cases funded by their own governments. At the same time, a process of localisation was taking place. It is still not unknown for expatriates to be involved in administrative training but is less frequently observed. Localisation has to a large extent removed expatriates from the scene, except for such activities as short-term consultancies or providing advice on training rather than actually doing the job. Face-to-face contact with the trainees is now largely the responsibility of indigenous staff. Many of them are well trained and experienced teachers, but there are others whose work could be improved through themselves receiving training or in other ways.

In some cases, it has proved difficult to recruit suitable people for training positions. For example, it is usually a mistake to recruit recent university graduates with little or no administrative experience. However, this is often done, sometimes because the posts concerned are not senior or attractive enough for the seasoned administrator, sometimes because the latter may in any case not have the requisite academic background. There is no escape from the conclusion that staff development programmes, aimed at making administrative trainers more effective, are a high priority need in many countries.

Another dilemma concerns the perceptions of the trainees themselves. In the 1950s and 1960s there was a general and understandable perception that training was worth receiving because there was a very good chance that significant and rapid promotion would result. This was particularly true where 'crash localisation' took place. In recent years, however, opportunities for upward mobility within the public services have been much more limited, thus making the benefits of attending a training programme less tangible and therefore less attractive to many. Thus, training can be seen as an activity not worth taking seriously, an attitude which can scarcely be said to provide the trainers with a great deal of encouragement. Making training interesting, enjoyable and worth while in such a context constitutes a major challenge for those with responsibilities in this field.

Evaluation of training is another area where improvement should be possible because not enough is generally being done at the moment. There are two main reasons why programmes should be evaluated. It helps to decide whether a programme should be continued or not; and (usually more importantly) evaluation can be a great help in indicating ways in which programmes can be improved. For example, an evaluation report might indicate that some topics should be dropped from the programme whilst others, hitherto not included, should be brought in. The value of various types of training methods might also be usefully analysed in such a report. In part, evaluation should be based on trainee responses (through discussion and survey, perhaps) but also on how trainer and the government agencies employing those attending perceive the value of the programme. Curriculum development can thus benefit greatly from well organised evaluation, as many training institutes have found. In some cases, however, resistance has taken place, often because the trainers themselves fear the criticisms of their performance which might be implicit in the results. There are other reasons, of course, but this seems to be the main one.

Morale in many training institutes is rather low. A number of factors seem to be involved here, including some points which have already been mentioned (e.g. poorly qualified trainers, negative trainee attitudes, inadequate linkages with national policy). However, another factor requiring consideration is that the leadership role within these institutions may not be up to the required standard. In too many cases the performance of this role is inadequate because top management lacks understanding and experience of training. Worse still, the Director/Principal may quite simply lack any serious sense of commitment to the job, being preoccupied with personal or 'outside' matters. Where this happens it is scarcely surprising that morale throughout the organisation sags, characterised, for example, by high rates of absenteeism, alcoholism, personal disputes (e.g. 'backbiting') and unwillingness to take any sort of initiative.

Finally, there are three types of manager or administrator who tend to be neglected by the arrangements which exist in many countries.

(1) There has been a tendency for the needs of more senior administrators to be ignored within the existing frameworks. However, it can be argued that Permanent Secretaries and the like also ought to have the opportunity to break away from their routine work, update their knowledge, and reflect on their experiences. This would not be training in the conventional sense. For example, secondment to industry or universities might be useful for such individuals so as to enable them to lose the staleness which so often adversely affects performance.

(2) There is the need to train professional/technical officers in managerial skills. For example, many countries have now adopted Primary Health Care as a policy. This has significant implications for medical work, and means in particular that doctors and nurses — especially the non-specialists in the field — need to acquire more managerial capacity than their professional training has probably given them. Here is yet another challenge for training institutions to face.

(3) There is the special case of public enterprises to be considered. In the past ten years, several surveys have been carried out by the International Association of Schools and Institutes of Administration and by the International Center for Public Enterprises in Developing Countries.[16] Several conclusions arising from this work stand out. Perhaps the main one is that Institutes of Public Administration by and large have not included public enterprise management within their programmes despite the growing importance of public corporations and similar bodies within the overall development strategies of a number of countries. This has resulted in the arrival of a number of training bodies to cater for the needs of specific enterprises. In the words of Delion, however, this has had results which have not been altogether satisfactory:

> Such a multiplication of internal training centres has indeed some positive aspects, but it is expensive, and runs the risk of favouring the more immediately practical aspects to the detriment of a more strategic teaching, the good of the firm over-shadowing the more general interest, and encouraging too great an autonomy with respect to the state.[17]

There are thus several gaps in present administrative training programmes which need to be filled, in addition to the other areas for improvement in performance which have already been noted.

Planning of human resources

What used to be generally known as 'manpower' planning is an important function of human resource management. Like several other of the functions under discussion in this chapter the effectiveness with which it is carried out could usefully be enhanced in many less developed countries. There are close parallels between this type of planning and financial planning in that both systems involve the making of forecasts in regard to expected availability of resources and what the needs are likely to be. Because of the way circumstances change, forecasts can never be completely accurate. This, however, does not mean that the exercise is likely to be a waste of time; but it does strongly suggest that administrators should interpret the findings of their planners with a great deal of caution.

Broadly speaking, it can be said that there are two types of human resource planning. First, there is what is sometimes known as the 'macro' approach which essentially is concerned with national forecasting of resources and requirements. For example, studies might be undertaken to make supply and demand forecasts on a nationwide basis for particular categories of personnel, for example vehicle mechanics, nurses, school teachers. Macro studies sometimes go further than this and look at all categories throughout the economy. Even in very small states this is a very substantial job as it embraces all organisations, private and public, and a very large part of the population. Secondly, there is 'micro' planning. This is applied to particular organisations, such as government departments, corporations, local authorities, firms. This is the type of planning which is of greater relevance to us because we are interested here in how governments plan their own human resources rather than how they plan for the entire economy of the country.

● Human resource planning for organisations

There are many elements to this type of planning. Reilly conveniently summarises the main ones:[18]

i) It is necessary to establish as clearly as possible what the objectives of the organisation are.

ii) Forecasting of future manpower needs has to be carried out, an exercise which requires an assessment of how effectively existing staff are being used (if they can be more effectively used it makes it less necessary to take on more staff).

iii) An assessment has to be made as to how far future needs can be met from within the organisation itself.

iv) Knowledge will have to be obtained concerning the resources which are likely to be generated from the schools, universities, technical colleges etc. Subjects, standards of attainment and so on will require analysis (e.g. numbers of Bachelors' degrees in physics or business administration).

v) Consideration should be given to the sort of incentives needed to attract appropriate personnel in the right numbers. Thus, salary figures need to be compared across jobs which require similar types of qualified personnel. Finally, account has to be taken of the various economic and political constraints existing, and which are bound to change from time to time. In states such as Oman, for example, where the economy depends on oil, falls in fuel prices may mean a reduction in the capacity of training and educational institutions to produce qualified people because the money available for such a purpose may no longer be enough.

Example: planning in the health sector

Obviously, this type of planning is complex and difficult. A full discussion of what is involved cannot be attempted here. However, it should be noted that it has frequently been ineffective for a number of reasons, among which may be mentioned the following points which have been observed for the health sector:[19]

i) The complexity of manpower needs is very considerable (individual skills and attitudes vary, work patterns cannot easily change, etc.).

ii) The planning of human resources is often not 'synchronised' with health plans. For example, a new hospital, completed at great cost with the assistance of foreign loans, may stand unused because of a lack of nursing staff.

iii) Instances of lack of co-ordination between planners and those responsible for the management of health programmes.

iv) Numbers are over-emphasised at the expense of qualitative issues, such as the relevance of educational programmes to health service needs.

v) Not enough attention is given to implementation, most planners tending to over-concentrate on formulation.

In the light of this by no means comprehensive list, it is clear that effort is needed to strengthen planning capacities. The need is not confined to health; other important sectors, notably agriculture, are also required to improve the quality of their human resource planning. The difficulties being faced, however, are such that dramatic break-throughs seem unlikely in the near future. Most countries, however, now accept the importance of these issues and steps are being taken to strengthen their planning systems. To this end, efforts are being made to train planners with appropriate skills and to create better ways of obtaining information about the requirement of organisations and the 'output' of educational and training bodies, such as schools, universities and polytechnics.

Staff appraisal

The focus in this section is largely on the individual officer, rather than the organisation as a whole. Staff appraisal systems (sometimes known as performance appraisal) generally try to fulfil several purposes but the essentials revolve around two points. First, there is the *need to look back* in order to see what an individual has or has not achieved over the previous year (the normal period of time used, although there can be others). Secondly, there is also a *need to look ahead* in order to see how the individual's work may best develop in the forthcoming period (e.g. the next year). Clearly appraisal is an important tool because potentially it can contribute much both to the performance of individual officers and indirectly to the performance levels attained by the organisation as a whole. In many countries this potential has not been fully realized.

Obviously the responsibility for appraisal lies with an individual's supervising officer who is expected to know enough about the officers he supervises. In the traditional bureaucratic system the supervisor prepares a confidential report (i.e. it is not seen by the officer who is the subject of it) which is submitted to the body in central government responsible for civil service personnel matters. The report may then be referred to for possible action (e.g. promotion, discipline, transfer, early retirement). This type of appraisal has the central weakness that it is largely a 'looking back' exercise and will only occasionally play a part in the development of the individual officer. Also, such reports may be treated lightly by the preparing officer. They will thus be superficial and inaccurate, rendering them of little use even as confidential reports.

A number of countries have been looking into ways of making staff appraisal a more open process, in which discussion can take place between reporting officer and 'reportee' to achieve a better general understanding of what the report should say and, preferably, provide a few pointers for individual development. Few countries, however, seem to have enjoyed much success in bringing about this type of reform of their staff appraisal systems. Resistance to such ideas by senior civil servants has been strong because they prefer to have their judgements about individuals protected by confidentiality, rather than expose themselves to question and, possibly, malicious criticism. The case for a more open approach, however, remains strong, because, as Fuller observes:

> In the past most civil services have used performance appraisal systems and forms which, like most traditional systems of financial control, have concerned themselves with measuring *inputs* instead of *outputs*. Not surprisingly this has led to the neglect of concern for

the effectiveness of manpower, its performance and measurement of that performance against organisational objectives and the tasks on which staff should be working to achieve those objectives.[20]

Once again, this case illustrates that a more developmental approach is possible but also shows that civil service resistance to reform remains a significant obstacle.

● *Management by objectives*
Closely related to the idea that appraisal should be an instrument of development is the approach commonly known as 'MBO' (management by objectives). It is linked to appraisal because it is concerned with ensuring that in the process of looking ahead and perhaps improving performance an individual will be helped greatly by being enabled to focus on a few realistic objectives at which to direct efforts. The idea is that goals or objectives should be jointly agreed between supervisors and supervised officers, bearing in mind two important points:

i)   There is no incompatability between overall organisational objectives and the views of the individual officer. This can be a considerable area of difficulty especially where there is little agreement on what the objectives should be.

ii) There is full account taken of the views of the individual officer. Normally this will involve discussion with him or her, sometimes going into a great deal of detail. Again, this can be difficult; supervising officers need suitably developed inter-personal skills to ensure that the discussions are conducted properly.

Research reported on by Fuller identifies in more detail what is required if MBO is to be a successful management innovation. He sees various staff needs requiring particular types of organisational responses. These are stated in Table 2, on page 160.[21]

The merit of this presentation of MBO is that it indicates that a number of factors are involved. There is, however, one further need. If objectives are to be really helpful, they should be measurable if at all possible. Fuller offers these two statements of objectives for comparison:

A   'to improve the operations of the department';
B   'to reduce the time taken to process appointments by 50% by the end of December 1986.'[22]

Statement A is vague and general; it is certainly not easy to measure, whilst statement B is clearly better on all counts.

MBO in practice
As with staff appraisal, the advantages of MBO, at least potentially, are considerable. In practice, however, only a limited amount of success

Table 2   Staff needs and organisational responses

Staff needs	Organisational response
'Tell me (or agree with me) what you expect from me.'	Clarification of departmental and unit objectives Establishing priority areas and tasks Developing improvement plans Job descriptions
'Give me an opportunity to perform.'	Organisational planning Resource allocation Delegation of authority
'Let me know how I am getting on.'	Control information Performance review Staff inspection Management services
'Give me help and guidance where and when I need it.'	Career development Performance review Training
'Reward me according to my contribution.'	Salary Potential review Succession planning Training

has been achieved. Few countries have made any serious effort to introduce it, mainly because time-honoured methods of administration are firmly entrenched in the minds of top bureaucrats, who sometimes fear that if they undertake innovations which have unpredictable results they may be in trouble with their political masters. An additional problem is that innovations of this type require much planning and training so that implementing officers fully know and understand what is involved. A lot of the rather half-hearted attempts which have taken place can be explained by the fact that these two functions were not well performed. The prospects for MBO, however, are not totally bleak. Kenya is an example of one country where it is still on the reform agenda, particularly in view of the need felt by the government of that country to motivate officers adequately through the setting of targets.[23]

Morale and motivation

These are two closely related ideas which are of considerable importance in the study of public administration. Definition of morale and motivation is difficult to achieve with precision. However, we are concerned, when using these terms, with the attitude of workers towards the organisation and the job they are doing within it. 'Morale' refers to the total attitude felt by the entire work force (i.e. from the most senior to the most junior) whilst 'motivation' is concerned with the feelings of individuals; it is about the desire on the part of an individual to do or achieve something, for example hunger motivates one to eat, promotion may motivate one to work harder. Obviously the relationship between the two is a close one because morale, in a sense, is a 'totalling up' or 'sum' of the motivations of individuals working for the organisation. Applying these terms in practice is difficult, not least because people tend to perceive the morale of their organisation differently. Some officers in a given department might have various reasons for seeing the morale of their staff as excellent, whilst colleagues working nearby might have good reasons for feeling quite the opposite. Attitudes to morale can also vary depending on the level one occupies within the hierarchy. Senior officers may regard morale as high but their juniors' view might be the opposite. Motivation is rather easier to discuss in a sense because it concerns individual attitudes. However, there are also complex issues to take into account; reference will be made to some of them in the account which follows.

Morale may be seen as a measure of the *health* of an organisation. It is often related to how well the organisation is achieving its objectives. However, in a number of organisations, particularly in the public sector, an added difficulty is that objectives tend to be unclear; hence there may well be confusion or uncertainty amongst officials, in itself a factor likely to contribute to low morale.

There are many different 'symptoms' or 'indicators' of morale. For example, it might be said that morale is 'high' when the staff are obviously enthusiastic about their work, are clearly putting in maximum effort, show that they are satisfied and work well together. On the other hand, 'low' morale is suggested by an obvious lack of effort, a high rate of absenteeism, non-co-operation at and between various hierarchical levels and disruptive behaviour (e.g. refusal to accept legitimate orders, drunkenness at work).

In many countries, there is a good deal of worry about the morale of the civil service. A recent report on the Kenya Civil Service, for instance, observes that despite the various recommendations which have been made from the early 1970s onward, 'there had been a significant deterioration in the morale and consequently in the efficiency of the civil service'.[24] This report saw many factors contributing to low morale — unsatisfactory performance evaluation, poor (often non-existent) career planning, lack of specific work schedules, various 'malpractices' (e.g. uncontrolled involvement in private sector activities by civil servants), poor staff deployment and inadequate incentives.[25] More seriously still, this report notes that 'in some instances promotions have been effected without due regard to merit, suitability, seniority and ability. This in our view contributes to low morale and general low performance of the civil service'.[26] Following on from this, the need is stressed for the application of management principles and techniques to put matters right (e.g. effective staff appraisal, clear work schedules, more emphasis on merit in deciding promotions). Arguments of this sort have been made about a number of other countries, for example India.[27] Gould and Amaro-Reyes, in their survey of less developed countries, emphasise the very real contribution which corruption can make to low morale. It can, for example, contribute to 'frustration', a clear indicator of low morale. They quote the case of Lebanon:

> The head of the Lebanese Civil Service Commission observed once that the Lebanese civil servant's inability to control corruption impels him to choose one of two options: the civil servant will either apply non corrupt standards and run the risk of becoming so alienated that he will eventually resign his position, or he will take advantage of his skills and position to enrich himself.[28]

Becoming 'alienated', if it becomes a widespread tendency in an organisation, must also count as a solid indicator of low morale. Corruption, however, is but one factor which has contributed to low morale in many less developed countries.

Where there are problems with morale in an organisation it is likely that the motivational levels of individual workers will be low. Where morale appears to be good, the individual levels of motivation will similarly be high. The concept of motivation is thus important to our understanding of morale in organisations.

• Studies of motivation

There is a substantial literature on motivation, especially from the USA. Much of this work raises complicated theoretical issues which will not be discussed here. There is, however, some agreement on a few points of relevance to less developed countries. The work of Douglas McGregor drew on the studies carried out by Maslow, Herzberg and others to suggest that a new approach to management was needed, certainly as far as the private sector in the USA was concerned.[29] His thinking on management has certainly had a lot of influence over the past thirty or so years, and although new approaches have been suggested his views still seem broadly valid, and may be of some relevance to less developed countries if sensitively applied.[30]

162

McGregor questions the validity of what he regards as the traditional concept of management, which he terms 'Theory X', an approach which emphasises 'top down' hierarchy and the exercise of authority. In many ways it resembles the style of management implied by Weber's bureaucratic model which, of course, also strongly emphasised the part played by authority in achieving organisational goals.

The assumptions behind this theory, according to McGregor, are as follows:

i) The average human being has an inherent dislike of work and will avoid it if he can.

ii) Because of this dislike, most people must be coerced, controlled, directed, threatened with punishment, etc. to make them put forth adequate effort towards the achievement of organisational objectives.

iii) The average human being prefers to be directed, wishes to avoid responsibility, has relatively little ambition and wants security above all.

It has been said that the scientific management movement ('Taylorism') tended to follow such assumptions with its stress upon specialisation, on establishing norms of production, designing equipment to regulate the pace of work and devise wage payments to reward good work and penalise the lazy.

McGregor advocates an alternative to this approach, one which he terms 'Theory Y'. This style of management is one which reflects the ideas of earlier management thinkers, such as Mayo, Maslow and Herzberg. Derived from this work, McGregor suggests the following alternative assumptions:

i) The expenditure of physical and mental effort in work is as natural as play or rest. That is, work may be a source of satisfaction; it is not inherently unpleasant and best avoided.

ii) Control and the threat of punishment are not the only means of bringing about effort directed towards the objective of organisations. If workers are committed to the objectives they can generally be expected to exercise self-direction and self-control.

iii) In the course of aiming to achieve organisational objectives individuals may fulfil such higher-level needs as 'self-actualisation'.

iv) The average human being, given the right conditions, may be able to accept responsibility and may even come to seek it.

Thus the task of management shifts its emphasis from authority (working *through* people) to an approach based upon the need to work *with* them. Management still has major responsibilities to perform: McGregor's approach does not mean that management can relax and allow people to do as they please. Leadership is still necessary but what McGregor is saying is that the *style* of leadership must change to one which is based more fully on the insights derived from human relations and motivation theories.

A further word of caution should be entered. McGregor's approach does not mean that the 'Theory Y' style should be adopted uncritically in all organisations. His ideas centre around the performance of the management function in the USA where, of course, the environment may well be quite different from that which prevails elsewhere. In addition, the style adopted has to be related to the purpose of the organisation being examined. 'Theory Y' may, for example, not work well for armies or organisations involved in disaster relief activities where immediate compliance with orders may be vital. Thus, management styles must be related to the *particular situation* being faced. As another major management thinker, Peter Drucker, has put it:

> The question the manager needs to ask is not, which theory of human nature is right? The question is what is the reality of *my* situation and how can I discharge *my* task of managing worker and working in today's situation?[31]

As far as the particular situation being faced in many less developed countries is concerned, it is clear that financial difficulties lie at the root of many of the problems. However, McGregor and others regard money as a relatively unimportant factor in motivation, basically because in countries such as the USA the salaries and wages paid are broadly adequate and as such they do not affect motivation. However, in many countries (e.g. Uganda, Sudan) civil service salaries are so low that it is difficult to see how better work performance can be achieved if nothing is done to increase them.

However, there could still be scope for the application of many of McGregor's ideas. He sees MBO, for example, as being one of several ways of applying a 'Theory Y' perspective to management; as we have seen, this is potentially a useful approach to apply in less developed countries. He also argues for better management communication and for the establishment of avenues for staff participation in decision making. In addition to McGregor, several writers have drawn attention to the value of this kind of improvement, including many of those who have observed the experience of less developed countries.

Participation

'Participation' has been referred to as an alternative to conventional forms of work organisation. According to Blunt, this term concerns the involvement of:

164

organisational members in a range of decisions varying from those associated with the running of the organisation itself through to those connected with designing their own work: it entails involvement in decision making by workers in matters which previously, have been regarded as the exclusive domain of those more senior to them in the organisation.[32]

The subject is a complex one because a number of objectives can be aimed at through participation, and different institutional arrangements may be adopted to achieve them. A study of worker participation conducted in nine countries (Algeria, Bangladesh, Guyana, India, Malta, Peru, Tanzania, Yugoslavia and Zambia) concluded that the range of objectives was such that four classifications could be made:[33]

i) *Political* — where, for example, it has been decided to transfer decision-making powers to workers for ideological reasons (e.g. Yugoslavia, Algeria, Peru, Tanzania).

ii) *Economic* — policies of workers' participation often aim to enhance economic development by increasing productivity (e.g. the cases of India and Malta).

iii) *Socio-cultural* — the idea of participation is often seen as desirable because it fits in with notions held by governments of the 'good society'.

iv) *The improvement of industrial relations* — workers' participation has often been seen as a way of generating a more co-operative way of working within organisations. This objective was the one which McGregor primarily had in mind, although much of what he had to say supports to some extent objectives 2 and 3 as well.[34]

As far as the institutional arrangements are concerned, there is one basic distinction to be made. On the one hand, there are systems in which real power is vested in workers' bodies (e.g. Works Councils); this means that workers' representatives make decisions on new investments, the development of new products, wage rates and so on. On the other hand, there are consultative or advisory forms where workers really only have the right to make their views known to management; they have very little by way of real power. Algeria has largely adopted the first type, Bangladesh and Zambia the second (the other countries under review seem to fall somewhere in between these extremes). Blunt accepts that the latter type is a very ambiguous form and shares the view that 'situations in which workers are offered full explanations of decisions already made by management' should be called 'pseudo participation'. 'Full participation', on the other hand, is said to exist only where power between managers and workers is at least equalised.[35]

The picture, however, is still more complicated because such a range

165

of possibilities exists. Somewhere in between the two extremes mentioned, for example, there is the 'quality circle' idea. Pioneered in Japan, and now adopted in several developed countries, this normally consists of small groups of people doing similar work, normally together, and reporting to the same supervisors and managers. The idea is for these groups to hold regular meetings on a voluntary basis to identify, analyse and solve problems. They are expected to recommend solutions to management. As far as possible the 'quality circles' implement changes themselves. If management is sufficiently supportive, these groups may contribute a great deal to productivity and harmony; they do not, however, involve the transfer of real powers to the workers.[36] Although many less developed countries have arrangements resembling this, few seem to have tried to adopt the idea systematically.

Attempts to introduce forms of workers' participation have often been problematic. The Indian case is a particularly interesting one because the history of these ideas in that country is a comparatively long one, going back to the 1920s. The indications there are that numerous difficulties still require solution:

> India also presents a picture where workers' participation has more stumbling blocks which lead to its weakness, than facilitating factors. In the first place, the Government and the policy makers are still not very clear about the concept and its modalities. The various experiments that were carried out in the past clearly indicate that the Government is still conducting trial and error experiment. This non-clarity of objectives grossly contributes to the basic weakness of the system of workers' participation in India. The mixed economy pattern of India, where private property interests still have predominance, poses another set of threats to participative efforts in this country. Besides these, the growing multiplicity of political parties and trade unions and their corresponding impact on industrial relations, also create difficulties in the implementation of workers' participation schemes. Professional management and workers remain largely ambivalent to the idea of workers' participation. On the whole, in India, workers' participation faces resistance at all levels, which makes the system perenially weak.[37]

Similar reports have been made about other countries. In Zambia, for example, there is said to have been a great deal of resistance to the idea by high-ranking officials.[38] Thus, as with other aspects of human resource management, workers' participation may be viewed as a useful idea which has not borne the expected fruit. It still, however, seems worth pursuing because, as Blunt points out, there are also examples of success to report, even in countries such as Zambia where most observers tend towards pessimism.[39]

166

Most of the literature on which this section has drawn is not specifically about the public service itself. The majority of the experiments and innovations which have taken place have been applied to public enterprises rather than to the public services.[40] The reasons for this emphasis are fairly clear. The relative autonomy granted to public enterprises makes for greater flexibility of management styles and structures, thus permitting innovation. At the same time, governments wanting to see workers' participation brought into industry can do so more easily by using public rather than private enterprise because the latter is harder to direct. Ironically, governments baulk at greater participation for workers in the civil service itself because of the constitutional and political sensitivities involved; for example the role and powers of Permanent (or Principal) Secretaries are not seen as readily alterable in order to give officers at a lower level more of a voice in decision making, especially where their views might clash with those of the political masters.

Management communication

Communication is another important area of human resource management. Effective participation, at whatever level, is partially dependent on being able to obtain valid information about the organisation. Communication is concerned with transmitting information between people in organisations. It has been defined as 'imparting or exchange understanding between persons or groups in and around the organisation.'[41] The main concern of this section is with *internal* communications within an organisation, not so much with how communication takes place with the world outside. As far as human resource management goes, there is one fundamental reason why communication is important. It applies (in varying degrees) to almost all situations and cultures: 'People will only give of their best if they know the reasons behind decisions that affect them.'[42]

Communication is often handled inadequately, leading to disruption of work, failure to achieve objectives and negative work attitudes. It can thus contribute, either negatively or positively, to morale. Its relevance for management has only recently gained recognition in less developed countries where, moreover, the difficulties may be greater because of linguistic and cultural differences which may be barriers to the communication process.[43] There are many facets of communication amongst which the following are of particular importance for most organisations:

a) face to face; formal and informal: this category can be further broken down into types (e.g. formal interviews — disciplinary, recruitment, etc., coffee-break discussions, briefing meetings);

b) group meetings, under which heading can be included committee work;

c) team briefings, e.g. where a manager addresses a team which has been established to carry out specific tasks;

d) conferences and seminars — these play an important part in the lives of many public servants;

e) publications and circulars — again often of considerable importance; well-written circulars can be extremely helpful, unclear ones often do more harm than good;[44]

f) correspondence — can be external (e.g. a letter to a donor agency) or internal (e.g. an office memo).

Enough has been said to indicate that communication skills are important tools needed by administrators in less developed countries as much as elsewhere, if not more so. For this reason, communication now seems to be gaining ground as an item to be included in administrative syllabuses.

Conclusions

The issues discussed in this chapter have put in less of an appearance in the literature of development administration than they might have done. The reason, perhaps, for this neglect is that human resource management is less directly linked to development policy than, say, rural development or public enterprise are. Political scientists often touch on human resource issues as part of the general analysis of whole political systems. This is not, however, the same as looking directly at how human resources are managed for purposes of development. Economists, too, have often mentioned personnel administration as a constraint to development plans but with rare exceptions, such as Waterston, they have not entered into the issues in detail.[45] Students of management, on the other hand, have perhaps shied away because of the political sensitivity of much of the subject matter. This is, for example, particularly true of public sector recruitment systems which cannot be properly analysed without taking into account the existence (often very marked) of corrupt practices and political interference.

This chapter has highlighted several key points. First, it is vital to acquire a full understanding of human resource management because its potential contribution to development is so immense. The second point that emerges is that techniques and processes developed in the West may not be applicable to all societies in precisely the same form. Those who wish to see change introduced need to be fully aware of the environment in which they are operating so as to maximise the chances of the transfer of systems being an effective exercise. These environmental considerations aside, however, our review of the main issues suggest that there is indeed scope for reform, much of it based on Western techniques and principles. Recruitment is a case in point. The merit principle, a fundamental of Weberian bureaucracy, has not always been applied. Often this has been for political reasons although other factors (nepotism, etc.) have also entered the picture. Where this has happened it has generally been to the detriment of effective administration. The need for persisting with the merit principle thus remains clear, even if its full acceptance requires more change from national leaders than they seem prepared to give. To introduce systems of recruitment which are more effective in filtering talent in the right direction remains then an urgent need.

Overall, to draw negative conclusions would be inappropriate. Much has been done, despite the constraints which so often appear to dominate the scene. Many senior civil servants are now considerably more conscious than they used to be of the need for reform. They do not always feel sure of how to go about it, nor do they always find support at high levels for what they wish to do. The road ahead is clearly not an easy one, but nor is it necessarily as impassable as some would have us believe.

Discussion questions

1 Draw up as comprehensive a list as possible of the various aspects of human resource management.

2 Prepare a memorandum of advice to your government on improving procedures for recruiting civil servants.

3 To what extent has administrative training often encountered difficulty? What measures might governments take to deal with these issues?

4 How can the various techniques of human resource management which have been discussed in this chapter contribute to improving the morale and motivation of civil servants in less developed countries?

9 Administrative Reform and Development

Introduction

Throughout this book our concern has not only been with describing and analysing the nature of bureaucracies as they try to tackle development. Much of what has been said has had a cautiously prescriptive element attached to it. It has been necessary to be cautious partly because public administration is not an exact science: it does not have formal laws to apply in the way that some other subjects such as physics and chemistry have; and partly because national cases vary so much. What works well in one place may not be appropriate elsewhere. It has been thought nevertheless desirable to be prescriptive because it is so obvious that improved performance is needed, sometimes quite desperately. The task then becomes one of suggesting some possibilities for desirable change, not one of 'laying down the law'. In this, the final chapter, we discuss more specifically a variety of aspects of administrative change in order to see how something may be done to make bureaucracies more effective.

The meaning of Administrative Reform

A useful working definition of administrative reform (AR) is to term it *induced, permanent improvement in administration.*[1] This, however, requires additional discussion and explanation.

(1) The word 'induced' is employed to indicate that we are talking about a form of administrative change which is deliberately brought about, not one which just happens by accident or without the making of any conscious effort. So, deliberate attempts to introduce better systems of recruiting civil servants (e.g. through the establishment of a

Public Service Commission) is an example of AR. Improvements in administration may happen because there is a change affecting the whole country, for example the ending of a civil war. That is not AR as we employ the term in this chapter. To clarify further, AR happens only when an institution (or perhaps an individual, e.g. the President of the country in question) decides that action is needed.

(2) The word 'permanent' carries the connotation that the changes introduced will be long-term, not just temporary. Obviously, in a changing and not very predictable world, reform cannot be expected to last forever but the term really should not be used to refer to any form of change which merely lasts for a matter of a few months. Indeed, it is probably not wise to describe administrative change as AR until a few years have elapsed, to enable judgement to be made about whether the changes made have 'taken root'.

(3) The third word requiring discussion within this definition is 'improvement'. Here there is even more difficulty involved. Simply put, to improve means 'to make better'. Of course, the problem here is that 'improvement' is (like beauty) in the eyes of the beholder. One man's improvement may be another man's deterioration or decline. Civil service recruitment again provides us with an appropriate example. To some, a system which more nearly guarantees merit recruitment may seem an improvement but not to those who benefit from nepotism, patronage and other non-bureaucratic ways of bringing people into the service. To the latter the reform proposed may be so damaging as to be viewed as very undesirable indeed. Thus, by using the word 'improvement' in our definition we are introducing an element of value judgement, i.e. we are bringing into the picture our own views about what is desirable change and what is not.

By way of clarifying terms, a further point needs to be made at the outset of our discussion. The meaning of 'reform' is quite distinct from the idea of 'revolution', which implies the total overthrow of old structures and systems (e.g. Russia 1917, China 1948), and their replacement by quite new ones. Revolution involves change throughout whole societies; reform is much less sweeping. When AR takes place, it aims to improve only the administrative system, perhaps in minor ways. It does not involve the overthrow of ruling classes and the creation of completely new social orders. AR may well, however, lead to social improvement as, for example, when a more efficient civil service is able to use its financial resources more effectively. In this way, the general public may benefit because it may be receiving better services (e.g. education, health) as a result. Also, revolution may lead to administrative change. The Chinese case, discussed later in the chapter, illustrates this.

●*Examples of administrative reform*

To express the meaning of AR more concretely it may be useful to provide some examples. One type, to which reference has been made in an earlier chapter, is decentralisation, whereby governments try to bring about improved administration over the relatively long term within the districts, provinces and so on. This type of AR is currently under way in a number of states in Africa, Asia and elsewhere.

Merit recruitment to the civil service has already been referred to in this chapter. Historically, it has been a very important type of AR in Europe and North America; and it represents a major area of concern currently in many less developed countries. Again, it clearly fits within the framework of our working definition of AR because it is deliberately introduced (**induced**), it is normally intended to be **permanent** and it is perceived by those who advocate it as being an **improvement** (even though many may not agree with them).

Another example is the establishment of systems intended to bring about administrative improvement through training. This would obviously fall within our definition of AR especially in cases where little or no training has been done previously, as in most of Africa where the creation of training institutions at around the time of independence would be a clear example of 'induced, permanent improvement'. Many countries have introduced government bodies with responsibility for management services (organisation and methods, work study, information technology, etc.). Such measures can also be counted as examples of AR.

When change is introduced with the aim of bringing about improved administrative performance, it is obvious that such efforts arise because people are discontented with the existing system — the 'status quo'. These feelings of discontent may be articulated by a number of different groups within society, some of which are bound to be more powerful than others. For the President to want change is quite different from a small peasant farmer who supports the opposition doing so, because the one is much more powerful than the other.

The initiators of reform

Some of the more important originators of AR may be:

The legislature

Members of Parliament may use parliamentary sessions to criticise the administration and make calls for reform. How effectively this is done depends, of course, on how knowledgeable the MPs are and also on the strength of the legislature within the political system as a whole.

The cabinet
Generally speaking this body has more power than the legislature and, in a sense, it may directly represent the views of the Head of State. It is thus much more likely to be able to instigate changes.

The bureaucracy
Again, much depends on levels of knowledge, not forgetting questions of power and influence — as with legislatures and cabinets. But it should also be borne in mind that bureaucrats are often unwilling to criticise themselves for obvious reasons of self-interest. This makes them unlikely to be advocates of AR.

'Outsiders'
Donor bodies may have a particular role here. The World Bank, for example, has been trying for some time to persuade governments to introduce reform and has been helping some of them with the 'nuts and bolts' of doing so.

The media
Again, this type of influence is external to the administrative system *per se*. However, the press, for example, by criticising the performance of administration may be a force for reform. A good example is corruption. Where there is a reasonably free press, newspaper attacks on corrupt bureaucrats may help bring about improvements. Unfortunately, most countries do not have media with enough independence to play this role effectively.

The difficulties

Enough has already been said to suggest that AR is a complex matter with a number of problem areas. In addition to what has already been mentioned, the following areas of difficulty merit discussion.

(1) There may be a lack of awareness of how bad the administration's performance is, or how improvements might be undertaken. In many countries there appears to be a fatalistic attitude of tolerance towards ineffective administration. Under such conditions the possibilities for AR are limited.
(2) The changes involved in AR may meet considerable resistance. This is a complex problem which could be discussed at greater length. However, bureaucracies themselves tend to dislike change, especially when their own interests are at stake. Corruption again presents a good example; reform may produce a cleaner administration but many

173

administrators may lose out in the process. Another fairly typical form of resistance is to be found where older civil servants resist changes proposed or demanded by their juniors. Again, this resistance may result from a desire for self-protection if older officers feel that AR represents a threat to them on the part of a younger generation which is better educated and impatient for promotion.

(3) Proposals for change may be too vague or confused to be easily put into practice. As a result, very little concrete change may result. Proposals for decentralisation often suffer from this sort of problem when they take the form of vague intentions and principles without going into any detail about how far powers are to be transferred from the centre to the districts. This and other examples of poorly framed proposals for AR serve to demonstrate the vital importance of ensuring that the measures proposed are spelt out in clearly implementable terms.

(4) A corollary of the last point is that those who are responsible for implementation may have very little understanding of what is supposed to be happening or of what has been proposed. This danger presents itself in three situations in particular: a) where the proposals are vaguely stated; b) where the ideas for AR originate from donors (e.g. the World Bank, USAID) with only marginal indigenous involvement at the planning stage; and c) where the staff responsible for implementation are poorly trained and/or lack appropriate qualifications for the tasks required of them. All three situations can, of course, be combined with regard to particular AR proposals, that is vaguely stated plans for AR may be originated by donors and require implementation by a poorly equipped staff — the worst possible way to go about bringing in changes.

(5) Mathur is quite right to provide this warning:

> What may work in one situation may be quite unworkable in another. Therefore, full consideration needs to be given to the unique situation in each country before any reform measures are introduced in the administrative system[2].

Unfortunately not all reformers bear this point in mind; the result is often failure.

Administrative reform and development policy

The need for reform has been increasingly recognized in less developed countries; in many it has been a long-standing concern. Earlier chapters of this book have referred to a variety of significant innovations, many of which can be referred to as examples of AR. The introduction of

174

new administrative institutions (e.g. training institutes, management services departments, public service commissions) which took place in most countries soon after independence, shows that interest in AR began some years ago.

The innovations which took place at that time, however, have only achieved partial success. Patterns of underdevelopment have not been removed; in a sense they have been accentuated in recent years because poverty and starvation have intensified dramatically, especially in parts of Africa (e.g. Mozambique, Sudan, Ethiopia). Clearly these conditions are not definite results of any single factor. International economic considerations have played a major role in all sorts of ways (declining terms of trade for products from less developed countries, exploitation by multi-national corporations, inappropriate aid policies, etc.), whilst physical/climatic phenomena also have to be included in the analysis, because drought has been such a significant feature in several countries. Political factors ought also to be considered. Countries such as Uganda which have experienced severely troubled political conditions have clearly experienced economic decline and difficulty as a result. But at least one other factor should be included within any analysis of these problems, and that is the performance of the bureaucracies themselves. Much was expected of them; indeed, they were regarded as the vanguard of the development effort. However, most observers are of the view that their performance has been a disappointment.

This does not mean, however, that there are no grounds for optimism. Current discussions about AR indicate that scope exists for improvement in many areas, and it is encouraging that many governments are increasingly aware of the problems being faced, even if the advice offered may be confusing and/or contradictory at times. Donor agencies have recently played a significant part in advising on AR (though they have not always called it that). An especially important role has been played by the World Bank, which has probably done more than any other body to bring a variety of AR-related issues close to the top of the development policy agenda. Thus, the administrative factors involved in development now have a greater prominence than they have had for very many years.

The case of the World Bank

There is nothing new in donors influencing patterns of AR in less developed countries. Many early aid policies had a pronounced AR focus, a point which has been demonstrated at various points in this book. The British, French and Americans have played important roles in promoting specific changes aimed at bringing about improved

175

performance. Training of various kinds has been offered, as Allen in particular has shown in her review of British and American activities in different parts of the world, whilst Dunsire has argued that the discipline of development administration grew out of US foreign policy concerns.[3] Apart from the United Nations, it was generally only national donors which took this sort of interest in the early days. The pattern has now altered somewhat; the World Bank has now taken the leading part. Furthermore, we now know far more than we used to about the development process because there is a body of documented experience on which to draw — much of this experience has informed the World Bank's thinking and policy prescriptions.

● The World Bank's controversial role

The World Bank is first and foremost a highly significant financial institution, especially as far as the less developed countries are concerned.[4] It is, however, not a bank in the normal sense. Rather, it is best regarded as a lending body specialising in development-related assistance. It has about 150 subscribing members, dominated in terms of voting power by the industrialised nations. Loans are made for development purposes at a variety of rates, there being a 'soft loan' facility which can be tapped by the poorest countries. It raises funds not only from its subscriptions but also by itself borrowing on the world markets. Its headquarters is in Washington, USA (see page 222), where most of its staff are concentrated, although it has recently adopted a policy of dispersing its staff to areas of the world where there are significant programmes and projects in which it has a financial interest. Because it is not an ordinary bank, its staffing requirements are not of the usual banking kind. Many of its staff have substantial expertise in development matters, several of them having previously worked as academic consultants or donor officials for their respective nations. Most of them come from the industrialised nations which tend to dominate the bank, but more effort is now being made to diversify so that less developed countries have a stronger representation.

The Bank's role in development has been a controversial one. It has been criticised from various quarters, partly for reasons mentioned already (e.g. dominance by the industrialised nations), because its influence is argued by some to be excessive, and still others feel its level of effectiveness of operations is too low. Thus, there are radical critics on the political left who see the Bank as being a mechanism through which less developed countries are in effect dictated to by the stronger capitalist nations, especially the USA. On the other hand, there is a more moderate school of criticism which broadly accepts the validity of the Bank's organising principles and objectives but which argues for a more effective style of performance. A good example of the first type of criticism, that of the radicals, is Payer's study of the Bank which reaches the conclusion that 'there are alternatives to the way the World Bank wants things done, and that there are people with technical expertise who are working on these problems and suggesting alternative solutions'. She goes on to indicate that in her view the Bank is not capable of taking a sufficiently radical stance because 'most of these alternatives require a challenge to the international corporations and to local elite structures of which the World Bank is not capable'. What is needed instead, she claims, is a 'socialist philosophy of development'.[5]

On the other hand, the more sympathetic or moderate critics see the problems of the Bank more as a challenge to its ability to be flexible and efficient. A recent book contains numerous pieces of advice to the Bank. In an 'open letter to the World Bank's new President', Feinberg sees four critical roles for the next few years — it should be a *coordinator* of global flows of capital, a *mediator* of political and economic differences between industrialised and developing countries, a *stabiliser* of the global economy and an *intellectual centre* for thinking about development. As Feinberg admits, these are not new roles for the Bank. In his view, they do, however, need reinforcement in order to promote better the effectiveness of the Bank's operations.[6]

Both these views of the World Bank's role are of relevance to the discussion which now ensues, one which concentrates specifically on questions of development administration. These questions have been of growing importance to the Bank in recent years. Lending policies are nowadays much more likely to be tied to some sort of administrative reform, as various states have discovered. The term 'structural adjustment' has come into substantial use during the 1980s. What the Bank precisely means by this has been the subject of some debate but essentially they have in mind a variety of reforms — of economic structures particularly — which are seen as necessary for development programmes to bear fruit. However, it is very clear that in a number of cases the reforms suggested are administrative or managerial in form. Loans for development purposes are now frequently granted on condition that structural adjustments occur — what is known as 'conditionality'. This has been the subject of some controversy, various critics seeing structural adjustment lending (SAL) as a way of exerting undue pressure on the recipient governments to undergo reform programmes which are unnecessary or even harmful. Privatisation is an example; its adoption as a policy where no viable private sector exists is unlikely to be a very effective option to follow. Payer criticises SAL for industry on the grounds that 'the recipient country will be expected to carry out important reforms in its economy, of a type consistent

177

with Bank demands through the years',[7] whilst Feinberg's support for the SAL strategy is an understandably cautious one. He points out that some Third World leaders (and not necessarily just the radical and/or socialist ones) are 'wary of the Bank's new enthusiasm for structural adjustment programs'.[8] Although he claims that leaders are rather more responsive than they were, he lists several complaints which they have been inclined to make about SAL:[9]

i) The Bank has tended to push simplistic, standardised formulas which are not always appropriate to the circumstances of the recipient countries.

ii) Too often the Bank staff handling the negotiations are too ignorant or arrogant to do so effectively.

iii) SAL programmes impose conditions which are often far too ambitious to meet within the time frame envisaged.

iv) The size of the loans on offer is frequently not commensurate with the risks involved.

Thus, there are all sorts of pitfalls. Much needs to be done, it would appear, to improve the quality of the dialogue between the Bank and the potential and existing recipients of its loans. The way this dialogue is handled needs to vary according to the circumstances to hand. On this point, Feinberg has an interesting comment to make:

> Bank missions must be especially circumspect with larger, more self confident clients, but they can sometimes be more assertive when a government lacks its own plans or analytical capabilities, or is internally divided, or heavily dependent on external donors for cash or for a high percentage of its public investment (as in much of Africa).[10]

These comments have another implication apart from requiring greater flexibility by World Bank missions. Clearly, if World Bank assertiveness can sometimes be justified then it also behoves recipients to approach their own negotiating task with a more aggressive and finely tuned approach to match that of the Bank — in itself a comment on administrative performance. The reference to Africa in the above quotation is particularly interesting because this part of the world has been of special interest to the Bank during the 1980s. Various reports have appeared suggesting how this assertiveness of the Bank's might be applied to the severe problems being faced by that continent, with a lot of mention made of administrative matters, (i.e. references to 'public sector management', 'managing reform' and so on).

● *The World Bank and African development*
Three reports on Africa appeared in the early 1980s which are of sufficient interest to justify detailed review of what they have to say

178

about the administrative factor in development.[11] Chapter 4 of the World Bank's 1984 report is the main focus here. However, because a number of references to management in Africa are to be found elsewhere in the report as well as in the 1981 (Berg) and 1983 reports it is necessary to go beyond a narrow discussion of just this one chapter. One reason for proceeding in this manner is because there does seem to be an emerging World Bank approach to management in Africa, the thrust of which can best be spelt out by a broadening of focus.

The report states that four themes are emerging world-wide as far as the management of development is concerned:

— Using pricing policy more widely in place of administrative controls to allocate resources.

— Reducing the burden on governments by greater use of community efforts and the private sector, so that governments can undertake their central responsibilities more efficiently.

— Giving more responsibility to managers of para-statals to operate their enterprises in a business-like manner.

— Avoiding discrimination against exporting.[12]

The report goes on to claim that these four major themes have been echoed in other reports published in Africa during the 1980s, for example by the African Development Bank, the Economic Commission for Africa and the governments of Kenya and Tanzania. Unfortunately, the quotations given from these latter reports hardly support the World Bank's claim, suggesting that perhaps there is not quite the emerging consensus that is implied.

Under the heading 'Public Sector Reforms', the report has a few interesting suggestions to make. The stress is on privatisation. It is seen to be desirable to reduce the burden of the public sector and 'encourage the private sector in a way that provides the services more efficiently and is consistent with national priorities'.[13] There is also talk of banning or severely limiting the growth of public employment. Rationalisation of public enterprises is also discussed on the grounds that the record in this sector is a dismal one. Like the earlier Berg Report, the 1984 authors are impressed by Senegal's public enterprise contracts, an arrangement by which public enterprises enter into negotiated agreements with the Senegalese Government. The contract describes 'the objectives government assigns to the para-statal as well as the resources it will provide and the degree of control which it will exercise. The company, in turn, promises certain results; performance is to be judged by indicators mutually accepted over a given period'.[14]

On public expenditure the emphasis is placed on improved funding for maintenance and operating rather than the initiation of new projects. There are also comments on the need for donors to bring less pressure to bear upon governments, since such pressures have in the past resulted in the taking on of commitments which governments cannot handle. Cuts in administrative services are also mentioned, although not with a high level of specificity. There are useful broad remarks on problems such as training, staff motivation and appointments under the general heading of 'Institutions'. This section also addresses the problems of agricultural extension services, where it emphasises the need for greater community involvement. Aid administration is also singled out for institutional reform, with stress placed on establishing clear linkages between donor activity and government planning and financial networks.

'Managing Policy Reform' seems to cover two interrelated concerns: the overall management of the reform process and the improved management of specific policies. The ensuing commentary will refer to both concerns.

●*The World Bank and Africa: a critique*
Six issues call for comment:

Planning and economic analysis
The various reports indicate that the institutionalisation of planning has a long way to go before a satisfactory stage is reached. It is particularly important that stress is placed on the improvement of linkages between the budgetary and planning processes — a clear-cut need in many states. Also the Berg Report stresses the need for improved screening of projects. Here again one can concur, with the caveat that some progress has been made in this direction in a number of African states. Two issues need more attention than the various World Bank Reports give them: the decentralisation of planning and the need to clarify how far central planning agencies have authority over other government agencies and para-statals. On both of these important issues the various reports under review are largely silent. Finally, the 1983 Report stresses the need for World Bank officials to be attached to planning agencies. The desirability of this idea obviously hinges on whether the overall World Bank strategy (with its various ideological undertones in the form of privatisation etc.) is acceptable.

Agricultural management
The bank rightly stresses the importance of agriculture. However, there are various points with which issue can be taken.
The Berg Report rightly states:

> All the evidence points to the fact that small holders are *outstanding managers* of their own resources — their land and *capital, fertilizer and water. They can be counted upon to respond to changes in the*

180

profitability of different crops and of other farming activities.[15] (my italics)

This being so, it seems useless to stress the need for more agricultural extension which is very costly in terms of staffing, transport, etc. Scarce resources for agriculture might be better used by improving the 'packages' for farmers, the infrastructure for delivery of produce, and so on, developing co-operative structures and promoting effective credit systems. By de-emphasising extension it is possible both to cut wasteful bureaucracy and to enable other measures to be taken which are likely to be more cost-effective. It is naive to assume that more advice to the farmers can be of any use when (a) the advice is often unhelpful, and (b) the farmer cannot act on advice given because of his resource constraints.

There is a particular need for detailed policy analysis on co-operative development. The Bank occasionally refers to this idea but without giving it the detailed attention it deserves. If there is to be a debureaucratisation of agriculture this may be the way to do it, but government support will still be needed, bearing in mind that co-operatives should not be mere extensions of the existing administrative apparatus. The tendency for this to happen has been observed in a number of countries. In this context donor assistance for bodies like Credit Unions and Co-operative Unions seems a significant need.

The para-statals
In this connection there is a strong World Bank thrust in the direction of privatisation. The reports have some helpful suggestions about what can be done to improve performance. Three stand out — making para-statals answerable to lower echelons of government, such as district authorities,[16] the Senegalese public enterprise contracts (already mentioned), and the establishment of 'organisational review bodies' for the parastatal sector.[17] This has been suggested for many countries but not often implemented.

In most cases, because of weakness of indigenous entrepreneurs, privatisation would amount to an invitation from less developed countries to multi-nationals, the negative consequences of which would probably be a significant weakening of planning, further cash outflows, a further skewing of development towards luxury consumption, the import of often inappropriate technologies and skills, and so on. In short, it seems premature to take the rather strongly anti-statist line of these reports.

The pruning of public bureaucracies
The World Bank seems correct on this issue in two respects: every country has to decide on its own priorities and overall there is a real

need for cuts. There should not be criticism of the Bank for not being very specific. One point to stress is that many public services contain a lot of 'deadwood' which should be removed. This would both reduce the burden on public finance and also create opportunities for graduates and other qualified people who have skills and knowledge to offer. However, the Bank seems to be broadly correct in calling for rationalisation and limiting expansion.

An issue not addressed by the Bank is the distribution of bureaucrats in the system. Perhaps such a study in a lot of states would show significant over-manning of some positions in the bureaucracy (e.g. central government clerical) and under-manning of others (e.g. rural clinical staff). This needs urgent and systematic attention.

Improving administrative productivity

Berg's comments here are helpful. Four requirements are listed:
a) improve the cost effectiveness of government manpower;
b) improve reward for performance;
c) make bureaucratic agencies more answerable to their clienteles;
d) gear reform measures to conditions in individual countries.
However, all three reports talk of the need for experimentation. Here there is a danger that needs recognition. Experimentation has taken place in a number of countries but without any real thought going into what is being aimed at. The results have often been chaotic. What needs emphasis is the need to work out how existing structures can operate more effectively. Experimentation should not be ruled out (a good example might be the Senegalese public enterprise contracts) but should be used more sparingly than the World Bank suggests.

Donor involvement

The report stresses the dangers involved in donors bringing pressure to bear on governments. Ironically the reports, taken together with the pattern of World Bank lending, can be themselves seen as a form of pressure. However, a revised formulation might be in order because a number of the Bank's criticisms are sensible — donors have too often been rigid where flexibility has been needed, they have failed to consider the recurrent cost consequences of projects, and so on. Thus, the Bank's reports serve to remind us that donor involvement, whilst very much needed, can be negative in its consequences. It should be stressed here that planning is often little more than a list of projects for submission to donor agencies. It should be considerably more than that if patterns of development are not to be mere reflections of the priorities of the donors. An indigenous policy-making capability which would, *inter alia*, counterbalance donor influence thus seems to be a very high priority need.

• The World Bank's Development Report for 1983: a review

The Bank's Development Report for 1983 (one of the regular series of annual reports looking at the global development scene) contains a wide ranging survey of various administrative questions, including a chapter devoted specifically to AR and development.[18] Many interesting insights are contained in a total of nine chapters devoted to what the bank calls 'Management in Development'. The approach adopted is to attempt generalisation wherever possible but to supplement this with a series of case-studies taken from individual Third World countries. In so doing, the authors seem to be aware of neglecting the uniqueness of individual countries, although not to the satisfaction of Murray who finds that the authors have a knowledge of a limited number of somewhat arbitrarily selected cases from which generalisations are confidently extended to all.[19] However, the value of this report lies largely in its capacity to stimulate thought and discussion about individual systems, which is not to say that it is by any means correct in everything it has to say about development management.

Three aspects of the report will be briefly reviewed here: its approach to privatisation and greater use of market mechanisms; its general comments on AR strategy; and the way it portrays success stories, not just failures.

Privatisation

The Bank clearly believes that most public sectors have become too big and that they are often grossly inefficient. Under most conditions, better results can be achieved by using the private sector/market forces more fully. Its advocacy of this point of view is cautious but firm:

> Though private management has much to contribute, it would be misleading to portray it as universally efficient. In poor countries, managerial capacity is weak in both the public and private sectors. However, the greater potential for competition and the ever-present possibility of bankruptcy exercises a discipline over private businesses that is lacking in the public sector. When services can be provided efficiently by small businesses, such as individual truckers, reliance on the private sector economises on management. Recognizing that, some governments have decided to reduce the size of the public sector while others are actively considering doing so.[20]

This succinctly presents the case for expanding the role of the private sector, de-emphasising the public sector in the process. To the Bank, a priority for AR should be to move firmly in this direction. SALs are one means by which this can be done. Set against this, however, there are other arguments to be stated such as those already mentioned regarding the World Bank's reports on Africa. To this can be added a point made by Murray who argues that even according to the Bank's own evidence (as presented in the 1983 report) our level of knowledge and understanding is not quite such that prescription can be propounded with unbridled confidence.[21] The implications seem clear: proposals for privatisation (or 'liberalisation') for any individual country should be the subject of close scrutiny, both to see what the possibilities are and, perhaps more importantly, to see what the adverse effects might turn out to be (e.g. greater control by multi-national corporations of a country's mining industry if attempted in a country such as Zambia, widespread unemployment if insufficient private capital turns out to be available as has been found in Tanzania).

Administrative reform strategies

The general comments made on AR reform strategies are of interest because they are somewhat unorthodox, in that some of them do not generally appear in the literature. The Bank suggests that experience demonstrates the validity of these main conclusions:

— Administrative reforms should concentrate on a few strategic institutions or functions, rather than be dispersed (and ineffective) across the board.

— Governments can simultaneously keep up pressures for gradual system-wide improvements particularly by incremental changes which increase official accountability and which reduce excessive coordination requirements or unproductive centralisation.

— Reform needs careful administrative planning and continuity in implementation — close attention to detailed procedures as well as the overall policy thrust.

— Non-bureaucratic interests must be included in the reform process to keep up pressure for accountability, to ensure that external criteria of efficiency and service are observed, and to see that the viewpoint of ordinary people is taken into account.

— There should be incentives for officials and agencies to help devise and execute reforms: otherwise their suspicion or hostility can quickly undermine results.[22]

These conclusions run counter to the conventional wisdom in a number of ways.

i)   They suggest that it is wrong to assume that reform should be comprehensive, arguing that better results can be achieved by interventions directed at specific and carefully chosen targets.

ii) They point out that co-ordination can be excessive, a notion which a number of governments and observers have all too frequently overlooked.

iii) The *planning* of AR is stressed, a useful emphasis because this

184

aspect is also often neglected, the results tending to be chaotic and to give AR a bad name. This has happened very often where decentralisation has been attempted in Africa.[23]

iv) Recognition is here given to interests outside the bureaucracy itself — a point which many potential reformers could be advised to consider carefully in formulating their proposals. Of course, the precise nature of these interests will vary from country to country, depending on the political system, the economy, etc. This, however, does not seem to detract from the validity of the point being made.

v) Finally, the idea of including incentives is useful because it has the potential to go a long way towards overcoming the problem of resistance (mainly bureaucratic) to AR which is found in many countries.

Success stories

The Bank's position is a comparatively optimistic one, bearing in mind its portrayals of cases of administrative success. It thus supplies an invigorating antidote to the general perspective found in the literature, which is dominated by discussions of failure. A few examples from a diversity of countries illustrate something of this optimism:

i) **Malaysia**'s National Institute of Public Administration is referred to as 'training that works' because it has 'developed a wealth of training methods', has sound systems of evaluation, is flexible to the needs of its clients, does not neglect top administrators and has systematic plans for the development of its own staff.[24]

ii) In the **Philippines** the National Irrigation Administration (NIA) has developed since 1976 an effective system of consultation with water users, with the result that needs have been more effectively met. Accountability has improved, whilst staff report greater job satisfaction.[25]

iii) **Bangladesh**'s example of personnel reform is said to demonstrate that 'persistence pays', a unified career service was created in 1980 and the 'unproductive' growth of the service has slowed down, despite considerable resistance from many public employees whose strikes and demonstrations 'nearly paralysed the administration'.[26]

iv) In **Senegal** the government is said to have negotiated 'contract plans' with five state-owned enterprises with 'promising' results in terms of performance. The main advantage seems to have been that these enterprises were obliged to plan their investments more thoroughly so as to demonstrate the justification for their requirements to the government. This case is interesting because it mentions what some might regard as an undesirable consequence of reform: the national airline was obliged to abolish services to certain remote areas.[27]

Learning from success: three case-studies

It is perfectly true, as a number of observers have pointed out, that a considerable amount can be gained from studying failure if the right sort of approach towards learning is followed. Many organisations fall down on this point, and may be characterised as poor learners from experience. However, there is also much to be gained from discussion of the relatively few success stories which are available for our analysis.[28] Three such cases have been selected for discussion here — The People's Republic of China's public health programme, Kenya's smallholder tea programme and Korea's experience with 'government invested enterprises'. They are discussed here only in outline form to bring out the main points of interest. More detailed analysis can be obtained from the sources quoted. They are not presented by any means as unqualified successes, which they are not, but because lessons can be derived from the positive results which have been observed. Two of them — the Chinese and Kenyan cases — have been mentioned briefly in the chapter on rural development.

●*The People's Republic of China — public health programme*
Before the 1949 Revolution, health care in China was very inadequate, the concentration of services being overwhelmingly in the urban areas. Very little attention was given to the needs of the peasants and to preventive medicine. There were, however, about half a million traditional practitioners who were not recognized by the modern health sector. By 1970 the picture had changed so substantially that 'China was being quoted as an example to the developing world of what could be done through social and organisational change in the field of public health'.[29] This was not done by a rejection of modern medicine altogether, as is sometimes assumed, but through a willingness to question some conventional assumptions held by ministry officials and by professionals trained within the Western medical tradition. This process of questioning was encouraged by the political leadership which was guided not so much by professional qualified advisors as by the need to give priority to the provision of adequate service to the peasants as opposed to the urban population.

This rural emphasis of the Chinese government is well illustrated by the notion of the 'barefoot doctor', an alternative to the conventional approaches which has been of some interest to a number of countries aiming to introduce primary health care strategies and policies. 'Barefoot doctors' are not medical practitioners in the usual sense. They are peasants who are given training locally for health work so that they can perform community health services on a part-time basis. Their work, together with the other medical services, emphasises the prevention of such diseases as malaria and schistosomiasis which were major health problems in China previously. Added to this, community participation in the planning and implementation of health programmes has been an important component, together with central co-ordination and direction. An example can be given from the finance field. A system of co-operative health care was introduced in the late 1960s, which imposed the payment of small fees by members of each of the country's communes, resulting in the establishment of a co-operative medical fund. Whilst this system was introduced by the centre, and co-ordinated by it, there was scope for significant variations at the local level.[30] These strategies to involve communities at the local level, with particular emphasis on the rural areas, required that supportive measures be taken to solve the manpower problems involved. Several measures were taken, including:[31]

a) greater use of existing medical personnel in the rural areas – a massive redistribution exercise, given the concentration of most of them in the urban centres,

b) the even more drastic decision to discontinue formal medical education so that it could be reformed to meet better the needs of rural people;

c) the unification of traditional and Western medicine so that each type had an effective role to play in the new system;

d) the 'barefoot doctor' idea to which reference has already been made.

Several writers on the Chinese case make the point that all these changes have been made possible by the wider social transformation (revolutionary in kind) which has taken place in China during the past forty or so years. Strong political commitment and support was essential for these reforms to succeed. MacPherson's comment sums up this point well – 'Health improvements in China came as a result of a strategy of total development not as a result of changes in the health services alone.'[32] China represents an example of a country where 'mobilisation of the masses' has clearly amounted to rather more than mere rhetoric. There have been enormous political costs involved, in terms of repression of dissidents and the like, and in recent years the regime's ideological stance has been a more pragmatic and westernised one. The health care system, however, remains a major achievement on which the present government can build. Frankenberg and Leeson observed some years ago that China might provide an alternative to the prevailing 'neo-colonialist pattern' of health care exemplified by the uncritical import of Western medical professional assumptions, attitudes and systems into so many less developed countries. They may still be proved right.[33]

•*Kenya Tea Development Authority*

The success of the Kenya Tea Development Authority (KTDA) has been noted by a number of observers. Its achievements are particularly interesting for three reasons. First, it constitutes one of the few success stories to emerge from the experience of *sub-Saharan Africa*, a part of the world which has suffered more than most from inadequate managerial performance. Secondly, it is a case of success by a *public enterprise*, again a rarity within the development administration literature. Thirdly, it focuses its activities on *rural development*, a policy area where the literature has tended to adopt a fairly negative tone in that the stories of failure far outweigh those which tell of success.

The achievements of the KTDA are well summarised by Lamb and Muller:

> In roughly two decades it has organised the planting of about 54,000 hectares of tea by some 138,000 smallholders, and has become a major processor and the largest exporter of black tea in the world. Smallholders produced 146,000 metric tons of green leaf in the crop year 1980/81, which was processed into approximately 33,000 metric tons of made tea, 85% of it for export. Smallholder tea exports, virtually non-existent before 1960, have accounted for about one-third of Kenya's annual tea exports since the mid-1970s, the remainder coming from long established commercially-owned tea estates.[34]

This achievement is all the more remarkable bearing in mind that Kenya's agricultural history before independence was dominated by the colonial assumption that tea was too sophisticated a crop for the African smallholder to grow.

A number of factors can be mentioned as contributors to the KTDA's success, several of them being managerial in kind. For example, four aspects of its institutional structure are mentioned by Lamb and Muller, all of which seem to have made a major contribution:

i)   A great deal of thought and care went into designing the organisational structure (this took place in the last years of colonial rule).

ii) Emphasis has been placed on the provision of services to the farmers in a comprehensive and integrated manner — this idea

188

was developed in the KTDA some time before it achieved acceptance elsewhere.

iii) The authority has developed a strong strategic planning capability to maintain its ability to innovate effectively.

iv) The pattern of managerial control is based on clear and uncomplicated objectives — to promote the smallholder tea industry.

Beyond these four major points, however, there are other factors to consider. The KTDA's autonomy has been well maintained. Political interference has not been absent but it has been limited to government representation on the authority's board.[35]

It can thus be concluded that the political environment has been unusually conducive to success. It has particularly benefited from having a large measure of financial autonomy. Another dimension is that of participation. Through a well organised structure of tea committees the farmers (i.e. the tea growers) have been given opportunities to state their views on aspects of the programme (e.g. pricing, collection of crops, tea factory performance, extension services). The *responsiveness* of the KTDA management to the ideas presented through those channels has contributed to the generally good relationship existing between the growers and the authority. This does not mean that the KTDA always accepts the views of the growers; that would be a very unrealistic perspective to adopt. However, the management clearly believes in two-way communication: where it rejects the views of growers it generally states clearly why this is so in a reasoned and understandable manner.

There is also the question of incentives. Here the KTDA has generally been dependent on the external market forces which affect prices for tea on the world market. However, this is not the whole story since the authority has choices about what it should pass on to the grower, and has used this as an opportunity to maximise the incentives for them to produce tea rather than go into other types of activity.

Another apparent contributor to success has been the performance of the KTDA's field staff. Because tea is a technically demanding crop it is important that the growers be well supervised and advised. To this end, the authority has made substantial investments in training and recruiting personnel so that there is an effective extension service operating in the field. However, the intention is gradually to cut back on extension because as the General Manager explained:

Once the number of tea growers stabilises and our extension staff have done their job of training the farmers, there is really no need to keep the field staff in the same strength. The farmers will need only minimal assistance. Our hope is that we can then revert most of the

189

field staff back to the Ministry of Agriculture from where they came in the first place.[36]

There is some evidence to suggest that the quality of KTDA's performance is also linked to various management policies and practices, such as well-designed record-keeping systems, incentives (e.g. housing), staff inspection, and the use of feedback on staff received from the growers themselves,[37] both through the tea committees and through the individual growers. The end result has been the establishment of 'an effective, disciplined extension service'[38] which has enabled a large number of Kenyan farmers to benefit from the world tea market which, at least until the early 1980s, was a favourable one. Thus, good management has made it possible for these farmers to maximise the advantages of climatic conditions (soil, rainfall, etc.) which in many parts of Kenya (e.g. Nyeri and Kericho Districts) are highly suitable for the growing of tea. This case-study, then, represents a good example of the manager as *enabler*, a function which seems to be increasingly in demand in Kenya as well as in other countries, as governments intervene in the economy less and less, but rather aim to assist the private sector to make use of the different opportunities which exist.

● *Republic of Korea — Government-Invested Enterprises*
A recent World Bank Discussion Paper by Young C. Park contains an analysis of the performance of public enterprises in this Far Eastern country.[39] It is mainly of interest because it contains a rare discussion of ways of achieving success in an area of management over which much gloom and despondency has loomed for years in a number of less developed countries.

Despite its emphasis on market forces and private entrepreneurship, Korea has a large public enterprise sector — often in partnership with the private sector. This sector includes a number of key products such as electricity, coal and telephone services, all of which are of strategic importance for the economy as a whole. By the late 1970s, clear disappointment with the performance of these bodies was being registered, much along the lines expressed in many other countries at the same time. As a result, a research effort was launched, utilising the government-sponsored Korea Development Institute (KDI). A wide range of problems were identified as a result of this research. Park[40] lists them as follows:
a) obscure and sometimes conflicting managerial goals;
b) the absence of both the accountability and the autonomy of management;

190

c) excessive government interference in day-to-day management without effective control over the results;

d) inadequate personnel and incentive systems;

e) complicated budget and procurement processes; and

f) inappropriate pricing and credit policies.

In other words, there was considerable inefficiency and muddle, a state of affairs akin to that being experienced in a number of other countries. Following on from this analysis, a number of reform proposals were made, culminating in the passage of the 'Government-Invested Enterprise Management Act' of 1983. Its main objectives were to increase managerial autonomy and accountability, and provide for effective control. To this end a number of very interesting innovations/reforms were included, among them being:

a) using Management by Objectives (MBO) for budget preparation;

b) giving enterprise managements better control over procurement, budgeting, and personnel policy;

c) providing for a 'two tier management organisation' with decision-making to be carried out by a Board of Directors, whilst the President of the enterprise is in charge of implementation;

d) simplifying and unifying the external auditing system;

e) eliminating business supervision by technical ministries;

f) creating an evaluation system, related to incentives.[41]

Park describes item f) of this list as the most important by far. Certainly it addresses a problem which has faced many such enterprises around the world (developed and otherwise) — *how best to evaluate performance*. The Korean system relates rewards/incentives and penalties to results derived from evaluation. High-level bodies of various kinds have been established with the specific purpose of carrying out evaluations, whilst the enterprises themselves have in response established their own evaluation units 'in-house'. The KDI which carried out the original research has had a key role in *the evaluation system*, the basic principles of which could be of interest to a number of countries.[42]

i) A distinction is made between the performance of the management (the subject of evaluation) and that of the company as a whole. For example, good management can reduce losses in a company running a deficit.

ii) Both short- and long-term performance should be considered.

iii) *Evaluation* should be confined to those variables within management's control (e.g. it cannot control tariffs applicable to the industry within which it is operating).

iv) Evaluation should be based upon notions of *public profitability*, duly recognizing that this is not the same as private profitability.

Whilst the system has not been devoid of problems (notably on how to make clear the difficult distinction indicated in point 4 above), the

191

results do seem to have been impressive. Managers are said to take the system seriously, because they give special attention to the various evaluation-of-performance indicators when making decisions. Linking rewards to performance provides *incentives* which are taken most seriously, and public enterprises now seem to be making a much more positive contribution to the Korean economy than they were doing ten years ago.

What are the reasons for this apparent success? Park lists several factors:[43]

i) There is a high degree of *political commitment.*

ii) The incentive system has appealed to Koreans not just because of the material rewards at stake but also because of the social status associated with achieving successful levels of performance. Of great importance is the financial 'extra bonus' determined by the 'ranking' of the enterprises. Those ranked 'outstanding' receive a sum equal to three months' 'extra' salary/wages, not insignificant as an inducement to improve performance. According to Park, however, *public recognition* (or status) is even more important in Korean culture.

iii) The system is *not too complex:* data requirements, for example, are simple.

iv) The high level of staffing of the enterprises — this was apparently less of a problem in Korea than it is in a number of other countries.

v) The contribution of 'private' experts (professors etc.).

vi) The cultural predisposition towards the competitiveness inherent in the ranking idea.

vii) The willingness of the authorities to implement the system flexibly, giving due recognition to enterprise-specific factors.

• *Commentary*

These three cases embrace quite different political systems in quite diverse parts of the world. Korea, from an ideological point of view, has more in common with the capitalist inclinations found in far away Kenya than with the communism of the nearby People's Republic of China. Certain themes, however, emerge from these cases in a way which serves at least to suggest what some of the crucial ingredients of success may prove to be.

i) In all three instances there was a *high level of commitment emanating from the political leadership.* In China, this commitment was quite aggressive in the 1960s (it is less so now). In the other two cases discussed it has been more muted but has nevertheless been consistently provided, thus maintaining the right balance

192

between public enterprise autonomy and central government control.

ii) A great deal of thought (involving some research) went into *designing the organisations* under review. This was particularly observable in the case of Korea (the role of the KDI) but was also very apparent in the other two examples given.

iii) The systems in all three countries were kept *as simple as possible*. Objectives were not highly complex and a lot of attention was paid to the need to make them as understandable as possible to those directly involved (farmers, managers, peasants, etc).

iv) A lot of thought went into appropriate provision of *human resources* to meet the organisational objectives. China virtually revolutionised its health care system by massive changes in staffing, whilst Kenya and Korea both took care to see to it that appropriate incentives were made available to staff.

v) It is probably very significant that what each country did was based on *the traditions and interests of the people being served*. The Chinese idea of integrating traditional medicine with modern ideas illustrates this. The Kenyan case shows that the KTDA was building upon pre-existing inclinations of the Kenyan peasantry to enter into small-scale agricultural production, whilst in Korea the system introduced into the government-invested enterprises seems to have fitted in well with cultural patterns in that country.

To the above points, which can be made about all three countries, there is another point to mention regarding Kenya and China. In both the programmes under review an effective balance was achieved between community institutions (communes, tea committees) and central co-ordination and control. This point is important because so often ideas of community involvement/participation are no more than empty rhetoric. The Korean case does not disprove its importance since there is little scope for community linkages for most government-invested enterprises.

These conclusions are merely suggestive of what might be done elsewhere. They are not presented as models of what ought to be done. What their presentation does perhaps achieve, however, is to indicate that there are some success stories worthy of discussion and that valuable lessons can be learnt from such a perspective.

The prospects for reform

Administrative systems are rarely static. Change takes place frequently, in a variety of forms and as the result of a variety of pressures. Earlier chapters of the book have also stressed the importance of change and have reviewed some attempts at reform by discussing particular case-studies drawn from a variety of countries in Africa and Asia. In doing so, it has been argued that reform is a highly complex process for which there are no magic solutions to which aspiring reformers can turn. However, there are nevertheless grounds for believing that the study of experience can indicate some useful lessons which may be applicable to a variety of countries.

The absence of magic solutions (or 'blueprints') can only be partially explained by pointing to the obvious enough fact that the environment of bureaucracy varies from one country to the other. Perhaps even more important is the complex network of interests which are involved, not only in pressing for change but also in terms of being affected by the consequences of it. In so many cases, somebody loses out in the course of the reform process. For example, in the Chinese health care case those with a vested interest in the continuation of the Western system were adversely affected by the sweeping changes which were brought in following the revolution in that country.

Resistance to reform often has to be overcome. Where major changes are being proposed (as in the Chinese case), success is unlikely to result without strong commitment on the part of the political leadership to override opposition. Thus, in studying any country's experience of administrative reform it is vital to consider fully all the factors involved, rather than assume that there are 'off the shelf' solutions readily available.[44] The latter approach has been tried often, and has been found wanting in a number of cases.

It is quite clear, however, that most countries in the parts of the world with which we are concerned are now much more aware of the need for administrative improvement than they were a few years ago. In the case of Africa, for example, the 'Lagos Plan of Action' (1980) illustrates this point well. This document was supposed to indicate ways of improving the levels of development achieved in Africa, but had very little to say about administrative factors.[45] Since that time, however, growing recognition of the importance of public sector management has occurred in most states, regardless of ideological orientation. It is not easy to specify precisely the origins of this change in perspective, but the general failure of development programmes to bring about real alleviation of poverty seems to have been an important factor, in that the poor performance of bureaucracy has often been interpreted as one of the major contributing factors.

•Administration and underdevelopment

Some observers go further than this to argue that administrators may actually contribute towards the perpetuation of underdevelopment

194

rather than acting as change agents aiming at reform.[46] It has been pointed out that bureaucrats often have strong economic interests (expressed through ownership of property, business activities, etc.) which do not coincide with development strategies directed at the needs of the less well-off members of society. These arguments are convincing ones, particularly if development is taken to mean greater benefits for the poor rather than concentrating on the privileged few. For example, Hirschmann is surely correct to point out that:

> The salaries received, at least by the upper echelons of civil servants, together with their better access to credit, enable many of them to become property owners through urban land purchases and house-building for residence or hire; the acquisition and development of farmlands and estates; and the launching or expansion of business ventures.[47]

This makes it likely that the bureaucrats will not be willing to endorse strategies which undermine their own economic positions. A few years ago this point was rather more important than it now is because the 1980s have seen a shift in development thinking towards a less egalitarian approach in which a large private sector is regarded as a positive element. In such a perspective, the economic interests of senior bureaucrats may be regarded as much less of an obstacle, and may even be seen as representing an opportunity for greater privatisation, because they often have the capital to put into business activity.

From the point of view of equality, this argument may be a hard one to stomach. However, there is no denying that the direction in which many countries are going is a capitalist one. Since very many capitalists in the Third World (especially in Africa) are closely linked to bureaucracy, some of the current ideas being propounded by the World Bank and other agencies may prove acceptable; they coincide with the interests of the 'bureaucratic bourgeoisie' in many countries. The position is rather different in countries of socialist inclination (e.g. Ethiopia, Tanzania). There, the external advice may well coincide with the preference of the bureaucrats but conflict with the views of the political leaders themselves.

A recent report[48] on Tanzania observed that the ex-President, Julius Nyerere, who is chairman of the ruling 'Chama Cha Mapinduzi' party, is trying to resist the dilution of that country's socialist path, a change in direction advocated by many external bodies (especially the International Monetary Fund) and accepted by many top figures, including many bureaucrats. The climate for reform thus varies somewhat from country to country. Nevertheless, there is now generally a more positive attitude towards pragmatic styles of reform which do not threaten significant

195

economic interests in the countries concerned. This suggests that the process of reform might turn out to be a fairly smooth one in countries inclined to the capitalist strategy, less in states which have opted for socialism. As a consequence of this it is likely that inequality will grow as class formation moves on apace. This raises extremely important questions about development policy in general, ones which require far more detailed discussion than is possible here.

● *Donor involvement*

Frequent reference in this book has been made to what is (often rather loosely) termed 'the donor community'. Particular attention has been given to the World Bank within the network of international bodies and states which are part and parcel of the 'aid business'. There is too little recognition in the literature of the importance of international factors in influencing governments to undertake administrative change. The detailed analysis, undertaken here of the World Bank in Africa, demonstrates some of the dimensions of this influence. There has, however, been mention made throughout the book of other forms of donor activity which have had implications for administrative systems. Both the Americans and the British have shown interest in this field. For less developed countries the problem here has been to assess how useful this assistance is likely to be, particularly in cases where Western principles and practices are being strongly emphasised. Dealing with this problem requires an indigenous administration which has the capability to assess the relevance of imported ideas for local conditions. This requirement is gradually being met; in most countries it is more than ever observable that uncritical acceptance of advice is unlikely to take place. The role of donors, however, is likely to increase in importance as concern about indebtedness and poverty grows. It is not likely that donors will simply 'wash their hands' as far as less developed countries are concerned, if only because they often have significant debts to recover and wish to see more effort put into improved management as a means to this end. In addition, there is, of course, a continuing real desire to eliminate (or at least reduce) poverty. To achieve that objective, too, there seems to be an acceptance of the need for some type of reform.

Conclusions

Discussion of what needs to be done in particular cases requires a greater willingness to question conventional wisdom than has often been practised in the past. Where little success is being achieved it is not enough merely to repeat time-honoured principles. Rather, it becomes of greater importance to question the assumptions which are made about all sorts of issues and, if necessary, reject them. The Chinese case is relevant here; the public health programme flowed from a readiness to reject the assumptions of the medical profession at the time. On the other hand, in discussing Africa we pointed out the folly of experimentation based on shallow thinking and superficial planning. The creation of confusion as a result of ignoring this point may be as big a danger as the uncritical acceptance of orthodox ideas.

It has also been a central concern in this book to present a balanced picture as far as administrative performance is concerned. This has inevitably led to quite a lot of discussion about the ways in which failure has occurred, simply reflecting the facts as far as most countries are concerned. However, to obtain a balanced picture as far as possible attention has been drawn to well-documented 'success stories'. World Bank material has been used a great deal here but there are other useful sources, to which reference has been made. Paul's work, for example, contains some particularly rewarding ideas, based upon such case-studies.[49]

Care has also been taken to ensure that over-generalisation does not occur. Repeated emphasis has been placed on the idea that every national system is unique and that a great deal of damage can be done by mindlessly assuming that ideas which have worked in one country can work in another. This argument has been applied particularly in instances where Western-based consultants recommend the taking of measures which have worked in USA, UK etc., without fully considering their workability in less developed countries.[50]

Finally, it is important to keep the role of administration in perspective. To blame the bureaucrats when programmes fail is usually only to see part of the truth, whilst to regard them as heroes when success is achieved can be an equally distorted view of reality. Administrators in less developed countries generally work in environments which are less conducive to effectiveness than do their counterparts in the more developed states. Agricultural officers can do little about falling crop prices in their districts when the determining factors are located in the USA, Europe and Japan. There is, too, generally little that can be done in the face of conditions of extreme drought or other forms of natural disaster. Much has been said, too, of the sometimes unhelpful nature of the political leadership in several national cases. All this makes administrative life difficult. It does not, however, necessarily make it impossible, as our numerous references to 'success stories' serve to demonstrate.

197

Questions

1   What are the main lessons to be derived from the 'success stories' discussed in this chapter?
2   In what ways may donors have negative impacts on administrative reform? What can be done to minimise these problems?
3   What obstacles stand in the way of devising a successful programme of socialist administrative reform in Third World countries?
4   Identify the main priorities for administrative reform in your own country. Give reasons for the choices you have made.
     What factors do you need to consider in order to implement successfully the reforms you are proposing?

References and Further Reading

Chapter 1

1 Good accounts of Weber's work are to be found in the following: Eugene Kamenka and Martin Krygier (eds), *Bureaucracy: The Career of a Concept* (Edward Arnold, London 1979), Martin Albrow, *Bureaucracy* (Macmillan, London 1970), Nicos P. Mouzelis, *Organisation and Bureaucracy* (Routledge and Kegan Paul, London 1967), Peter M. Blau, *Bureaucracy in Modern Society* (Random House, New York 1987) and David Beetham *Bureaucracy* (Open University, Milton Keynes, UK, 1987).

2 See B. C. Smith, *Decentralisation: The Territorial Dimension of the State* (Allen and Unwin, London 1985), especially ch. 8 for a discussion of various countries.

3 See J. Suret-Canale, *French Colonialism in Tropical Africa* (G. Hurst, London 1971), M. Crowder (ed.), *Colonial West Africa: Collected Essays* (Cass, London 1978), especially Crowder's own essay '"Indirect Rule" French and British Style'.

4 J. D. Hargreaves (ed.), *France and West Africa* (Papermac, London 1969) pp. 210–214.

5 *Ibid*, pp. 211–212.

6 Quoted in A. H. M. Kirk Greene (ed.), *The Principles of Native Administration in Nigeria* (Oxford University Press, Oxford 1965) p. 149.

7 *Ibid*, pp. 70–71.

8 Walter Rodney, *How Europe Underdeveloped Africa* (Bogle l'Overture, London 1972).

9 Lord Hailey, *Native Administration in the British African Territories (pt. 5)* (HMSO, London 1953), pp. 13–16.

10 See B. B. Schaffer, 'The deadlock in development administration' in Colin Leys (ed.), *Politics and Change in Developing Countries* (Cambridge University Press, Cambridge 1969) pp. 177–211.

11 See A. L. Adu, *The Civil Service in Commonwealth Africa* (Allen and Unwin, London 1969), ch. 7. Also Richard Symonds, *The British and their Successors* (Faber, London 1969).

12 Robert K. Merton, 'Bureaucratic Structure and Personality' in Merton *et al.* (eds) *Reader in Bureaucracy* (Free Press, New York 1952), pp. 361–371.

13 E. Mayo, 'Hawthorne and the Western Electric Company' in D. S. Pugh (ed.) *Organisation Theory* (Penguin, Harmondsworth 1985) pp. 279–292.

14 Blau (1987), ch. 3.

15   Mayo (1985), p. 291.
16   Schaffer (1969), p. 190. A useful set of essays reflecting this writer's concerns is found in *Public Administration and Development* (October/ November, 1986).
17   See, for example, Goran Hyden, *No Shortcuts to Progress* (Heinemann, London 1983) and Richard Sandbrook, *The Politics of Africa's Economic Stagnation* (Cambridge University Press, Cambridge 1985). David K Leonard, 'The Political Realities of African Management' in *World Development* (July 1987) takes a slightly more optimistic view.
18   Issa G. Shivji, *Class Struggles in Tanzania* (Heinemann, London 1978).
19   See for example, *North — South: A Programme for Survival* (Pan, London 1980) — otherwise known as the 'Brandt Report' and Giovanni A. Cornia, Richard Jolly, Frances Stewart (eds) *Adjustment with a Human Face* Vol I and II (Clarendon Press, Oxford 1987 and 1988).
20   See A. H. Hanson, *Public Enterprise and Economic Development* (Routledge and Kegan Paul, London 1965) for a review of the main factors contributing to this tendency.
21   R. B. Fitch and M. Oppenheimer, *Ghana: End of an Illusion* (Monthly Review Press, New York 1966).
22   See *Handbook of World Development: The guide to the Brandt Report* (Longman, Harlow 1981) p. 3.
23   See *Ibid*, p. 68/69, for general background on the Bank.
24   For example, World Bank, *Accelerated Development in Sub-Saharan Africa: An Agenda for Action* (World Bank, Washington 1981).
25   See, for example, Rodney (1972) and Shivji (1976) Also, David Hirschmann, *The Administration of Planning in Lesotho* (Department of Administrative Studies, University of Manchester 1981) ch. 3, Rene Dumont, *False Start in Africa* (Andre Deutsch, London 1966).
26   As argued by Sartaj Aziz, *Rural Development: Learning from China* (Macmillan, London 1978).
27   A useful concise source on Cuba is Gordon White, *Cuban Planning in the mid-1980s* (IDS, Brighton 1985).
28   Dudley Seers, 'The Meaning of Development' in Norman T. Uphoff and Warren F. Ilchman (eds), *The Political Economy of Development* (University of California Press, California 1972), pp. 123–128.
      Ann Seidman, 'Changing Theories of Political Economy in Africa' in Christopher Fyfe (ed.) *African Studies since 1945: A tribute to Basil Davidson* (Longman, London 1976), pp. 49–65.
29   Seidman, *ibid*, pp. 61–62. She is referring to E. C. Edozien, 'The Development Decade in Africa, a Preliminary Appraisal', *Nigerian Journal of Economic and Social Studies*, (March 1972) pp. 77–92.
30   Seers (1972), p. 123.
31   Seidman (1976), p. 54.

Chapter 2

1   D. E. Apter, *The Politics of Modernisation* (University of Chicago Press, Chicago 1965), G. A. Almond and J. S. Coleman, *The Politics of the Developing Areas* (Princeton University Press, Princeton 1960).
2   Alec Nove, *An Economic History of the USSR* (Allen Lane, London 1972).

3   For a full discussion of 'ujamaa' see Goran Hyden, *Beyond Ujamaa in Tanzania* (Heinemann, London 1980).

4   This issue is discussed in detail by Colin Leys, *Underdevelopment in Kenya* (Heinemann, London 1975).

5   Aristide Zolberg, *Creating Political Order* (Rand McNally, Chicago 1966). On Asia, see Hugh Tinker, *Reorientations: Studies on Asia in Transition* (Pall Mall, London 1965) and *Ballot Box and Bayonet: People and Government in Emergent Asian Countries* (Royal Institute of International Affairs, London 1964).

6   Zolberg (1966), p. 150. On Africa in general, see William Tordoff, *Government and Politics of Africa* (Macmillan, London 1984). See also Christopher Clapham, *Third World Politics: An Introduction* (Croom Helm, London 1985).

7   Woodrow Wilson, 'The Study of Administration', *Political Science Quarterly* (June 1887) pp. 481–506.

8   Ladipo Adamolekun, *Politics and Administration in Nigeria* (Spectrum, Ibadan 1986). David Potter, *India's Political Administrators* (Clarendon Press, Oxford 1986) illustrates this point well for India.

9   F. Ridley and J. Blondel, *Public Administration in France* (Routledge and Kegan Paul, London 1969).

10 Issa Shivji, *Class Struggles in Tanzania* (Heinemann, London 1976).

11 Jonathan Lynn and Anthony Jay (eds), *The Complete Yes Minister* (BBC books, London 1984).

12 Peter A. Hall, 'Policy Innovation and the Structure of the State: The Politics Administration Nexus in France and Britain', *The Annals of the American Academy of Political and Social Sciences* (March 1983), pp. 43–59.

13 Martin Krygier, 'Weber, Lenin and the reality of socialism' in Kamenka and Krygier (eds) *Bureaucracy: the Career of a Concept* (Edward Arnold, London 1979), pp. 66–70.

14 Cherry Gertzel, *The Politics of Independent Kenya* (Heinemann, London 1970), ch. 5.

15 For example, see A. H. Hanson (with Janet Douglas), *India's Democracy* (Weidenfeld and Nicholson, London 1972), especially ch. 5.

16 A useful account of the African experience is Philip Mawhood (ed.) *Local Government in the Third World: The Experience of Tropical Africa* (John Wiley, Chichester 1983).

17 Ferrel Heady, *Public Administration: A Comparative Perspective* (Prentice Hall, Englewood Cliffs 1966) pp. 67–68.

18 Olatunde Odetola, *Military Regimes and Development* (Allen and Unwin, London 1982) p. 80.

19 Adamolekun (1986), especially ch. V.

20 Odetola (1982), p. 185.

21 Republic of Kenya, *African Socialism and its Application to Planning in Kenya* (Government Printer, Nairobi 1965).

22 *Ibid*, p. 17.

23 *Ibid*, p. 12.

24 *Ibid*, pp. 2–3.

25 Julius K. Nyerere, *Ujamaa: Essays on Socialism* (Oxford University Press, Oxford 1971).

26 K. D. Kaunda, 'Humanism in Zambia' in B. de Gaay Fortman (ed.), *After Mulungushi* (East African Publishing House, Nairobi 1969) pp. 12–13.

201

27   *Ibid*, p. 16.
28   *Ibid*, p. 23.
29   For additional reading, see Joel S. Barkan and John J. Okumu, *Politics and Public Policy in Kenya and Tanzania* (Praeger, New York 1979), Ben Turok, *Development in Zambia* (Zed, London 1979), S. Quick, 'The Paradox of Popularity in Zambia' in M. Grindle (ed.), *Politics and Policy Implementation in the Third World* (Princeton University Press, Princeton 1980), Goran Hyden, *No Shortcuts to Progress* (Heinemann, London 1983), especially Ch. 3. See also Crawford Young, *Ideology and Development in Africa* (Yale University Press, New Haven 1982).
30   See Gavin Kitching, *Development and Underdevelopment in Historical Perspective* (Methuen, London 1982) for a fuller account of these arguments. Young (1982), is also very useful on dependency, as is Vicky Randall and Robin Theobald, *Political Change and Underdevelopment* (Macmillan, London 1985) ch. 4.
31   For a discussion of this case see Colin Leys (1975). He argued in this book that Kenya's dependence on foreign capital made the likelihood of independent development slight, a view he later revised.
32   Kitching (1982), p. 176.

Chapter 3

1   For further discussion, see A. Waterston, *Development Planning: Lessons of Experience* (Johns Hopkins Press, Baltimore 1979) ch. VI.
2   Waterston, *ibid*, pp. 516–17.
3   By way of illustration, see Colin Leys, 'The Analysis of Planning' in Leys (ed.), *Politics and Change in Developing Countries* (1969), pp. 247–275. Many economists, of course, recognize the importance of political factors. A good example is Tony Killick, *Policy Economics* (Heinemann, London 1981) especially ch. 3.
4   Waterston (1979), ch. IV.
5   Goran Hyden, *No Short Cuts to Progress* (London 1983) especially p. 65.
6   Two World Bank reports on Africa are of relevance here. See the World Bank, *Toward Sustained Development in Sub-Saharan Africa: A Joint Program for Africa* (Washington 1984) and the World Bank, *Accelerated Development in Sub-Saharan Africa: An Agenda for Action* (Washington 1981). The latter report is often referred to as the 'Berg report' after its principal author, Elliot Berg.
7   Waterston (1979), ch. VIII and IX. A more recent study is Lapido Adamolekun *Public Administration: A Nigerian and Comparative Perspective* (Longman, Harlow 1983), especially ch. II, mainly on the Nigerian experience, whilst a useful general discussion is contained in Diana Conyers and Peter Hills, *An Introduction to Development Planning in the Third World* (John Wiley, Chichester 1984), ch. 9. Also useful is P. Ndegwa, L. P. Mureithi, R. H. Green (eds), *Management for Development: Priority Themes in Africa Today* (Oxford University Press, Oxford 1987).
8   Dennis A. Rondinelli and G. Shabbir Cheema, 'Implementing Decentralisation Policies: An Introduction', in Cheema and Rondinelli (eds), *Decentralisation and Development* (Sage, Beverley Hills, 1983) p. 11.
9   Conyers and Hills (1984), pp. 222. Several useful accounts of problems

arising from overcentralised planning in Asia and the Pacific are to be found in Hidehiko Sazanami (ed.) *Local Social Development Planning: Towards a Trainer's Training Course* (UNCRD, Nagoya Japan, 1984).

10 The World Bank (1981) p. 34.

11 Nimrod Raphaeli, Jacques Roumani, A. C. MacKellar, *Public Sector Management in Botswana: Lessons in Pragmatism* (World Bank Staff Working Paper no. 709, Washington, 1984), p. 5.

12 *Ibid*, p. 2.

13 W. Reilly, 'District Development Planning in Botswana' *Manchester Papers on Development* (Department of Administrative Studies, Manchester University, 1981), p. 55.

14 Useful discussion of the range of problems faced by the small states of the Commonwealth is to be found in Commonwealth Secretariat, *Vulnerability: Small States in the Global Society* (Commonwealth Secretariat, London 1985).

15 C. J. Davies, *Administrative Control Systems: Project Monitoring in Malaysia* (Development Administration Group, University of Birmingham, 1981).

16 *Ibid.*, p. 10.

17 Mavis Puthucheary, *The Politics of Administration: The Malaysian Experience* (Oxford University Press, Kuala Lumpur 1978) p. 48. Important texts on the earlier post-independence years are M. J. Esman, *Administration and Development in Malaysia* (University Press, Cornell 1972) and G. Ness, *Bureaucracy and Rural Development in Malaysia* (University of California Press, California 1967).

18 *Second Malaysia Plan 1971–1975* (Kuala Lumpur 1971), p. 1, quoted by Puthucheary, *ibid*, p. 62.

19 Davies (1981), p. 14.

20 *Ibid*, p. 18.

21 Yash Ghai, 'Law and Public Enterprise in Tanzania' in Ghai (ed.), *Law in the Political Economy of Public Enterprise – African Perspectives* (Scandinavian Institute of African Studies, Uppsala, Sweden 1977), p. 211.

22 Waterston (1979). On Tanzania in the 1960s, useful material is available in R. C. Pratt, 'the Administration of Economic Planning in a newly independent state', *Journal of Commonwealth Political Studies* (March 1967).

23 Shivji, *Class Struggles in Tanzania* (London 1976).

24 Andrew Coulson (ed.), *African Socialism in Practice* (Spokesman, Nottingham 1979).

25 Shivji (1976).

26 Hyden (1983). Although this book is on Africa in general, much of his argument is based upon Tanzanian examples. See also his *Beyond Ujamaa in Tanzania* (London 1980).

27 The United Republic of Tanzania, speech by the Minister of Finance, Ndugu C. D. Msuya (MP), 'Introducing the Estimates of Public Revenue and Expenditure for the Financial Year 1985/86 to the National Assembly on 13th June, 1985' (English version) (Dar es Salaam 1985).

28 Adamolekun (1983) is an excellent source. See also Odetola, *Military Regimes and Development* (London 1982), especially pp. 127–134 and M. J. Balogun, *Public Administration in Nigeria* (Macmillan, London 1983).

29 Adamolekun (1983), p. 162–3.

Chapter 4

1   Michael Lipton, 'Financing Economic Development', in Dudley Seers and Leonard Joy (eds), *Development in a Divided World* (Penguin, London 1971), p. 268.; Naomi Caiden and Aaron Wildasky, *Planning and Budgeting in Poor Countries* (Wiley, New York 1974) and Richard L. Kitchen, *Finance for the Developing Countries* (John Wiley, Chichester 1986) are useful general sources.

2   Useful case-study material is available from Peter Marris and Anthony Somerset, *African Businessmen* (Routledge and Kegan Paul, London 1971), Andrew Beveridge and Anthony Oberschall, *African Businessmen and Development in Zambia* (Princeton University Press, Princeton 1979) and Adebayo Adedeji (ed.), *Indigenisation of African Economies* (Hutchinson, London 1981).

3   On co-operatives, see Goran Hyden, *Efficiency vs. Distribution in East African Cooperatives* (Nairobi, E. A. Literature Bureau, 1973) and Peter Worsley (ed.), *Two Blades of Grass* (Manchester University Press, Manchester, 1971).

4   *Encyclopedia Britannica* vol. 3 (Chicago 1977) p. 441.

5   Peter N. Dean, 'Programme and performance budgeting in Malaysia' in *Public Administration and Development* (vol. 6, 3, 1986) p. 268. This section draws heavily on this article.

6   *Ibid*, p. 269. This list of problems is derived from Joon Chien Doh, 'An interim evaluation of programme and performance budgeting in Malaysia', *Tadbiran Awan* (Public Administration), November–December, 1972).

7   Dean (1986), p. 279.

8   *Ibid*, p. 286.

9   Kingdom of Lesotho, *Report of the Auditor-General* (Maseru, 1982).

10 *Ibid*, p. 4.

11 *Ibid*, p. 2.

12 *Ibid*, p. 5.

13 *Ibid*, p. 8.

14 *Ibid*, pp. 11–12.

15 *Ibid*, p. 15.

16 *Ibid*, pp. 103–4.

17 *Ibid*, p. 117.

18 Waterston, *Development Planning: Lessons of Experience* (1979), ch. VII, Caiden and Wildasky (1974), especially ch. 8, World Bank, *Toward Sustained Development in Sub-Saharan Africa* (Washington 1984) ch. 5.

19 Caiden and Wildasky (1974), p. 244.

20 *Ibid*, p. 244.

21 Raphaeli *et al.*, *Public Sector Management in Botswana: Lessons in Pragmatism* (1984).

22 Quoted in *ibid*, p. 17.

23 World Bank (1984), p. 41. On the Bank's role see Richard E. Feinberg *et al.*, *Between Two Worlds: The World Bank's Next Decade* (Transaction, New Brunswick 1986).

24 The Work of Teresa Hayter is of particular interest here. See Teresa Hayter, *Aid as Imperialism* (Penguin, Harmondsworth 1971). More recently, she has authored *The Creation of World Poverty* (Pluto, London 1981).
    For a different view, taking Kenya as a case-study, see Gerald Holtham

and Arthur Hazlewood, *Aid and Inequality in Kenya* (Croom Helm, London 1976).

25 Guy Arnold, *Aid in Africa* (Kogan Page, London 1979) p. 209. See also Reginald Herbold Green, 'Third World Debt Renegotiation 1980–1986 and After: procedures, paradigms and portents' (IDS, University of Sussex, DP 223, December 1986).

26 Arnold (1979), p. 222.

Chapter 5

1 M. P. K. Sorrensen, *Land Reform in the Kikuyu Country* (Oxford University Press, Nairobi 1967) pp. 41–2.

2 See Uma Lele, *The Design of Rural Development: Lessons from Africa* (World Bank, Washington 1975) for a detailed review of many such programmes in a variety of parts of Africa.

3 On NGOs, see Goran Hyden, *No Shortcuts to Progress* (1983) ch. 5, and a special issue of *World Development* (Autumn 1987).

4 A good overview in Robert Chambers, *Managing Rural Development* (Scandinavian Institute of African Studies, Uppsala 1974) ch. 1. For a more positive account see Samuel Paul, *Managing Development Programmes: The Lessons of Success* (Westview, Boulder 1982).

5 The World Bank has strongly advocated privatisation of some rural development activity. See The World Bank, *Toward Sustained Development in Sub-Saharan Africa* (Washington 1984), p. 37.

6 Joseph W. Elder, 'Cultural and Social Factors in Agricultural Development' in Norman T. Uphoff and Warren F. Ilchman (eds), *The Political Economy of Development* (1972).

7 See, for example, the work of Thoden van Velzen and David Leonard on Tanzania and Kenya, respectively. H. U. E. Thoden van Velzen, 'Staff, Kulak and Peasants' in L. Cliffe, J. S. Coleman and M. R. Doornbos (eds), *Government and Rural Development in East Africa: Essays on Political Penetration* (Martinus Nijhoff, The Hague 1977) and David K. Leonard, *Reaching the Peasant Farmer* (University of Chicago Press, London 1977).

8 See Lele (1975), ch. 4.

9 This analysis is partly derived from M. A. H. Wallis, *The Politics and Administration of Rural Development in Kenya: A Case Study of the Kericho District* (Ph.D. Thesis, University of Manchester 1974) ch. 6.

10 Chambers (1974), ch. 3.

11 A useful source is Oscar Gish, *Planning the Health Sector* (Croom Helm, London 1975).

12 Government of Lesotho, *Primary Health Care in Lesotho* (Maseru 1978) p. 7.

13 This requires an exploration of the political and economic dimensions of health policy. For example, See David Sanders with Richard Carver, *The Struggle for Health: Medicine and the Politics of Underdevelopment* (Macmillan, London 1986), Ronald Frankenberg and Joyce Leeson, 'Health Dilemmas in the Post-Colonial World: Intermediate Technology and Medical Care in Zambia, Zaire and China' in Emanuel de Kadt and

Gavin Williams (eds), *Sociology and Development* (Tavistock, London 1974).

14   The same point is argued by Norman T. Uphoff, John M. Cohen, Arthur A. Goldsmith, *Feasibility and Application of Rural Development Participation* (Rural Development Committee, Cornell University 1979), p. 250.

15   Susan B. Rifkin and Raphael Kaplinsky, 'Health Strategy and Development Planning: Lessons from the People's Republic of China', *Journal of Development Studies* (9(2), 1973) provides a useful account.

16   Gish (1975).

17   For a recent discussion of various cases see J. P. Vaughan and D. Smith, 'The District and Support for Primary Health Care: The Management Experience from Large Scale Projects', *Public Administration and Development* (6/3/1986). It looks at cases from Ghana, India, Iran, Korea, Philippines, Thailand and Zaire.

18   Details of this case-study have been obtained from Dick Stockley, 'Primary Health Care in Teso, 1980–1984' in Cole P. Dodge and Paul D. Wicke, *Crisis in Uganda: The Breakdown of Health Services* (Pergamon, Oxford 1985). The chapter by Klaus K. Minde and Israel Kalyesubula entitled 'The Delivery of Primary Health Care in Uganda Today: Some Problems and Opportunities' in the same volume is also useful.

19   Robert J. Saunders and Jeremy T. Warford, *Village Water Supply: Economics and Policy in the Developing World* (Johns Hopkins, Baltimore 1976) p. 3.

20   Great Britain, Colonial Office, *Community Development: A Handbook* (London 1960) p. 3. The best source for the conventional theory of CD is T. E. Batten, *Communities and their Development* (Oxford University Press, London 1971).

21   On the Kenya case, see M. A. H. Wallis, *Bureaucrats, Politicians, and Rural Communities in Kenya* (Department of Administrative Studies, Manchester University 1982), especially ch. 3. Useful general criticism is found in Bernard Schaeffer, 'The Deadlock in Development Administration' in Colin Leys (ed.), *Politics and Change in Developing Countries* (1969) pp. 203–6.

22   Wallis (1982) refers to the Kenya case in some detail.

23   *Ibid*, pp. 41–42.

24   Two useful discussions of evaluation and monitoring are Peter Oakley and David Winder, 'The concept and practice of rural social development: current trends in Latin America and India', *Manchester Papers on Development* (Department of Administrative Studies, Manchester University 1981) and D. M. E. Curtis and J. R. Watson, *Review: simple evaluation techniques for district and field officers* (Development Administration Group, Birmingham University 1984).

25   Joseph Mullen, *Training for Integrated Rural Development* (Department of Administrative Studies, Manchester University 1986), p. 6. A useful general discussion is found in N. T. Uphoff, J. M. Cohen, A. A. Goldsmith (1979).

26   Mullen (1986), p. 6.

27   Uma Lele's book (1975) contains numerous good examples for Africa whilst the work of Robert Chambers, to which reference has also been made, is also of considerable value (1974).

28   James R. Sheffield (ed.), *Education, Employment and Rural Development* (E. A. Publishing House, Nairobi 1967). For detailed general discussion

of SRDP the best source is Walter O. Oyugi, *Rural Development Administration: A Kenyan Experience* (Vikas, New Delhi 1981).

29   Oyugi, *ibid*. Also useful are two evaluation reports on SRDP — Institute for Development Studies, University of Nairobi, *Occasional Paper no. 8* (1972) and *Occasional Paper no. 12* (1975). A British adviser's account is given in J. W. Leach 'The Kenya Special Rural Development Programme', *Journal of Administration Overseas* (April 1974). See also Uma Lele (1975), ch. IX.

30   John M. Cohen and Richard H. Hook 'District Development Planning in Kenya' (Harvard Institute for International Development, 1985), especially pp. 17—18.

31   See, for instance, Akhter Hameed Khan, *Ten Decades of Rural Development Lessons from India* (E. Lansing, Michigan State University, 1978), *Tour of Twenty Thanas* (Bangladesh Academy for Rural Development, Comilla 1971).

32   Mullen (1986), p. 18.

Chapter 6

1   Republic of Kenya, *Review of Statutory Boards* (Government Printer, Nairobi, 1979), p. 2.

2   A. G. N. Kazi, 'Economic Performance of Public Enterprises' in United Nations, *Economic Performance of Public Enterprise: Major Issues and Strategies* (UN, New York 1986) p. 35.

3   For Zambia see, for example, B. de Gaay Fortman (ed.), *After Mulungushi* (Nairobi 1969). On Tanzania, a useful source is Yash Ghai, 'Law and Public Enterprise in Tanzania' in Yash Ghai (ed.), *Law in the Political Economy of Public Enterprise* (1977).

4   A. M. Mufti, 'Experience of Public Enterprises in Pakistan' in United Nations (1986), p. 54.

5   A. H. Hanson, *Public Enterprises and Economic Development* (Routledge and Kegan Paul, London 1966) especially ch. 11.

6   On the TVA it is still worth reading Philip Selznick's classic study *TVA and the Grass Roots* (Harper Row, New York, 1966). On the Damodar valley, a valuable source of description and analysis is R. E. Hamilton, 'Damodar Valley Corporation: India's Experiment with the TVA model', *Indian Journal of Public Administration*. (January—March, 1969).

7   See N. S. Carey-Jones *et al.*, *Politics, Public Enterprise and the Industrial Development Agency* (Croom Helm, London 1974).

8   Kazi (1986), p. 33.

9   See for example, Goran Hyden, *No Short Cuts to Progress* (1983), pp. 102—3.

10   On Zambia, see Ben Turok, *Development in Zambia* (Zed, London 1979), especially ch. 4 and ch. 5.

11   This information is obtained from S. S. Khera, *Management and Control in Public Enterprise* (Asia Publishing House, London 1964), ch. 9.

12   Republic of Kenya (1979).

13   For a comprehensive directory see The Commonwealth Secretariat, *Training for Public Enterprise Management* (Commonwealth Secretariat, London 1981).

14   See especially Robin Fincham and Grace Zulu, 'Labour and Participation

207

in Zambia' in Turok (1979). A useful source on industrial relations in Zambia's mines is Robert H. Bates, *Unions, Parties and Political Development* (Yale University Press, New Haven and London, 1971).

15 Quoted by Khera (1964), p. 188.
16 Fincham and Zulu (1979).
17 On Tanzania, see Hanson (1965); Ghai (1977), pp. 232–7.
18 A finding of student research projects carried out at the National University of Lesotho in 1983 and 1984.
19 Ghai (1977), p. 215.
20 See, for example, Andrew Coulson (ed.), *African Socialism in Practice*, ch. 12.
21 This discussion is largely derived from B. Mramba and B. Mwansasu, 'Management for Socialist Development in Tanzania — the case of the National Development Corporation in Tanzania', *The African Review* (January 1972) pp. 29–47.
22 *The World Development Forum*, (Washington 30 November, 1986) p. 1.
23 Paul Cook, 'Liberalisation in the Context of Industrial Development in LDCs' (University of Manchester, International Development Centre paper 8602, no date), p. 16. He quotes these figures from G. Cowen, 'The American perspective on privatisation', presented at a seminar organised by Deloitte, Haskins and Sells, London, 16 October 1985. On Asia, see Asian Development Bank, *Privatisation: Policies, Methods and Procedures* (Manila 1985).
24 Hyden (1983), ch. 4.
25 World Bank, *Accelerated Development in Sub-Saharan Africa* (Washington 1981).
26 *Ibid*, p. 37.
27 John F. H. Purcell and Michelle B. Miller, 'The World Bank and Private Capital' in Richard Feinberg *et al.*, *Between Two Worlds: The World Bank's Next Decade* p. 119.
28 The World Bank, *Annual Report* 1985 (Washington 1985), p. 143.
29 *Ibid*, p. 137.
30 Ann Seidman, 'The Need for an Appropriate Southern African Industrial Strategy' *Conference on The Southern African Economy after Apartheid* (University of York, 1986), p. 51. See also the paper presented to the same conference by Robert Davies, entitled 'Nationalisation, Socialisation and the Freedom Charter'.
31 A good example of the sort of work that is required is *The Role of Public Enterprises in Development in Eastern Africa* (IDS, University of Nairobi, 1982). It contains papers on Ethiopia, Kenya, Tanzania and Uganda. On the KTDA see G. Lamb and S. Muller, *Control, Accountability and Incentives in a Successful Development Institution* (World Bank, Washington 1982). Also valuable is Praxy Fernades, *Managing Relations between Governments and Public Enterprises* (ILO, Geneva 1986).
32 On Senegal, see World Bank (1981) p. 39.

Chapter 7

1 The main texts of interest are H. Maddick, *Democracy, Decentralisation and Development* (Asia Publishing House, Bombay 1963), B. C. Smith, *Field Administration: An Aspect of Decentralisation* (Routledge and

Kegan Paul, London 1967), B. C. Smith, *Decentralisation: The Territorial Dimension of the State* (1985) and Philip Mawhood (ed.), *Local Government in the Third World* (John Wiley, Chichester 1983).

2   Numerous examples could be given. Of particular interest and importance are the papers contained in G. Shabbir Cheema and Dennis A. Rondinelli, *Decentralisation and Development* (Sage, Beverley Hills 1983). This volume contains numerous references to recent literature on participation and development.

3   B. C. Smith, *Decentralisation* (1985), pp. 20−1.

4   Maddick (1963).

5   Smith (1985), p. 21.

6   For example, Republic of Kenya, *Development Plan 1970−1974*, (Government Printer, Nairobi, 1970) p. 174. Botswana's development plans since the early 1970s have placed substantial emphasis on local government.

7   M. Bhattarcharya, *Essays in Urban Government* (World Press, Calcutta 1970) pp. 1−2.

8   This account of British colonial policy is largely a summary of Nelson Kasfir, 'Designs and Dilemmas: An Overview' in Mawhood (1983) pp. 27−28.

9   *Ibid*, p. 27.

10 M. W. Norris, *Local Government in Peninsular Malaysia* (Gower, Farnborough 1980) p. 14.

11 Philip Mawhood, 'Applying the French model in Cameroon', in Mawhood (1983), p. 185.

12 Apart from Mawhood, *ibid*, useful discussion of the francophone case − with references − can be found in O. M. Laleye and S. Bamidele Oyo, 'An Overview of Recent Trends in Anglophone and Francophone West Africa' in *Planning and Administration* (Spring 1987). This was a special issue on local government in Africa.

13 See Malcolm Wallis 'Local Government and Development in Southern African States: Botswana and Lesotho Compared' in *Planning and Administration, ibid*.

14 A good general source is Kenneth Davey, *Financing Regional Government* (John Wiley, Chichester 1983).

15 Dennis A. Rondinelli and G. Shabbir Cheema, 'Implementing Decentralisation Policies: An Introduction' in Cheema and Rondinelli (eds) (1983), p. 30.

16 Walter Ouma Oyugi, 'Local government in Kenya: a case of institutional decline' in Mawhood (ed.) (1983), p. 134.

17 Wyn Reilly, 'Decentralisation in Botswana − Myth or Reality?' in Mawhood (ed.), *ibid*, pp. 158−161.

18 Philip Mawhood, 'Decentralisation and the Third World in the 1980s' in *Planning and Administration* (Spring 1987) p. 12. Within this tradition he includes Henry Maddick (see reference 1).

19 *Ibid*, p. 17.

20 Harry J. Friedman, 'Decentralised Development in Asia: Local Political Alternatives' in G. Shabbir Cheema and Denis A. Rondinelli (eds) (1983), pp. 43−4. The research Friedman draws on is more fully reported in Susan G. Hadden, 'Controlled Decentralisation and Policy Implementation: The Case of Rural Electrification in Rajasthan', in Merilee S. Grindle (ed.), *Politics and Policy Implementation in the Third World* (Princeton University Press, Princeton, 1980).

21 Friedman, *ibid*, pp. 46–49.
22 Herbert Kaufman, *The Forest Ranger* (John Hopkins, Baltimore 1967) is the classic study of this phenomenon. See chapter 3 for a discussion of what he calls 'capture' in the organisation he analyses, the US Forest Service.
23 See references to Smith's work in reference 1.
24 Smith (1985), p. 152.

Chapter 8

1 See D. C. Pitt and B. C. Smith, *The Computer Revolution in Public Administration* (Wheatsheaf, Brighton 1984) for a discussion of these issues with special reference to the British case. See also R. B. Davidson, *Information Technology in the Third World* (Department of Administrative Studies, University of Manchester 1983) and Ray Souder and Nicholas Damachi, 'Introduction of Computers to Management in Development Countries' in U. G. Damachi and H. D. Seibel (eds), *Management Problems in Africa* (Macmillan, London 1986).
2 The World Bank has been particularly forthright in advancing this view in recent years.
3 W. N. Wamalwa, 'The Role of Public Service Commissions in New African States', in Rwyemamu and Hyden (eds), *A Decade of Public Administration in Africa* (E. A. Literature Bureau, Nairobi 1975) is a very useful source of historical background on PSCs whilst A. L. Adu, *The Civil Service in Commonwealth Africa* (1969), ch. 8, is a good discussion of the principles behind their establishment.
4 Wamalwa (1975), p. 55.
5 *Ibid*, p. 59.
6 David J. Gould and Jose A. Amaro-Reyes, *The Effects of Corruption on Administrative Performance: Illustrations from Developing Countries* (World Bank, Washington 1983), p. 28. This publication is also a valuable source of references on corruption in general. See also Kenneth Kernaghan and O. P. Dwivedi (eds), *Ethics in the Public Services: Comparative Perspectives* (International Institute of Administrative Sciences, Brussels: 1983).
7 Gould and Amaro-Reyes, *ibid*, p. 22.
8 Useful general sources are Richard Symonds, *The British and their Successors* (Faber, London 1969), which also has some discussion of the other colonial powers (e.g. France, Belgium) and Bernard Schaffer (ed.), *Administrative Training and Development: A Comparative Study of East Africa, Zambia, Pakistan and India* (Praeger, New York 1974).
9 Geof Wood 'Administrative Training in Zambia' in Schaffer (1974), p. 214.
10 Zoe Allen, 'From Shirt-Sleeve Diplomacy and Localisation to Aid for Development Administration: The Foreign Support element', *ibid*, p. 109. Allen's chapter is particularly valuable because it documents the role played by foreign aid in these processes.
11 David C. Potter, *India's Political Administrators* (1986) especially ch. 5.
12 Allen (1974) and Andrew Dunsire, *Administration* (Martin Robertson, London 1973) ch. 8 are useful sources.

13 Wyn Reilly, *Training Administrators for Development* (Heinemann, London 1979), p. 30. This book contains much valuable discussion of training in less developed countries.

14 Republic of Kenya, *District Focus Strategy for Rural Development* (Government Printer, Nairobi 1987). See also UN, *Curricula Design for Management Development* (Report of an Expert Group Workshop in Tanzania), (New York 1982).

15 See Reilly (1979), ch. 5 and Schaffer (1974), especially ch. 4. It is of interest that suggestions for the improvement of teaching methods have been circulating for some considerable time; for an early piece of advocacy see Adebayo Adedeji (ed.), *Problems and Techniques of Administrative Training in Africa* (University of Ife Press, Ife, Nigeria 1969), especially part 3. On the use of different training methods for public enterprise managers see Hiten Bhaya, *Methods and Techniques of Training Public Enterprise Managers* (International Center for Public Enterprises in Developing Countries, Ljubljana, Yugoslavia, 1983).

16 Andre G. Delion, *Education and Training in Public Enterprise Administration* (International Association of Schools and Institutes of Administration, Brussels 1984) and Irshad H. Khan, Shahiruddin Ali and Stane Mozina, *Management Training and Development in Public Enterprises* (International Center for Public Enterprises in Developing Countries, Ljubljana 1982) report most of these findings.

17 Delion, *ibid*, p. 24.

18 Reilly (1979), p. 44.

19 P. Hornby, D. K. Ray, P. H. Shipp, *Guidelines for Health Manpower Planning* (WHO, Geneva, 1980). pp. 29–32 provide a useful list, on which this section is based. This book contains very valuable information on techniques and procedures for planning, as does L. Richter, *Training Needs: assessment and monitoring* (ILO, Geneva 1986).

20 Colin Fuller, *Personnel Management and Staff Development* (Department of Administrative Studies, University of Manchester 1985) p. 55. On general principles see Paul Pigors and Charles A. Myers, *Personnel Administration: a point of view and a method* (McGraw Hill, Kogakusha 1977) ch. 16.

21 Fuller, *ibid*, pp. 55, 56. Most of the research Fuller has in mind has been conducted in industrialised states. This author, however, has substantial experience of civil services in LDCs. Although not much MBO research has been carried out in LDCs, it has had its influential advocates and commentators. See for example the 'Ndegwa Report': Republic of Kenya, *Report of the Commission of Inquiry* (Public Service Structural Remuneration Commission) (Government Printer, Nairobi 1971), especially pp. 89–90. The recommendations on MBO contained in this report were, however, not implemented to any great extent. See Republic of Kenya, *Report of the Civil Service Salaries Review Committee* (Government Printer, Nairobi 1985) p. 26. For an interesting case-study of an industrialised state's experience of MBO see John Garrett, *Managing the Civil Service* (Heinemann, London 1980), pp. 134–6.

22 Fuller, *ibid*, p. 56.

23 Republic of Kenya (1985) p. 26.

24 Republic of Kenya (1985) p. 21. Kenya has adopted a very honest and open approach to these matters, setting an example which other countries could valuably follow.

25 *Ibid* pp. 22–3.
26 *Ibid* p. 27.
27 S. P. Verma and S. K. Sharma, *Managing Public Personnel Systems: A Comparative Perspective* (IIPA, New Delhi, 1985), p. 165.
28 Gould and Amaro-Reyes (1983), p. 33.
29 Useful sources are Victor H. Vroom and Edward L. Deci (eds), *Management and Motivation* (Penguin, Harmondswcrth 1975). This collection contains extracts from the work of Maslow (chapter 2), Herzberg (chapter 7), Likert (chapter 14). Taylor (chapter 20) and McGregor (chapter 22). See also Charles B. Handy, *Understanding Organisations* (Penguin, Harmondsworth 1976), especially ch. 2 and ch. 4. Another useful collection is D. S. Pugh, *Organisation Theory* (Penguin, Harmondsworth 1985), especially ch. 18, 19, 20.
30 Very little writing on motivation in LDCs exists especially as far as the public sector is concerned. One example is George Itsu Imany, 'A Study of Motivational Needs of Mid-Level Managers in the Nigerian Civil Service', *African Administrative Studies* (Tangier), 27, 1986. A useful discussion is to be found in Peter Blunt, *Organisational Theory and Behaviour: An African Perspective* (Longman, London 1983), especially ch. 4.
31 Peter Drucker, *Management Tasks, Responsibilities, Practices* (Harper and Row, New York 1974) p. 235. Quoted in Pigors and Myers (1977), p. 10.
32 Blunt (1983), p. 159.
33 Krishan C. Sethi *et al.*, *Workers' Self Management and Participation in Developing Countries* (International Center for Public Enterprise in Developing Countries, Ljubljana 1983) pp. 41–2. Also useful is Ukandi G. Damachi, 'Workers' Participation in Management' in Damachi and Seibel (1986).
34 Vroom and Deci (1975), ch. 22.
35 Blunt (1983), p. 159. He refers here to another useful book: C. Pateman, *Participation and Democratic Theory* (Cambridge University Press, London 1970).
36 For detailed discussion of Quality Circles see M. Robson, *Quality Circles* (Gower, Aldershot, 1982).
37 Sethi (1983), pp. 70–1.
38 *Ibid*, p. 73. On Zambia, see also Blunt (1983), p. 176–8 and R. Fincham and G. Zulu, 'Labour and Participation in Zambia' in B. Turok (ed.), *Development in Zambia* 1979).
39 Blunt (1983), p. 177. He contrasts his own work in Zambia with the more pessimistic views of Fincham and Zulu.
40 The International Centre for Public Enterprises in Developing Countries in Yugoslavia has done a valuable service by producing a number of case-studies. See, for example, *Workers' Self Management and Participation in Practice* (International Center for Public Enterprises in Developing Countries, Ljubljana 1986). This volume, for example, includes detailed case material on The Sri Lanka Ports Authority, The National Bank of Commerce in Tanzania and Zambia's ROPHD (Refined Oil Products). These cases are well worth detailed study.
41 Quoted in a circular issued by the Society of Local Authority Chief Executives in UK (no date, no page numbers).
42 *Ibid*.

43   Very little has been written about the LDCs in this context. Useful material is, however, to be found in Ronald F. Clarke, *Communication for the Manager and Administrator* (Department of Administrative Studies, University of Manchester 1984).

44   For written communication in general, see Sir Ernest Gowers, *The Complete Plain Words* (Penguin, Harmondsworth 1970).

45   Albert Waterston, *Development Planning* (1979) ch. VIII.

Chapter 9

1   Gerald Caiden, *Administrative Reform* (Allen Lane, London 1970) pp. 8–11 discusses the issue of definition. See also a special volume of *Development and Change* (Vol. II, 1970–1, no. 2), which is devoted to the study of AR.

2   Hari Mohan Mathur, *Administering Development in the Third World* (Sage, New Delhi 1986) p. 81.

3   Zoe Allen, 'From Shirt-Sleeve Diplomacy and Localisation to Aid for Development Administration: the foreign support element' in Schaffer (ed.), *Administrative Training and Development* (1974). Andrew Dunsire, *Administration* (1973) ch. 8.

4   Details are taken from *Handbook of World Development: The Guide to the Brandt Report* (Longman, Harlow 1981) pp. 68–9.

5   Cheryl Payer, *The World Bank: A Critical Analysis* (Monthly Review Press, New York and London 1982) p. 372.

6   Richard E. Feinberg and contributors, *Between Two Worlds: The World Bank's Next Decade* (1986), pp. 5–6.

7   Payer (1982), pp. 153–4. When this book was published SAL had not become as important as it is now and Payer makes little reference to it.

8   Feinberg (1986), p. 11.

9   *Ibid*, p. 12. See also Giovanni Andrea Cornia, Richard Jolly, Frances Stewart (eds), *Adjustment with a Human Face* Vol. 1 (1987). This UNICEF study, whilst not specifically focused on the World Bank, is a valuable review of the social implications of adjustment policies in general.

10   *Ibid*, p. 13.

11   The three World Bank reports referred to are *Accelerated Development in Sub-Saharan Africa* (Washington 1981) — often known as the 'Berg' report after the main author, *Sub-Saharan Africa: Progress Report on Development Prospects and Programmes* (Washington 1983) and *Toward Sustained Development in Sub-Saharan Africa* (Washington 1984).

12   World Bank (1984), p. 34.

13   *Ibid*, p. 37.

14   World Bank (1981), p. 39.

15   *Ibid*, p. 35.

16   *Ibid*, p. 35.

17   *Ibid*, p. 39.

18   World Bank, *World Development Report 1983* (Washington 1983).

19   David J. Murray 'The World Bank's perspective on how to improve administration', *Public Administration and Development* (Vol. 3, 1983) p. 295.

20   *World Development Report 1983*, p. 51.
21   Murray (1983), p. 294.
22   *World Development Report 1983*, p. 124.
23   See special issue of *Planning and Administration* (Spring 1987).
24   *World Development Report 1983*, p. 108.
25   *Ibid*, p. 93. This analysis predates, of course, the overthrow of the Marcos regime in 1986.
26   *Ibid*, p. 110.
27   *Ibid*, p. 79.
28   A useful theoretical discussion of this point is to be found in Samuel Paul, *Managing Development Programs: The Lessons of Success* (1982).
29   *Ibid*, p. 79.
30   *Ibid*, p. 89.
31   *Ibid*, p. 85.
32   Stewart MacPherson, *Social Policy in the Third World* (Wheatsheaf, Brighton 1982) p. 12. See also S. B. Rifkin and R. Kaplinsky, 'Health strategy and development planning: lessons from the People's Republic of China; *Journal of Development Studies* 9 (2), 1973.
33   Ronald Frankenberg and Joyce Leeson, 'The Sociology of Health: Dilemmas in the Post-colonial world: Intermediate Technology and medical care in Zambia, Zaire and China' in Emanual de Kadt and Gavin Williams (eds), *Sociology and Development* (1974), p. 274.
34   G. Lamb and S. Muller, *Control, Accountability and Incentives in a Successful Development Institution* (World Bank, Washington 1982) p. 1.
35   World Bank, *World Development Report 1983*, p. 78.
36   Quoted by Paul (1982), p. 59.
37   Lamb and Muller (1982), pp. 42−3.
38   Paul (1982), p. 61.
39   Young C. Park, *A System for Evaluating the Performance of Government Invested Enterprises in the Republic of Korea* (World Bank, Washington 1986).
40   *Ibid*, p. 5.
41   *Ibid*, p. 7.
42   *Ibid*, pp. 15−16.
43   *Ibid*, pp. 31−3.
44   For a recent discussion which draws attention to the complexities of change, see Geoffrey Lamb, *Managing Economic Policy Change: Institutional Dimensions* (World Bank, Washington 1987).
45   Aliou S. Diallo, 'Note on the Lagos Plan of Action', *Africa Administrative Studies* (No. 22, 1983).
46   David Hirschmann, 'Development or Underdevelopment Administration? A Further Deadlock', *Development and Change* (July 1981).
47   *Ibid*, p. 471.
48   The *Independent* (London), 30 December 1987.
49   Paul (1982).
50   Useful discussion on this point referring to Asia and East Africa is to be found in Gabino A. Mendoza, 'The Transferability of Western Management Concepts and Programs, an Asian perspective' and Jon R. Moris 'The Transferability of Western Management Concepts and Programs, an East Africa Perspective'. Both appear in L. D. Stifel, J. S. Coleman, J. E. Black (eds), *Education and Training for Public Sector Management in Developing Countries* (Rockefeller Foundation, New York 1977).

Guide to Further Reading

This guide lists those items likely to be particularly useful for the reader who wishes to explore the literature in more depth. It is by no means a comprehensive list, but familiarity with a large number of these sources would certainly lead to a greatly enhanced understanding of the issues with which we are concerned in this volume. All of the items listed contain references of their own, and in some cases reading lists, from which readers can obtain additional guidance on the literature available.

- **•***Bureaucracy and development administration* (chapter 1)
David Beetham, *Bureaucracy* (Open University, Milton Keynes 1987) is a clear account of this concept. See especially chapter one of this book. Richard Symonds, *The British and their Successors* (Faber, London 1969) remains a useful discussion of the administrative implications of the transfer of power in the Commonwealth. On the work of Elton Mayo, it is useful to sample a piece he wrote himself — 'Hawthorne and the Western Electric Company' in D. S. Pugh (ed.) *Organisation Theory* (Penguin Harmondsworth 1985) pp. 279–92. Richard Merton's essay 'Bureaucratic Structure and Personality' in Merton *et al.* (eds), *Reader in Bureaucracy* (Free Press, New York 1952) is a classic piece of elegant analysis.

Norman T. Uphoff and Warren F. Ilchman (eds), *The Political Economy of Development* (University of California Press, California 1972), although somewhat dated, contains much useful material, especially the essay by Seers. On the development crisis of the 1980s, the ideas contained in the Brandt Report are still of interest — *North — South: A Programme for Survival* (Pan, London 1981) has masses of useful information. More recently, Giovanni Andrea Cornia, Richard Jolly, Frances Stewart (eds), *Adjustment with a Human Face Vols I/II* (Clarendon Press, Oxford 1987, 1988) is a UNICEF commissioned study which explores very thoroughly the social implications of world economic trends. Volume II contains case-studies of Botswana, Brazil, Chile, Ghana, Jamaica, Peru, Philippines, South Korea, Sri Lanka and Zimbabwe.

215

• *The political environment* (chapter 2)
Christopher Clapham, *Third World Politics: An Introduction* (Croom Helm, London 1985) is a good clear account which includes examples taken from a number of countries in the Third World. Ladipo Adamolekun, *Politics and Administration in Nigeria* (Spectrum, Ibadan 1986) is a valuable in depth analysis of an important African state. David Potter, *India's Political Administrators* (Clarendon Press, Oxford 1986) is probably the best study available of the relationships between politics and administration in an Asian state. On the early years of independence and the latter days of colonialism, Aristide Zolberg, *Creating Political Order* (Rand McNally, Chicago 1966) remains an excellent study of West Africa, whilst Hugh Tinker's *Ballot Box and Bayonet: People and Government in Emergent Asian Countries* (Royal Institute of International Affairs, London 1964) is in many ways a parallel study focused on South Asia. More recently, William Tordoff, *Government and Politics in Africa* (Macmillan, London 1984) is a full survey of the politics of that continent. Olatunde Odetola, *Military Regimes and Development* (Allen and Unwin, London 1982) looks at African military interventions in politics and development. On ideology, a useful general discussion of Africa is Crawford Young, *Ideology and Development in Africa* (Yale University Press, New Haven 1982) which discusses the question of dependency. On which also see Gavin Kitching, *Development and Underdevelopment in Historical Perspective* (Methuen, London 1982) – especially chapter 6 and Vicky Randall and Robin Theobald, *Political Change and Underdevelopment* (Macmillan, London 1985), especially chapter 4.

• *Development planning* (chapter 3)
Although the information it contains is now quite dated, Albert Waterston, *Development Planning: Lessons of Experience* (Johns Hopkins, Baltimore 1979) remains a most valuable text because of its comprehensive coverage of the administrative issues involved in planning. Diana Conyers and Peter Hills, *An Introduction to Development Planning in the Third World* (John Wiley, Chichester 1984) is excellent, whilst P. Ndegwa, L. P. Mureithi, R. H. Green (eds), *Management for Development: Priority Themes in Africa Today* (Oxford University Press, Oxford 1987) has a good chapter focusing on planning and has useful points to make about administrative factors. A book which concentrates on Asia and the Pacific is Hidehiko Sazanami (ed.), *Local Social Development Planning: Toward a Trainers' Training Course* (Nagoya, Japan 1984). As its title implies, it contributes to our understanding of the training implications of local planning. Chapters 1 and 10 of Dennis A. Rondinelli and G. Shabbir Cheema (eds) *Decen-*

tralisation and Development (Sage, Beverley Hills 1983) are helpful. On Botswana, Nimrod Raphaeli, Jacques Roumani, A. C. MacKellar, *Public Sector Management in Botswana: Lessons in Pragmatism* (World Bank, Washington 1984) is a good source. On Malaysia, Mavis Puthucheary, *The Politics of Administration: The Malaysian Experience* (Oxford University Press, Kuala Lumpur 1978) usefully highlights the political factors involved in planning, whilst Goran Hyden, *No Short-cuts to Progress* (Heinemann, London 1983), although about Africa in general, has much to say on Tanzania. On Nigeria, a good source is Ladipo Adamolekun, *Public Administration: A Nigerian and Comparative Perspective* (Longman, Harlow 1983), especially chapter 11.

●*Financial management* (chapter 4)
Richard L. Kitchen, *Finance for the Developing Countries* (John Wiley, Chichester 1986), is a comprehensive textbook. Naomi Caiden and Aaron Wildasky, *Planning and Budgeting in Poor Countries* (Wiley, New York 1974) is a good review of the interrelations between planning and finance. Peter Worsley (ed.), *Two Blades of Grass* (Manchester University Press, Manchester 1971) is a very good study of co-operatives, without focusing very specifically on financial issues. Peter Dean's article on Malaysia in *Public Administration and Development* (vol. 6, 3, 1986) is a very interesting case-study. On aid, there are several sources. The World Bank, *Toward Sustained Development in Sub-Saharan Africa* (Washington 1984), looks closely at issues arising from the utilisation of aid — see ch. 5. Teresa Hayter's *The Creation of World Poverty* (Pluto, London 1981) presents a radical viewpoint. On indebtedness, a condensed account worth reading is Reginald Herbold Green, 'Third World Debt Renegotiation 1980–1986 and After: procedures, paradigms and portents' (IDS, University of Sussex, DP 223, December 1986).

●*Bureaucracy and rural development* (chapter 5)
Uma Lele, *The Design of Rural Development: Lessons from Africa* (World Bank, Washington 1975) is a detailed review of numerous programmes in Africa. Joseph W. Elder, 'Cultural and Social Factors in Agricultural Development', in Norman T. Uphoff and Warren R. Ilchman (eds), *The Political Economy of Development* (University of California Press, California 1972) provides an excellent overview. David K. Leonard's *Reaching the Peasant Farmer* (University of Chicago Press, London 1977) is an extremely interesting case-study of extension services in Kenya. On health, probably the most valuable recent source is David Sanders with Richard Carver, *The Struggle for Health: Medicine*

and the Politics of Underdevelopment (Macmillan, London 1986). On water supplies, Robert J. Saunders and Jeremy T. Warford, *Village Water Supply: Economics and Policy in the Developing World* (Johns Hopkins, Baltimore 1976) is a full study. Peter Oakley and David Winder, 'The concept and practice of rural social development: current trends in Latin America and India', *Manchester Papers on Development* (Department of Administrative Studies, Manchester University 1981) is valuable both because it looks at the issue of community participation and because it discusses evaluation and monitoring. Also from Manchester University is Joseph Mullen's *Training for Integrated Rural Development* (Department of Administrative Studies, Manchester University 1986). This handbook is a valuable overview but also contains a concise discussion of the Comilla experience in Bangladesh (pp. 15–18). A practical guide to reviewing the performance of rural development programmes is to be found in D. M. E. Curtis and J. R. Watson, *Review: simple evaluation techniques for district and field officers* (Development Administration Group, University of Birmingham 1984). On NGOs, a special issue of *World Development* (Autumn 1987) contains numerous relevant contributions, especially those by Fernandez (mainly on India), Korten (mainly on Asia generally) and Van der Heijden (on NGO autonomy and relationships with donors). Drabek's editorial 'Overview' article is also worth consulting.

●*Public enterprises* (chapter 6)
A. H. Hanson's *Public Enterprise and Economic Development* (Routledge and Kegan Paul, London 1965) is so thorough and analytically excellent that its dated empirical material only partially detracts from its value. A comparable study, reflecting the circumstances of the 1980s, is urgently needed. An important and very readable contribution is Praxy Fernandes, *Managing Relations between Governments and Public Enterprises* (ILO, Geneva 1986). On Africa, Yash Ghai (ed.), *Law in the Political Economy of Public Enterprises* (Scandinavian Institute of African Studies, Uppsala 1977) is quite wide ranging despite the specialised focus implied by its title. N. S. Carey-Jones *et al.*, *Politics, Public Enterprise and the Industrial Development Agency* (Croom Helm, London 1974) looks at one particularly important type of enterprise and contains valuable material on a number of countries. A United Nations publication, *Economic Performance of Public Enterprise: Major Issues and Strategies* (UN, New York 1986) has an Asian perspective, being based on a workshop held in Pakistan. John F. J. Purcell and Michelle B. Miller, 'The World Bank and Private Capital' in Richard Feinberg *et al.*, *Between Two Worlds: The World Bank's Next Decade* (Transaction, New Brunswick 1986) is useful on

218

privatisation. Goran Hyden, *No Shortcuts to Progress* (Heinemann, London 1983), ch. 4, looks at arguments in favour of reducing the size of the public enterprise sector in Africa. On Asia, a publication by the Asian Development Bank — *Privatisation: Policies, Methods and Procedures* (Manila 1985) — contains detailed analysis and includes case-studies of Japan, the UK, Republic of Korea, Malaysia, Thailand, Bangladesh, Pakistan and Sri Lanka. Also see Paul Cook and Colin Kirkpatrick (eds), *Privatisation in Less Developed Countries* (Wheatsheaf, Brighton 1988) for a well-balanced discussion of privatisation.

●*Local government and field administration* (chapter 7)
The work of B. C. Smith is particularly important. See especially his *Decentralisation: The Territorial Dimension of the State* (Allen and Unwin, London 1985). Dennis A. Rondinelli and G. Shabbir Cheema (eds), *Decentralisation and Development* (Sage, Beverley Hills 1983) contains a number of references to literature on participation and development and has two particularly good essays on decentralisation in Asia (ch. 2 and 3). Philip Mawhood (ed.), *Local Government in the Third World* (John Wiley, Chichester 1983) has several interesting African case-studies, as does a special issue of *Planning and Administration* (Spring 1987). M. W. Norris, *Local Government in Peninsular Malaysia* (Gower, Farnborough 1980) is an interesting account of an Asian experience. On financial issues, Kenneth Davey, *Financing Regional Development* (John Wiley, Chichester 1983) is a good general survey. On personnel, there is no general source to suggest but most of this literature contains discussion of recruitment and other issues. Of considerable historical interest is H. Maddick, *Democracy, Decentralisation and Development* (Asia Publishing House, Bombay 1983).

●*The management of human resources* (chapter 8)
U. G. Damachi and H. D. Seibel (eds), *Management Problems in Africa* (Macmillan, London 1986) is a useful general text although much of its focus is on the private sector. Peter Blunt, *Organisational Theory and Behaviour: An African Perspective* (Longman, London 1983) is also a good source on Africa. S. P. Verma and S. K. Sharma, *Managing Public Personnel Systems: A Comparative Perspective* (IIPA, New Delhi 1985) is a good general survey, providing coverage of both developed and less developed countries, as does Colin Fuller's *Personnel Management and Staff Development* (Department of Administrative Studies, University of Manchester 1985). On corruption and related ethical issues, see Kenneth Kernaghan and O. P. Dwivedi (eds), *Ethics*

in the Public Service: Comparative Perspectives (International Association of Schools and Institutes of Administration, Brussels 1983). On general theories, apart from Blunt's work, the following are valuable: Victor H. Vroom and Edward L. Deci (eds), *Management and Motivation* (Penguin, Harmondsworth 1975); Charles B. Handy, *Understanding Organisations* (Penguin, Harmondsworth 1976); and D. S. Pugh, *Organisation Theory* (Penguin, Harmondsworth 1985). All three of these books are sources of information on the ideas of key writers such as McGregor and Herzberg. For material on more specific issues, readers should consult the chapter references, but mention should be made of Wyn Reilly, *Training Administrators for Development* (Heinemann, London 1979), which not only contains much valuable discussion of training in less developed countries but also touches on other issues such as human resource planning.

•*Administrative reform and development* (chapter 9)
On administrative reform in general, Gerald Caiden, *Administrative Reform* (Allen Lane, London 1970) remains an excellent source. Also of considerable value is a special volume of the journal *Development and Change* (vol. II−2, 1970−1971) which is devoted to the study of administrative reform. The articles by Dror, Cohen and Moharir are particularly interesting. Dror presents a broad analysis of a number of the strategic issues involved in undertaking reform. Cohen, using India as an example, draws attention to some of the human factors involved, whilst Moharir provides a case-study of the same country. Hari Mathur, *Administering Development in the Third World* (Sage, New Delhi 1986) has a lot of interesting discussion of administrative reform, especially chs. 1 and 4. Much of the empirical material it contains is based on the Asian experience. On the World Bank, Cheryl Payer, *The World Bank: A Critical Analysis* (Monthly Review Press, New York and London 1982) provides a comprehensive radical critique, whilst Richard E. Feinberg *et al.*, *Between Two Worlds: The World Bank's Next Decade* (Transaction, New Brunswick 1986) provides a coverage which is more up-to-date and rather more sympathetic to the World Bank's approach. The Bank's own reports should also be consulted. Especially useful is *The World Development Report 1983* which is focused on management issues. On 'success stories' Samuel Paul, *Managing Development Programs: The Lessons of Success* (Westview, Boulder Colorado 1982) is invaluable. It contains numerous interesting case-studies of various programmes in India, the Philippines, Kenya, Indonesia, China and Mexico. Geoffrey Lamb, *Managing Economic Policy Change: Institutional Dimensions* (World Bank, Washington 1987) is a useful recent World Bank view, whilst David Hirschmann's

article 'Development or Underdevelopment Administration? A Further Deadlock' in *Development and Change* (July 1981) presents an alternative view.

Key journals

There are a number of journals which regularly contain articles on the topics discussed in this book. Some of the most valuable ones are:

Public Administration and Development (London). This journal is concerned with 'the practice of public administration where this is directed to development in Third World countries'.

International Review of Administrative Sciences (Brussels) — 'on a wide range of topics related to public administration'. This regularly includes contributions on the Third World.

Development and Change (The Hague). A development studies journal, often containing public administration-related articles.

Community Development Journal (Oxford). Mainly focuses on the Third World.

The Asian Journal of Public Administration (Hong Kong) 'seeks to promote the study, research and dissemination of information on public administration in the region'.

Public Enterprise (Ljubljana, Yugoslavia). Concentrates on public enterprise management and policy in the Third World.

Manchester Papers on Development (Manchester). Another development studies journal, but with a strong public administration thrust (now renamed *Journal of International Development*).

Planning and Administration (The Hague). This journal usually has a high Third World content.

Journal of Modern African Studies (Cambridge). In the absence of a regular African public administration journal, a useful source.

World Development (Oxford). A useful inter-disciplinary journal on development which often contains articles on public administration topics.

Useful addresses

In addition to the ordinary publishers there are a number of organisations which regularly produce useful publications, some of which have been used in the course of preparing this book. The addresses of some of the key ones are:

221

United Nations
Sales Section
New York   NY10017
USA

Development Administration Group
University of Birmingham
P.O. Box 363
Birmingham   B15 2TT
UK

Institute of Development Policy and Management
University of Manchester
Crawford House
Precinct Centre
Manchester   M13 9QS
UK

International Labour Office
CH — 1211
Geneva 22
Switzerland

The World Bank
1818 H Street, N.W.
Washington DC
20433
USA

Commonwealth Secretariat
Marlborough House
London   SW1Y 5HX

International Institute of Administrative Sciences (and International
Association of Schools and Institutes of Administration)
1 Rue Defacqz, bte 11
B-1050 Brussels
Belgium

African Association of Public Administration and Management
P.O. Box 60087
Addis Ababa
Ethiopia

International Centre for Public Enterprises
P.O. Box 92
Ljubljana
Yugoslavia

Index

absorptive capacity, 16, 55, 73
accountability: public, 106–8, 121
administration: area, 79; of
    development planning, 55–6; and
    foreign aid, 151; and IRD, 96–7;
    and politics, 24–7; and
    underdevelopment, 194–6
administrative: district, 6;
    institutions, 9; obstacles, to
    planning, 49–50; productivity,
    182; training centres, 150
administrators: and dependency,
    38–9; field, 139–40, 150, 154–5
African development: and World
    Bank, 178–84
African economies: World Bank
    classification, 74–5
African Socialism, 32–7; in Kenya,
    33–4
Africanisation, 33
agricultural extension workers,
    84–6; and management, 87,
    180–1
agriculture: administration of,
    82–7, 180–1; credit, 84; farmer
    participation, 86; inputs,
    distribution of, 83; research in,
    85; and rural development, 77, 81
aid: and dependency, 37–40, 73,
    75; dispensability, 75–6;
    organisations, 73; and Third
    World, 15; utilisation, 16; see also
    donor bodies; donor finance
apartheid: and South Africa, 53
AR, administrative reform, 170–98;
    prospects for, 193–6; strategies,
    184–5
Arusha Declaration (1967), 34, 55,
    102

auditing, 66–9; in Lesotho, 67–9
autonomy: in local government,
    133–4

Bangladesh: Comilla Model, 98;
    personnel reform, 185
Berg Report: on Africa, 119, 180
Botswana, 51; and development
    planning, 52–3; and finance,
    71–2; MFPD in, 71; Rolling
    Plans System, 71–2
British: in Botswana, 72; and
    colonial administration, 5–6,
    127–8
budgeting, 64–5; in Malaysia, 65–6
bureaucracy, 1–5; critics of, 10–13,
    16–20; effectiveness, 15–16; and
    military rule, 31–2; pruning of,
    181–2; and reform, 173; and
    social inequality, 13; and society,
    20
bureaucratic bourgeoisie, 13, 26–7,
    195
bureaucrats, 1–4; and development
    crisis, 13–15; dominance by, 25,
    26; experience of, 25; and internal
    politics, 22; self-interests of, 18,
    19, 26; training of, 149–55; see
    also administrators
Burkina-Faso: administration in, 7

capitalism, 2, 17; and development,
    14–15; and reform, 195–6; in
    Zambia, 36
CD, Community Development,
    92–6; and local government, 124
centralisation: and local authorities,
    29–30, 125–6; over-, 136
charismatic administration, 2

223

chieftainship, 4; and local
government, 134; in Zambia, 35
China: and local government, 126;
health care in, 186−8; socialist
model, 17
class: analysis, 37; issue, 37
colonial administration, 8; and field
administration, 140
colonialism, 5−9
Comilla Model, Bangladesh, 98
communication management,
167−8
community, 193; see also CD
comprador, 39
computer: use of, 3; and human
resources, 142−3
conditions of service, 111−12
contracts: operating, 104; tendering
for, 68
co-operative societies, 79, 98, 181
co-ordination: in community, 193;
lack of, 81; in planning, 98
corruption: and auditing, 66, 68, 69;
and CD, 96; control of, 162; and
recruitment, 148; and reform, 173
crash localisation: in training,
149−50, 154
credit, 63; unions, 63
customary administration, 2, 6, 7

debt servicing, 60, 73−5
decentralisation, 98, 99, 122−3,
137, 140, 180; of finance, 89; and
PHC, 89
deconcentration, 122−3, 135, 140
dependency: politics of, 37−40
denationalisation, 117, 118
development, 18, 32; administration,
8−9, 11; and AR, 174−5; crisis,
13−15, 115; and growth, 17−20;
and ideologies, 36−7; and
politics, 22−4; and the State,
14−15
development planning, 41−58; in
Botswana, 71−2; and finance,
59−76; implementation of, 50,
71; and state ownership, 102; see
also under planning
devolution, 122−3
district, 123, 127; administrators,
137, 150; Commissioner, 6, 127,
128
donor bodies, 16, 196; influence of,

73, 75−6, 182, 196; and reform,
173, 175−86
donor finance, 72−6; and SRDP, 97
economic: analysis, 42−3, 180;
development, 22−4, 37−40;
nationalism, 39; planning, 8,
42−58
economies: of affection, 118, 119;
income level, 74; market, 118;
mixed, 45−7
education: adult, and CD, 92, 94
evaluation: of performance, 191
expatriates: in administration, 9; in
Botswana, 72; and planning, 48,
52
expertise: lack of indigenous, 116

field administration, 122, 135−40
finance: and development planning,
59−76; and local government,
129−31
financial institutions, 61−3
foreign aid, 1; for capital projects,
59−60; and training, 151−2; see
also donor bodies
foreign exchange: shortage, 115
foreign influence: and dependency,
38−9
French: and colonial administration,
6; commune administration,
128−9

GDP, Gross Domestic Product:
growth of, 18
Ghana: and cocoa crisis, 15; leaders
of, 23
growth: and development, 17−20

harambee: and CD, 95; self-help
clinics, 87
health care: in China, 186−8; sector
planning, 157; see also under PHC
hierarchy: of bureaucracy, 3; and
individuals, 3; and military rule,
31
human resources: management, 80,
142−69; planning, 112, 155−7,
193; see also personnel
management
Hyden, Goran: and
denationalisation, 118−19

ideologies, 32−9; and local

224

government, 126
ILO, International Labour
Organisation, 113
IMF, International Monetary Fund:
and dependency, 37
incentives: to performance, 185,
189, 192
independence: effects of, 9−10;
expectations from, 13−14; and
politics, 22
India: administration in, 5−7, 29;
development planning in, 41;
green revolution in, 82; local
government in, 127; personnel
management, 109; public
corporations in, 104; worker
participation in, 112−13, 166
industrial relations, 112, 165
industrialisation: critics of, 78
industry: state ownership, 36; see
also nationalisation
information: from field officers, 136;
and financial management, 70; for
planning, 44, 115
inputs: for planning, 43
institutionalised instability: of
states, 24
international conflicts: and
bureaucracy, 16
interventionism, 14
IRD, integrated rural development,
96−8; in Bangladesh, 98; in
Kenya, 97−8

job: analysis, 148; creation, and
unemployment, 143

Kenya, 8, 28−9; African Socialism
in, 33−4; development, 38; and
local government, 132; MBO in,
160; 'mixed' economy, 36; para-
statals in, 101, 102; and rural
development, 78; SRDP in, 78,
97−8
Kenya Tea Development Authority,
86−121; success of, 188−90
KIA, Kenya Institute of
Administration, 152
Korea: Development Institute in,
190−2

labour relations, 145
land tenure: and agricultural

development, 83−4
Latin America: and dependency,
38; and military rule, 30
legal rational authority, 2, 3
legislatures, 27−8; and bureaucracy,
27−30; and reform, 172
Lesotho: auditing in, 67−9; local
government problems, 129;
planning, 114
liberalisation, 117
loans, World Bank, 176−8; and
conditionality, 177; soft, 176
local authorities: bureaucracy of,
29−30
local governmnet, 122−34; 'classical
model', 133
localisation, 9−10, 149−50, 153; see
also crash localisation

macro planning, 156
Malaysia, 51, 185; budgeting in,
65−6; development, 38;
development planning, 53−5;
local government in, 128; plural
society, 53
management: and administration,
21; and agricultural extension
workers, 87; autonomy, 121;
personnel, 109−13, 131−2
manpower: morale of, 80; planning,
80; shortage, 80; see also human
resources
markets: accessibility of, 82
MBO, management by objectives,
159−60, 191
merit recruitment, 4, 110, 169, 172
micro planning, 156
military-bureaucratic complex, 31
military rule: and bureaucracy,
30−2
morale: indicators of, 161; in Kenya
Civil Service, 161; of staff, 144,
160−2, 167
motivation: of staff, 144, 160,
studies of, 162−4
multinational corporations: and
development, 14−15
nationalisation: in Kenya, 33; in
Tanzania, 34, 46, 102; in Zambia,
102
NGOs, non-government
organisations, 79
NICs, newly industrialising

225

scarcity of, and planning, 48; *see also* human resources
rhetoric: and local government, 125
Rolling Plans system: in Botswana, 71–2
rural: depopulation, 77; poor, 78; populism, 32, 34, 37
rural development: bureaucratic role in, 79–100; Comilla Model, Bangladesh, 98; integration in, 47; lack of co-ordination, 83; and PHC, 87–91; problems of, 79–82; SRDP, Kenya, 97–8; and village water supplies, 91–2

SAL, Structural Adjustment Lending, 119, 183
salary administration, 144
savings, private: level of, 60
self-actualisation, 163
Senegal: contract plans, 185–6
socialism: African, 32–7; and bureaucracy, 17, 19; European, 33; in Kenya, 33–4; in Tanzania, 34–5, 55–6; in Zambia, 35–6
spheres of competence, 2–3
staff: appraisal and management, 144, 158–60; morale and motivation, 144, 160–4; needs, 160; participation and communication, 144; probation, 144; promotion, 144; transfers, 144
standard of living: and development, 18
state: capitalism, 36; companies, 104; ownership, in mixed economy, 45; *see also* public enterprises
statutory boards, 103
structural adjustment, 177; lending (SAL), 177–8

Tanzania, 36, 51 bureaucratic bourgeoisie, 26–7; and development planning, 55–6; National Development Corporation, 116–17; and nationalisation, 101–2; and reform, 195; Ujamaa Socialism, 23, 34–5, 126; worker participation, 112

taxation, 60–1; administration of, 1; and colonialism, 8; and local government, 130; and the private sector, 46
Taylorism, 163
teachers: and training, 153
technical expertise: in Botswana, 52; and human resources, 142–3; in Nigeria 56; and planning, 42
tendering: for government contracts, 68
Third World: and aid, 15; and bureaucracy, 4, 10, 12–13; dependence by, 17; and development planning, 41–58; and military rule, 31–2; parliamentary control in, 28–30; political changes in, 22
trained incapacity, 10
training: aid for, 176; in CD, 94, 96; difficulties in, 151–5; evaluation, 154; of field officers, 136; institutions, 172; materials, lack of, 152–3; of personnel, 144, 149–55; in public enterprises, 110–11; worth of, 154
tribal divisions: in states, 24
Trinidad: and development, 18

Uganda: bureaucracy in, 2, 25, 26; primary health care in, 90–1
Ujamaa Socialism: in Tanzania, 23, 34–5, 126
UN: aid from, 15
underdevelopment: and reform, 194–6
unemployment, 143
urbanisation: 'exploding cities', 77
USAID, United States Agency for International Development, 15, 125

village government: *see* local government
village leadership: and agricultural development, 84

water: and rural development, 91–2
Weber, Max: analysis of bureaucracy, 2–5, 10–11, 110, 145, 163
WHO, World Health Organisation, 88

Wilson, Woodrow: doctrine of, 25–7
women: Groups, and CD, 93–4; in PHC, 91; role of, 152
worker participation, 112–13
World Bank: in Africa, 178–84; aid from, 15, 73; and AR, 175–86; view on bureaucracy, 16–17, 19, 125; and dependency, 37; Development Report, 1983, 183–6; and financial planning, 70; loan controversy, 176–8; and

privatisation, 119–20; role of, 176–7
written records: of bureaucracy, 3

Zambia, 36; Humanism, 35–6, 126; industrial relations, 112; local training in, 150; and nationalisation, 101–2; rural population of, 77; worker participation in, 112, 113, 166
Zimbabwe: mixed economy, 46

WORK FROM SHED

HOXTON MINI PRESS

Above: The Shed by Hufft, USA (p.221).
Right: Garden Office by All in One Design
& Build, UK (p.121).

Left: Writer's Studio by WT Architecture, UK (p.107).
Above: Tiny Atelier by Ryuji Kajino and
Malubishi Architects, Japan (p.248).

George Bernard Shaw outside of
his shed in the garden of his home
in Hertfordshire, UK, July 1946.

INTRODUCTION

Think of a shed, and you'll probably think of something made of wood. Think a bit more, and you might visualise somewhere personal, a retreat from the world, from where great literature or world-changing inventions might emanate, or where private passions can be cultivated. Someone might invent cold nuclear fusion in a shed, polish their collection of garden gnomes, or build a model of Salisbury Cathedral out of matchsticks. Seen from the outside, sheds tend to be generic and anonymous; inside, they are idiosyncratic and individual.

A shed might be something like the one pictured left, where George Bernard Shaw wrote his Nobel-Prize-winning plays, built on a pivot so it could rotate to follow the course of the sun – at once eccentric, intimate and cosmic. It might be the pine-bark-and-plywood *cabanon* that Le Corbusier built for himself on some rocks above the Mediterranean, its dimensions calculated to be the minimum necessary for him to eat, sleep and work. 'I have a chateau on the Côte d'Azur,' was his description of this modest structure. 'It's extravagant in comfort and gentleness.'

There is a connection between sheds being mostly wooden and their being places of invention. Their construction is typically simple and visible – you can see the nails and boards, both inside and out – which gives them an aura of honest making. You feel close to the person who put your shed together and, like the writers, artists and potters who have commissioned many of the structures in this book, you feel inspired to create something yourself. Wood shows wear, weather and the passage of time. There is a sense of the organic: timber is natural, sheds (as in potting sheds, garden sheds) are places of growth. Again, the spirit is one of creation.

Now consider the popularity of putting wood-burning stoves inside sheds, of which you'll see examples in this book – handsome objects with cylindrical flues rising through the ceiling. There's a frisson here that comes from the apparent fire hazard – you're burning the stuff that gives you shelter! Creation comes twinned with destruction. You can imagine yourself in a pioneer's cabin: that there's nothing but bears and snow outside, with only planks and logs keeping you from extinction, even if there's really nothing more threatening than urban foxes and the neighbours' cats.

All of which explains the flourishing of sheds and shed-like places, and the never-ending resourcefulness with which

9

architects, designers and their clients re-imagine this typology. With the 'sheds' presented here, pleasure in craft is embellished with features you don't get in your basic version: high ceilings, clever plans, the encounters of materials artistically considered.

There might, as in TDO's Forest Pond House (p.126), be a big, well-placed window that connects the user with light and nature. In their Room in the Garden (p.46) in Putney, south west London, Studio Ben Allen adapted standard framing techniques to make a refined polygonal vault. Standard timber cladding might be substituted, as on The Writing Room (p.35) by Neighbourhood Studio or Studio Bark's Holloway Lightbox (p.28), by playful shingles or tiles.

Many are highly bespoke projects, the polar opposite of flat-packed structures from B&Q, where the unique preferences of clients are interpreted by aspiring young architects. Some, such as Bert's Boxes (p.123), offer something between the standard and the individual: they come in a fixed range of types and sizes, which you can then customise to suit your own tastes.

With most of the sheds in this book there is some fiction at play. They have to follow the building regulations, which complicates the nails-and-planks directness of the shed. I am writing these words in such a space myself, a house extension by 6a architects clad inside with white-painted softwood and outside with jarrah boards reclaimed from old railway sleepers. Between them is a thick but invisible layer of modern building products – insulation, damp proof membranes – that keep me warm and dry, for which I am grateful. It looks a bit shed-like, but the design and construction have come quite a long way from their inspirations. The point here is not to recreate 'shed-iness' right down to the drafts and damp, but to enjoy that sense of making.

Some of these projects, such as Sonn studio's Terrazzo Studio (p.70), use materials that are heftier than wood. These too have travelled far from their origins. They forego a shed's air of ephemerality and movability – the feeling that it might be picked up and carried off – but they retain the spirit of retreat and freedom, of opening up possibilities that the conventions of a typical house inhibit.

If part of the joy of sheds is about elemental simplicity – a single room, four walls and a roof – it can also be about giving free rein to invention. They can be your own personal version of the follies that 18th-century aristocrats built in the landscape gardens of their country houses. They can be fantastical as well as functional, something like Platform 5's Shoffice (p.12), an elliptical tube which looks like an improbable timber spaceship. Noah meets *Star Trek*, you might say. This is not something you would build if pure practicality were your only aim.

There are additional explanations than

the poetry of sheds for their appeal. One is
the planning policies in a city like London,
which tend to be less restrictive about
discreet works in back gardens than about
more publicly visible projects. Another is the
rise of working from home. Whatever the
long-term ramifications of the pandemic, it
seems likely that, for those whose jobs allow
it, the advantages of avoiding a five-day-a-
week commute won't be easily forgotten. In
which case we can expect the range of ideas
to continue to grow.

'People bother me,' said Shaw of his
shed, 'I came here to hide from them.' He
called the shed 'London', so that unwanted
visitors to his Hertfordshire home could
be told that 'he's gone to London'. Some
guests were welcome, however, such as
the occasional Hollywood star, or the press
photographers who would burnish his
image as a hermit-genius by photographing
him outside his humble wooden structure.

You don't have to be as grumpy as the
old playwright to enjoy a nice shed, but you
can appreciate the range of experiences
he got out of this tiny structure. It was,
for him, a reclusive hideaway, a place of
creation and a display of his life and values.
For all its modesty, the 'shed' is a structure
that runs many gamuts.

Rowan Moore,
Architecture critic

11

SHOFFICE

A shed and an office combined and innovated

LONDON, UK

Designs for this hybrid 'shoffice' required close collaboration between architects Platform 5 and their structural engineer, Morph Structures; the result is a magnificently sculptural build that swoops and swirls into the back garden of a 1950s terraced house in St John's Wood. The bold wooden curve hugs an office with oak-lined interiors and built-in storage, before flowing into a terrace that leads on to the garden. Two skylights – one glazed, one open – flood the space with natural light and further blur the line between inside and out. The lightweight structure is formed of two steel ring beams with timber ribs and a plywood outer layer, and was largely prefabricated before being constructed onsite to minimise disruption; in fact, its final shape is so organic, you could almost imagine it had grown here.

Architects: Platform 5 Architects
Build cost: approx. £90,000/$120,000
Footprint: 7m²/75ft²

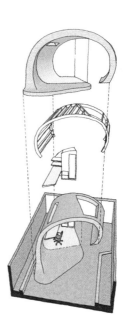

The structure's swooping form
and snug layers of glass, steel
and timber give it a remarkably
organic quality – reminiscent
of a beached seashell.

DECORATED SHED

A modern take on the classic silhouette

LONDON, UK

'Garden sheds have changed,' says architect Rodrigo Moreno Masey – looking at the one he has created for his own garden, you'll no doubt agree. Although the exterior is designed to echo a traditional shed, with reclaimed oak cladding and a classic pitched roof, you won't find a cobweb-covered lawnmower or ageing paint tins inside. Instead, the space can function as an office, a gym, a library or a cinema. The structure's roof and exterior walls blend together seamlessly thanks to the uninterrupted flow of timber, and the interior, though cleanly decorated, is warm and welcoming and full of practical storage. Its tiled floor extends into a patio, while a glazed garage door rolls up over the ceiling, allowing one wall to be almost entirely open and creating a playful merging of indoor and out. With a grey wall primed for the projector on movie nights, this garden room is an evolution in shed-escapism.

Architects: MorenoMasey
Build cost: £50,000/$68,000
Footprint: 28m²/301ft²

The architect and owner of this shed, Rodrigo Moreno Masey, wanted it to feel like a distinct, separate space for his young family, rather than just an extension of their home.

THE BUNKER

An inner-city retreat from the capital's chaos

LONDON, UK

This sunken studio was built as the Brexit debate raged on across the UK; the client affectionately dubbed it 'The Brexit Bunker', saying it provided an escape from the political climate. The entire exterior is clad in naturally weathered steel, lending it an industrial look, but the interior's warmth and brightness is created by birch plywood cladding. Insulated walls keep the space warm, while also muffling the sound of trains which pass close behind the client's garden, and built-in storage doubles as a set of steps leading up to a small platform under the skylight: intended as a space for the client to sit, look up and be able to imagine they are in the countryside. Across the floor, a deep oriel window overlooking the garden offers a sunny reading spot – the final tranquil touch to this bespoke bolthole, where talk of referendums is forbidden.

Architects: RISE Design Studio
Build cost: £145,000/$197,000
Footprint: 41m²/441ft²

The rusted steel exterior of The Bunker was inspired by the railway line that runs directly behind it; yet inside, the space has been designed to block out all interference from the surrounding city.

WRITER'S SHED

A fairy-tale retreat with a woodburning stove

LONDON, UK

The architects describe their brief for this project as 'a fairy-tale hut at the bottom of the garden'. The client wanted the shed to reflect his passion for children's literature and mythology, and to provide him with a space where he could escape the city and immerse himself in his work. The result (clad in wooden shingles rather than gingerbread) perfectly balances whimsy and function. At the front, a partially enclosed veranda constructed with warm cedar seems to glow at night as the light from the interior shines through, while a chimney and log store add to the story-book feel. Inside, quirky shelving hugs the shape of the stove pipe, while the woodburning stove casts a fittingly flickering light across the room.

Architects: Weston, Surman & Deane
Build cost: £32,000/$43,000
Footprint: 15m²/161ft²

Bookshelves form the focal point of this shed: their whimsical positioning around the chimney flue provides a refined take on a tumble-down, fairy-tale cabin.

HOLLOWAY LIGHTBOX

A photography studio behind bespoke tiles

LONDON, UK

The clients, a photographer and a screenwriter, who commissioned this garden build were looking for a space that could function as a photography studio as well as a writing room. With a focus on making the most of the natural light, the architects designed a pitched roof with a large south-west facing skylight. The angle of the roof matches that of the sun's rays as it sets, flooding the studio with elusive golden-hour light. Inside, the built-in storage can be moved around at will, providing different photography backgrounds while keeping the space clutter-free. Large sliding doors open on to the garden, making the studio feel even more spacious. Inspired by the clients' professions, the architects handmade more than 1,200 different-coloured tiles from a mix of waste timber fibres and cement for the exterior cladding, creating its playful, pixelated effect.

Architects: Studio Bark
Build cost: £30,000/$41,000
Footprint: 21m²/226ft²

FAYE & DANIEL'S PLACE

Material-led design in a space to work and play

LONDON, UK

This garden structure makes extensive use of a material perhaps more often associated with sprawling palaces than terraced houses in south London: marble. The architects were inspired by the dappled light cast by the surrounding trees to create this marbled studio, and also designed a marble-clad extension to the clients' home at the same time. They opted for a combination of light-coloured Arabescato marble with a dark grey Bardiglio, combined with large expanses of glazing that lend the hard-angled structure a warmth and lightness. In summer, the bi-folding windows can be fully opened, making the space feel like an extension of the garden. During the week, the studio functions as a home office, but when the weekend comes, the in-built cupboards open up to reveal a well-stocked bar: transforming it into a space for socialising.

Architects: Alexander Owen Architecture
Build cost: approx. £45,000/$61,000
Footprint: 16m²/172ft²

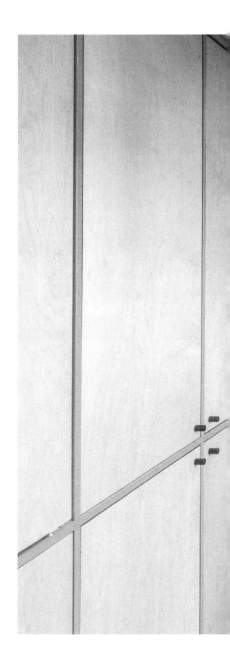

The architects chose the materials for this build for their ability to be used in an almost 'raw' state, purposefully balancing the organic warmth of timber with the natural coolness of marble.

THE WRITING ROOM

A versatile space for an outdoor enthusiast

LONDON, UK

When Neighbourhood Studio were approached by an actor who wanted to replace his dilapidated garden shed with a structure that would provide space for writing, relaxation and storage for his surf gear, they responded to the brief with this clever L-shaped design that manages to separate a small area into three distinct spaces. One side is taken up with a comfortable armchair, while the other incorporates a writing nook and a generous amount of externally accessible storage for surfboards and bikes. The two sides wrap around a terrace with built-in outside seating, while a woodburning stove ensures the room feels cosy in winter. The timber cladding creates a sense of warmth and gives a 'cabin in the woods' feel, as requested by the client, making it a peaceful escape for when he can't hit the (rather distant) waves.

Architects: Neighbourhood Studio
Build cost: £25,000/$34,000
Footprint: 22m²/237ft²

35

CEDAR CABIN

A sleek studio celebrating timber

LONDON, UK

As part of a renovation project that saw a fully glazed dining room and kitchen extension added to the rear of their house, these clients also commissioned a small garden studio as a place to retreat and work from home. A set of basalt stones leads you through the garden to the cedar-clad cabin, where the architects continued their theme of impressive glazing by incorporating an innovative corner window. Inside, the walls, ceiling, desk and storage are all pink plywood, and the built-in cupboards' holes in place of handles give a simple, smooth finish. The corner desk hugs the window, looking back towards the house, while a small stained-glass panel in the door adds a pop of colour and personality to this understated space.

Architects: RISE Design Studio
Build cost: £45,000/$61,000
Footprint: 8m²/86ft²

The clients of this cabin requested a pane of stained glass inspired by the work of American architect Frank Lloyd Wright – RISE Design Studio had one created by bespoke glass makers, Leadbitter Glass.

DANIEL HEATH'S GARDEN STUDIO

A self-built studio adorned with illustrations

LONDON, UK

Wallpaper and textile designer Daniel and his wife Laura, an author and colour consultant, embarked on this build because Daniel's previous workspace had become so full of equipment and materials he was struggling to find room to draw. They opted to construct their new studio themselves, ordering a kit from Dunster House that consisted of hundreds of pieces they had to 'post' through their bathroom window and into the back garden, thanks to a hard-to-navigate corridor. The main build took three to four days but, once lockdown hit, Daniel used the sudden overspill of free time to add decking, along with a salvaged brick patio and raised beds. He also created a series of illustrations, referencing the surrounding planting, that were then engraved on to reclaimed slate and used to clad the exterior. Inside, inspired by his previously overcrowded workspace, Daniel has kept the interior clean and minimal to leave plenty of space for sketching and thinking.

Architects: Dunster House/Self-build
Build cost: £5,000/$7,000
Footprint: 17.5m²/188ft²

Daniel was so inspired by the raised
beds his wife Laura planted out
around their studio that he wanted
to keep the feeling of foliage year
round, and immortalised it via
illustrations engraved into slate.

A ROOM IN THE GARDEN

A flat-packed escape pod with fluid functions

LONDON, UK

This playful garden structure can act as a workspace, a playroom, a spare bedroom – and everything in between. Designed to provide a quiet haven for clients Jonnie and Rachel (who have two young children), its form was inspired by a traditional folly, and its jewel-toned exterior designed to blend in with the surrounding garden.
The double doors can be flung open in summer, while underfloor heating and airtight insulation make it a cosy hideaway in winter. Geometry is at the heart of this build: the octagonal wall structure connects to a hexagonal roof, which frames a square skylight. Inside, there's a desk, shelving, and a reading nook that folds out into a bed. Perhaps the pod's most impressive feature, however, is that it arrived flat-packed – all parts having been fabricated on a CNC machine – so the clients could assemble it themselves. It can also be easily dissembled and moved, should the need arise, making its possible uses almost endless.

Architects: Studio Ben Allen
Build cost: £35,000/$48,000
Footprint: 15m²/161ft²

46

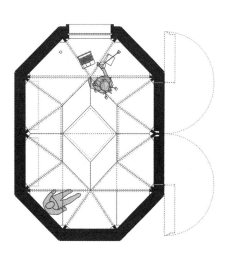

Each element of the structure was digitally cut by a CNC machine and designed to interlock seamlessly, pushing this technology to its limits to allow for innovative, easy self-assembly.

THE LIGHT SHED

A co-working space suffused with sunlight

LONDON, UK

When architect Richard John Andrews decided to design a low-cost studio space for his expanding practice, he had two key things in mind: natural light and collaborative working. Built in his back garden, which is accessible only through his house, it was essential that the studio materials were lightweight and in small-enough pieces to carry through his home before being assembled onsite. The timber frame is clad in corrugated, black fibreglass panels, punctuated by sliding doors. Inside, there is built-in shelving and desk space for two to three people, so collaborators can come and share ideas. The highpoint of the project, though, is its polycarbonate roofing. Richard was keen to avoid direct light and glare: the polycarbonate plastic ensures the space is filled with diffused natural light for a relaxing working environment. Happily, Richard notes, the roof material he chose also creates the ideal conditions for aphids, attracting many birds to the garden.

Architect: Richard John Andrews
Build cost: £12,500/$17,000
Footprint: 16m²/172ft²

GREENWICH GARDEN STUDIO

*A reclaimed-brick reading room
with a living roof*

LONDON, UK

The client for this build, a writer, wanted to create
a new home office in his cramped and overgrown garden,
which housed a derelict washhouse. MW Architects
met this challenge by transforming the garden into a
compact courtyard and using the retaining walls of the
old washhouse as the basis for the new studio. The space
incorporates a reading room and a small shower room,
separated from each other by a plywood-clad partition
with built-in shelving and a desk. The architects also made
use of bricks rescued from the washhouse's demolition and,
in a further nod to its humble origins, installed a sedum
green roof to echo the mossy, weed-covered exterior of the
original outbuilding. A large skylight ensures the space's
brightness, while a comfortable chair, precisely positioned
to give a view over the courtyard, provides a spot for
drinking coffee and untangling plots.

Architects: MW Architects
Build cost: £42,000/$57,000
Footprint: 10m²/108ft²

54

NESTLE STUDIO

A camouflaged, light-filled haven in which to paint

LONDON, UK

With a growing family and space at a premium, these clients asked Mustard Architects to create a painting studio in their back garden with two key requirements: they needed plenty of natural light, and they wanted to retain the mature silver birch that stood right where the studio was supposed to go. The result is this subtle structure, which wraps around the treasured tree and has multiple, angled windows. The studio is covered in vertical cladding in untreated western red cedar – over time, this will turn grey, echoing the silver birch. Intending that the studio should eventually blend into its surroundings, the architects also introduced a feathered edge to the top of the cladding, to create the illusion that the studio is fading into the surrounding planting. Inside, the walls are birch-faced plywood while the floor is concrete: tough enough to cope with the inevitable splashes of paint.

Architects: Mustard Architects
Build cost: approx. £75,000/$101,000
Footprint: 35m²/377ft²

57

With its abundance of south-facing windows, the architects were mindful of ensuring this studio wouldn't overheat in summer; the surrounding trees provide vital shade as well as appealingly dappled light.

MANBEY POD

A self-built kit studio using natural materials

LONDON, UK

Constructed from one of Studio Bark's innovative 'U-Build' kits, this space was designed to function as an extra family room, storage area and textile studio. Nestled in the clients' back garden under a mature maple tree, the interior is clad in birch plywood for a uniform finish, with skylights to provide extra light. Keen to make the build low-energy and eco-friendly, the architects used natural, UK-sourced materials for the kits, including natural wool insulation and wood from British forests. The exterior cladding is western red cedar – its herringbone pattern a nod to the textiles that will be created within. Putting it all together was, the client says, surprisingly easy: 'If you can assemble flat-pack furniture, you can do this – although, thankfully, there's no Allen key involved.'

Architects: Studio Bark
Build cost: £18,000/$24,000
Footprint: 17.5m²/188ft²

MY ROOM IN THE GARDEN

A prefab office module to suit tiny spaces

LONDON, UK

Just as they do with their groundbreaking Minima Moralia artists' studio (p.90), architects Tomaso Boano and Jonas Prišmontas intend this compact garden office to make a statement. Inspired by the surge in working from home sparked by the Covid-19 pandemic, and the way that many people found their already-crowded homes overtaken by work, they created these affordable 'pocket spaces': tiny office modules that can sit in even the smallest of gardens. They are easy to assemble and can be built in just one day, with a timber frame and corrugated, clear polycarbonate cladding to ensure the space is full of natural light. Just 2.5m (8ft) high to avoid the need for planning permission, they are wonderfully unobtrusive, with the option of varying the interior or even adding on extra modules to suit your needs. Could these little pods be the future of home working?

Architects: Boano Prišmontas
Build cost: from £5,000/$6,800
Footprint: 4.3m²/46ft²

62

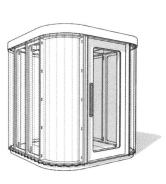

Designs for the home-office pod
aimed to minimise material waste
by making each component an
efficient, standard size – and each
module is designed, manufactured
and pre-assembled within the UK.

CLAIRE & TOM'S GARDEN STUDIO

A serene, separate workspace for two new parents

LONDON, UK

Anyone with young children will know (or may only dream of) the benefits of having a quiet place to work that's both near their home and very much separate to it. Neuropsychologist Claire and designer Tom were originally considering an extension to their two-storey Victorian home, but with the arrival of their twin baby girls decided to create this garden studio. The structure, which is west-facing to catch the afternoon light, is slightly sunk into the ground to aid its discreetness, while the cosy hammock chair that hangs from its timber canopy is perfectly placed for an opportune nap. Inside, the walls and ceiling are lined with oiled birch plywood, and the blue terrazzo-patterned rubber flooring has taken inspiration from the local Victoria line underground trains. Outside, the primary-yellow aluminium window frame, tractor-green walls, sedum roof and simple geometric shapes make the studio feel suitably playful for this young family.

Architects: Zminkowska De Boise Architects
Build cost: £40,000/$54,000
Footprint: 10.5m²/113ft²

Clients Claire and Tom initially asked the architects to investigate extending their mid-terraced house, but eventually settled on a garden studio to ensure separation between work and home life.

TERRAZZO STUDIO

A tropical-feel oasis with a secret workshop

LONDON, UK

Inspired by a research trip to Mexico, Tim Robinson –
architect and owner of Sonn studio – designed and
built this studio space as a personal sanctuary in the
garden of his one-bed flat. Lush tropical planting
surrounds the structure and is echoed in its forest-green,
bespoke terrazzo cladding, which hugs the exterior and
complements the grey aluminium-framed glass walls.
Inside, the light-filled studio has a cork desk running
the length of one side, while cupboard space cleverly
hides a foldaway bed. Linen curtains can be pulled out of
a concealed slot to transform the workspace into a private
guest bedroom. The microcement flooring (a cement-based
coating that mimics polished concrete) extends through
the full-length sliding doors and on to a drinks terrace
outside with seating and palm trees – perfect for enjoying
a margarita after a day's work. At the rear, the ridged
cladding conceals a secret door to a second room: a hidden
workshop, with space for tools and a workbench, lit from
above by a skylight.

Architects: Sonn
Build cost: £25,000/$34,000
(materials only)
Footprint: 14m²/151ft²

The studio's cladding conceals the door to its secret workshop space, while a waterbutt to the side of the building collects rainwater for the workshop sink.

RUG ROOM

A weathered steel haven with a secret garden

LONDON, UK

Building a garden studio for this client's rug-making business provided a challenge for architect Nic Howett, as the garden itself (at the back of a Victorian terrace) is rather slender and can only be accessed via the house and an awkward, narrow staircase. The resulting steel-clad plywood structure was transported into the garden in small pieces (each less than 2.5 x 1.25m/8 x 4ft) and constructed onsite. The architect actually made a feature of the narrow space available by positioning the studio not-quite-at-the-end of the garden, creating a 'secret' second garden beyond the studio's back door. Inside, there is space to work, read and – of course – make rugs, with a work table and shelves for books and fabric. The exterior is clad in Cor-Ten steel, a metal that's designed to weather with a rust-like appearance over time, without needing to be painted. In the relatively short time that the Rug Room has been in place, the Cor-Ten has taken on an autumnal, rusty hue that makes it feel as if it's been there for years.

Architect: Nic Howett
Build cost: £25,000/$34,000
Footprint: 9m²/97ft²

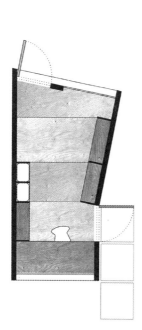

CORK STUDY

A compact, practical workspace for two creatives

LONDON, UK

Creating a shared workspace for a musician and a seamstress in a small area might have been a tall order, but this cork-wrapped studio managed to tick all its new owners' boxes. With limited space and a desire to create something that felt in keeping with the surrounding garden, the architects opted for the innovative cork cladding because it is sustainable and weatherproof, but also provides all-important sound insulation while keeping the interior snug. The sedum wildflower roof blends into the greenery around it, making the studio almost invisible from above. Inside, the couple have a desk each, plus plenty of shelving and storage, with all the furniture cantilevered off the walls to make the most of the limited room. The oak-framed door can be slid entirely out of view to allow the study to open directly on to the garden in warmer weather, making the space feel bigger than it really is.

Architects: Surman Weston
Build cost: £45,000/$61,000
Footprint: 13m²/140ft²

POTTING SHED

*A cost-effective creative project
using reclaimed materials*

LONDON, UK

With a limited budget, creating this studio for a ceramicist
and keen gardener called for an inventive and resourceful
approach. The client was looking for a warm, inviting
space that could meet all the practical needs of a maker's
studio and provide room for gardening tools. The design
was built around (and adjusted to suit) the salvaged
materials they were able to source: ex-display windows
and doors with minor cosmetic defects provided the basis,
while the plywood that clads the internal and external
walls is made up of offcuts that would otherwise have gone
to waste. The result is a pleasing patchwork effect that
lends a quirky feel to this little studio. The exterior's
clean lines, matt-black finish and low-rise pitched roof
were inspired by local east London factories. Its position,
hugging a mature apple tree, makes the most of an
underutilised space at the edge of the garden. It's the ideal
spot for both potting plants and making pots.

*Architects: Grey Griffiths Architects
Build cost: £15,900/$21,600
Footprint: 18m²/194ft²*

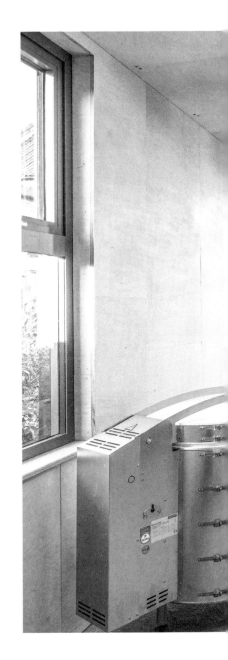

Though the ceramicist who commissioned this build primarily needed a workshop, she didn't want the design to be constrained to this typology: the space can also function as a comfortable office and snug.

SE5 GARDEN LIBRARY

Innovation prompted by building restrictions

LONDON, UK

The clients who commissioned this build, a growing family, were seeking a study, a spare room and more storage space, but adding an extension to their flat was far too complex. The architects still had to tackle a number of restrictions to create this studio – in particular, the need to leave a 1m (3ft) boundary around the build – but the result of their resourcefulness is a brilliant balance of playfulness and functionality. The foundations were cast in concrete, and the wooden sheets that had been used for the cast were then repurposed to make the ceiling beams. As you peer up through them, an elevated library is revealed. The building materials were deliberately kept simple and unadorned – concrete, plywood, simple valve taps – but the space still has a warm and friendly aesthetic thanks to the family's brightly coloured books. Raised planters outside conceal extra storage underneath, cleverly making the very best of the boundary area, while leaving plenty of floorspace available for play.

Architects: Turner Architects
Build cost: approx. £60,000/$80,000
Footprint: 30m²/323ft²

MINIMA MORALIA

*A manifesto for the affordable
studio of the future*

LONDON, UK

When is a shed not a shed? When it's a political statement,
of course. This small pop-up studio was created by Tomaso
Boano and Jonas Prišmontas to highlight the way that
London's sky-high rents and cost of living are damaging
the creative industry. 'Creativity should not be linked to
social status,' they say, and here they have aimed to create
a model for what a financially accessible studio might look
like. With a steel frame, OSB fittings and foldable walls
made from panels of polycarbonate cladding, the unit is
low cost and compact. The translucent walls allow the
artist working within to connect with their surroundings,
while the folding canopy, window and skylight allow them
to open up or close the space as much as they desire. Keep
an eye on the horizon: these clever little pods could be
popping up all over the city before long.

Architects: Boano Prišmontas
Build cost: £6,000/$8,000
Footprint: 4m²/43ft²

CLERKEN-WELL ROAD

*A tranquil home office with
its own timber terrace*

LONDON, UK

Built with a focus on efficiency, openness and flexibility, this home office doubles as a spare bedroom thanks to a built-in, fold-down bed. Clad in the same western red cedar that forms the surrounding decking and outside seating area, it blends in seamlessly to the terrace on which it stands, with small, shuttered windows that look across to the main apartment as well as a large picture window providing views over the city. With built-in shelving and space for a large desk, it's an ideal working environment – and, best of all, there's a projector for transforming the terrace into an outside home cinema. All that's missing is a popcorn machine.

Architect: Hannes Wingate
Footprint: 13m²/140ft²

93

In summer, the timber terrace that connects the client's office to their two-bed apartment is a perfect spot for a sunny lunchbreak.

LONDON TOWNHOUSE SHED

A quiet working escape lined with books

LONDON, UK

This garden studio was built for book designer Kate. She and her partner were starting a family and she needed a separate space to focus on work away from the main house. Clad in western red cedar with a sedum roof, the shed sits at the rear of the garden where it blends in with the surrounding greenery and red brickwork. Inside, the walls and ceiling are lined with birch plywood, with a feature wall showing a graphic book print. All the furniture was customised by the architects to suit Kate's needs: there is a large desk (which ingeniously incorporates a pull-out electric piano), as well as a comfortable seating area for reading or relaxing, with fold-away tables so she can meet with clients. The front wall is fully glazed with sliding doors that open on to the garden and face the house, visually linking the space to the family's other rooms, while a slight overhang from the roof creates a mini sheltered patio.

Architect: Lia Kiladis
Footprint: 18.5m²/199ft²

DWELLING UNIT FOR MUSICIANS

A music-studio-meets-shed made by robots

BRISTOL, UK

You might expect a shed built by robots to be all futuristic metals and flashing lights, but the focus of this one is sustainability and affordability, and that means timber. Using Automated Architecture's unique system, modular structures composed of timber building blocks are constructed by machine (and then put together onsite by local craftspeople), and can be adapted almost limitlessly to the client's needs. This space was created for a musician couple – a double bassist and a cellist – who were looking for a home office and rehearsal studio. The floor-to-ceiling windows, skylight and glazed door allow for lots of natural light, but a clever paper cellulose insulation system still gives that all-important acoustic insulation. The roof is made from EPDM (a non-toxic, recyclable rubber), and the flooring is rubber, too. All in all, this automated design has been perfectly tuned.

Architects: Automated Architecture
Build cost: £15,000/$20,000
Footprint: 10m²/108ft²

The timber building blocks can be
disassembled and reassembled for
other completely different uses,
adhering to the principles of
circular design.

ROOM

*A personally designed space
with distinctive cladding*

MANCHESTER, UK

With a creative job and young children, a dedicated – and
separate – workspace was understandably desirable for
Tim Denton, who runs his own design and build studio
in Manchester. Not only does this garden room provide
him with an escape where he can work undisturbed, it
also allows him to close the door on his work at the end
of the day for uninterrupted family time. In fact, he got so
much enjoyment from his shed that he decided to launch it
as a product, using his build as the prototype for a prefab
garden office that's easy for anyone to adapt to their needs.
The exterior of his studio is clad in unusually shaped
shingles inspired by a trip to Chile, but Tim wants to offer
customers the option of a bespoke pattern for their own
sheds. The insides are lined with wood for a natural finish,
while large windows keep the space connected to the
garden – perfect if, like Tim, you like to spend your coffee
breaks pottering around the flowerbeds.

Architect: Tim Denton
Build cost: £24,000/$33,000
Footprint: 12.25m²/132ft²

On a research trip to Lemuy Island
in Chile in 2010, Tim fell in love with
the villages' timber buildings clad
in all sorts of patterns and shapes,
and was inspired to create his own
modern shingles for his shed.

WRITER'S STUDIO

*A 19th-century glasshouse
given a new lease of life*

EDINBURGH, UK

Before WT Architecture designed this studio, the two writers for whom it was created had been working in a delipidated Victorian glasshouse in their garden, putting up with its leaky roof and constant drafts. With a brief to retain the original footprint but revitalise the glasshouse, the architects created this 21st-century space. The Douglas fir timber frame and beams echo the branches of the trees above, adding to the feeling of being outside created by the largely glass structure. Described by the architect as a writing studio and 'sitooterie' (a Scottish term for a place you can sit outside), it features a woodburning stove surrounded by a raised seating area, as well as the all-important desk. Not only does the desk provide a space for writing, it's also a vital part of the structure, sitting on the brick walls of the original glasshouse and extending beyond them to create a larger area while retaining the original footprint.

*Architects: WT Architecture
Build cost: £42,000/$57,000
Footprint: 10m²/108ft²*

The clients' new overhanging
writing desk forms a cantilever
which supports the timber frame
and glazed canopy so that they
appear to be suspended over the
original Victorian brick walls.

THE STUDIOS

A pair of matching, low-maintenance workspaces

SUFFOLK, UK

The couple who commissioned these garden studios – a painter and a sculptor – intended to use them as a retreat rather than year-round workplaces, so the architects set out to create spaces that would need minimal upkeep. The larger was designed for the painter to work on huge canvases, while the sculptor wanted a slightly smaller workplace. The result is these non-identical twins, with huge windows and skylights through which to enjoy the surrounding gardens and slanted roofs that channel rainwater into a nearby pond. The clients' family historically worked in the construction of corrugated iron buildings in the early 1900s – the studios' fibre-cement cladding is a nod to this history, as well as to the style of local farm outbuildings.

Architects: SOUP
Footprints: 40m²/431ft² and 60m²/646ft²

SCULPTURE CABIN

*A whimsical structure
for deep work and meditation*

PREFABRICATED IN THE UK & IRELAND

The bold geometry of this cabin would make a striking addition to any garden – and, indeed, it can: Koto offer their prefabricated structure as both an off-the-shelf and a bespoke design that can be used in a variety of spaces. The structure is made of entirely natural materials: an essential design choice for its creators. They were inspired by Japanese design and the idea of wabi-sabi, which celebrates the transient nature of life and the beauty in imperfection. The light-coloured interior walls contrast with the charred timber exterior, and their unusual angles bounce light around the space. Both inside and out, there's something rather magical about these pods.

Architects: Koto
Build cost: from £30,000/$41,000
Footprint: approx. 5.5m²/59ft²

At first glance, the degree to which the cabin appears wedged into the ground gives the illusion it fell from the sky.

TWO PAVILIONS

*A retreat reached by tunnel
and a rustic sculptor's studio*

EAST SUSSEX, UK

Not one shed, but two, this remarkable pair of structures
has enabled the clients to significantly expand their living
space. The first pavilion (pictured right), described as a
'hermitage', is a guest suite with an oak-lined bedroom,
bathroom and kitchenette in a simple concrete building
on the banks of a manmade lake. A large window opens
on to a deck hanging over the water, but the only way
to access the suite is via a 40m (131ft) galvanised steel,
subterranean tunnel that runs back to the main house,
giving it a uniquely cut-off feel. The second is a sculptor's
studio (pictured overleaf), built on the remains of a
dilapidated 18th-century farmhouse with walls consisting
partly of the original brick and partly polished concrete.
The steel roof has a generous overhang to create sheltered
outside workspaces, while four enormous windows look
out over the surrounding marshlands.

Architects: Carmody Groarke
Build cost: £500,000/$680,000
Footprint: 36m²/388ft² (guest suite)
and 80m²/861ft² (studio)

The long, wild grasses of the marshes which surround the sculpture studio (pictured opposite) are expected to grow up around the building until, eventually, only the weathered steel roof will be visible.

GARDEN OFFICE

A contemporary take on the traditional wooden cabin

ESSEX, UK

The architects of this smart little office studio were briefed with designing something that would sit unobtrusively in their client's garden, so as not to bother the neighbours on either side. They responded by creating this cedar-clad cabin that blends in with the surrounding trees – their choice of wood also added a personal touch for their Canadian client, reminding her of home. Cedar silvers with age, so over time the cabin will become increasingly subtle. Double doors lead into a cosy space with a small woodburning stove, while the built-in desk and shelving provide plenty of room for work and storage but still leave enough floorspace for the studio to be adapted for other uses, such as a home gym or reading spot.

Architects: All In One Design & Build
Build cost: £55,000/$75,000
Footprint: 10m²/108ft²

BERT'S BOXES

Adaptable structures finished with handmade materials

PREFABRICATED IN THE UK

Architects Box 9 Design teamed up with tile and interiors company Bert & May to create this range of eco-friendly, prefabricated 'boxes'. The Study Box (pictured left) offers a simple, customisable office space with full-height windows, but the company also make three other styles: the Studio Box (pictured overleaf, which houses a sleeping or living space, in-room bath and separate shower room), the One-Bed Box and the Two-Bed Box, both of which also have kitchens. The boxes can be fully adapted to suit the client, with an often-updated range of reclaimed or handmade choices for flooring and interior and exterior wall cladding, plus – of course – tiles. There's even the option to add a woodburning stove or a pergola and decking, perfect for a post-work sundowner.

Architects: Box 9 Design/Bert & May
Build cost: £27,500/$37,000
Footprint: 9m²/97ft²

UK-based handmade-tile specialists
Bert & May have collaborated
with Box 9 Design to offer many
vibrant, bespoke flooring options
for the cabins.

FOREST POND HOUSE

A woodland hideaway for all ages

HAMPSHIRE, UK

The architects of this build were tasked with creating a dual-purpose space: a children's den that could also function as a waterside meditation room in which to destress and think creatively. Inspired by the juxtaposition of the dark forest and the calm, light water, this small structure is timber-framed and finished with plywood, copper and glass. One end cantilevers over the pond, with the flooring arranged in steps that create a bench for sitting and gazing out through the window – a tranquil spot in which to contemplate new ideas. To the rear, the exterior walls are dark and angular, painted with chalkboard paint to encourage the children to draw on the building. Inside, the rising floor is matched with a ceiling that shrinks down at one end, creating an *Alice-in-Wonderland* feel where one corner is child-sized. It's a joyful and inventive space equally suited to meditation and play.

Architects: TDO
Build cost: £7,500/$10,000
Footprint: 6m²/65ft²

REED HOUSE: GARDEN STUDIO

A marshland workspace inspired by fishermen's huts

SUFFOLK, UK

Husband-and-wife design team David and Henrietta Villiers created this subtle studio as part of a full-house renovation of their home in Aldeburgh, on the edge of Suffolk's coastal marshes. Drawing inspiration from local boatyards, they clad the exterior of the studio in folded aluminium, which reflects the light that bounces off the pond opposite. A large window occupies most of one wall and looks out over the pond, while a wall of translucent polycarbonate at one end softly illuminates the warm birch plywood interior. Picture rails run along the walls for displaying artwork, and there's plenty of space for large desks where the couple work. With the deliberately overgrown garden leading on to the marshes beyond, the space feels fully enclosed in nature, yet the couple's commute is simply a short walk across their garden.

Architects: Studio Pond
Build cost: £50–60,000/
$68–82,000
Footprint: 38m²/409ft²

ESCAPE POD

An adaptable, rotating garden room

PREFABRICATED IN THE UK

With its egg-shaped structure and cedar shingle cladding, the Escape Pod looks a little like a bee hive or a pinecone. The Gloucestershire-based creators of this pleasingly organic form, Dominic Ash and Jeremy Fitter, say they wanted to create 'beautiful, unusual outdoor structures'. Dominic's background is in furniture building, while Jeremy studied civil engineering, specialising in treehouses. Built on a rotating raised platform, their prefabricated pod can be spun around to catch the sun or change its view. The interior meanwhile is fully adaptable, with a choice of underfloor heating or a woodburning stove, and a variety of layouts to suit a wide range of home-workers' needs: a circular bench and table for a social space, two desks for an office, one desk and a day bed for the perfect artist's studio. There's even the option of adding a raised double bed to turn it into a glamping pod – complete with a circular skylight through which to watch the stars.

Architects: Podmakers
Build cost: from £20,200/$30,200
Footprint: 7m²/75ft²

Podmakers use innovative CNC milling and making techniques to achieve the curved form of their garden structure.

MYRTLE COTTAGE STUDIO

A hidden sanctuary surrounded by wildlife

SOMERSET, UK

With something of a bird-hide feel about it, this remarkable garden studio is built into the undulating landscape: it blends in almost seamlessly with the surrounding gardens, helped along by a heavily planted roof and pre-patinated copper cladding, which gives it an earthy hue. Inspired by the idea of a 'ha-ha' (a slightly sunken structure that marks a boundary without spoiling the view), this embedded space provides a place for working, sleeping, sewing and playing guitar. Inside, an oak-lined storage wall incorporates a sofa bed and woodburning stove, while there's also a copper-and-concrete wet room. The large windows provide views of passing wildlife, and regular visits from a local family of deer are proof that the architects have achieved their aim of creating a structure that all but disappears.

Architects: Stonewood Design
Build cost: £139,000/$189,000
Footprint: 30m²/323ft²

The studio's windows were thoughtfully placed so as to frame striking views across the surrounding Avon valley.

ABANDONED TRAILER

Design that breathes fresh life into an old structure

GHENT, BELGIUM

This quirky office space was once a disused trailer: bought by a young family from a local building site, where it had once been used as a temporary site office, for just €50 (£42/$57). The clients asked architect Karel Verstraeten to create a design that would transform it into somewhere to work and rest, as well as offering an extra play space for their two sons. Once designed, the family carried out the work themselves. The exterior was clad in strips of oak, and a 1m (3ft) domed window was added, giving a submarine-like feel and allowing them to enjoy the view of the surrounding meadows. Inspired by the classic curved roof, the interior was clad in plywood with each corner rounded off. Wooden runners attached to the walls at different heights allow planks to be moved around to create a desk, seating or even a bed, ensuring the hideaway remains supremely practical.

Architects: Karel Verstraeten/FELT
Build cost: approx. €5,000/£4,200/$5,700
Footprint: 8m²/86ft²

143

144

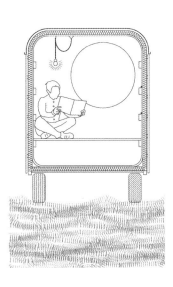

GARDEN ROOM

*A lantern-like hideaway
encased in translucent shingles*

EAST FLANDERS, BELGIUM

Architect Indra Janda created this unusual structure at her parents' home to function as a multi-use space for dining, work, relaxation and more. The wooden frame is covered with semi-transparent polycarbonate shingles, arranged in an overlapping pattern so that they look almost like scales: an effect amplified by frameless windows and a roof that is flush with the walls, creating one continuous, harmonious shape. Inside, the space is full of soft light, and its cladding means that it stays cool in summer yet warm in winter. When lit from inside for evening entertaining, the whole structure glows, lending a magical feel to the garden.

*Architects: Atelier Janda Vanderghote
Build cost: €35,000/£29,500/
$40,000
Footprint: 45m²/484ft²*

In daylight, the Garden Room's wooden skeleton casts shifting shadows against the translucent cladding, so its appearance changes subtly throughout the day.

THE FOREST HOUSE

A composer's studio made from salvaged materials

OISE, FRANCE

The brief for this build was to turn an old tool shed into an 'intimate, isolated and independent space' where the client, a composer, could focus on his work and create new music. With a limited budget and an aim to use entirely ecologically-sound components, the architects sourced glass and steel for the structure from the remains of a demolished factory nearby, as well as wooden off-cuts from the closest sawmill. The floor-to-ceiling windows offer views over the vegetable garden, and a mature oak tree provides extra shelter. The area above where the client's desk sits is entirely glazed, thanks to a corner window leading into a skylight, while a subtle sofa bed offers a spot to rest while waiting for inspiration to strike.

Architects: JCPCDR Architecture
Build cost: €10,000/£8,400/$11,400
Footprint: 24m²/258ft²

TINI
OFFICE

A ready-made office hidden among the trees

MADRID, SPAIN

Tini specialise (as their name suggests) in making diminutive, prefabricated modules that come ready to use. For this build in Madrid, they customised one of these structures to create a garden office designed to sit unobtrusively among the many trees in their client's garden, with expansive windows to give the feeling of being out in nature. The frame and exterior are Cor-Ten steel: the warm, rusty colour of which helps the office blend in with its surroundings. Inside, the walls are lined with poplar OSB – a plywood-like, versatile building board – with a thick layer of recycled cotton insulation in between. Poplar and local pine have been used for the fittings and cabinets, while the custom-made chairs and mid-century furnishings provide an aesthetic finish, as do the smart red frames of the sliding doors. The whole thing was lowered into the garden by crane, with minimal construction done onsite. It's a place to work, rest and watch the garden's wildlife.

Architects: tini (tinyhome.es)
Build cost: €56,200/£47,000/$64,000
Footprint: 22m²/237ft²

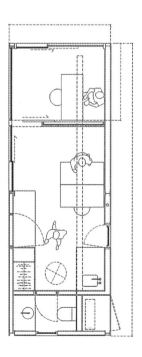

156

ARTIST'S STUDIO

*A prefabricated studio
with a unique format*

GIRONA, SPAIN

The artist who commissioned this garden studio had a
very specific brief: he wanted to work as close to his home
as possible, without being able to see it. He also needed to
be able to paint in natural light, excluding the option of a
fully enclosed box, so the architects took up the challenge
by creating this unusual, cross-shaped structure. To
minimise disruption, it was prefabricated in a workshop,
then assembled onsite, where it shares the garden with an
enormous ash tree. Featuring a double-height workspace
in the centre with surrounding single-height 'wings' that
house storage and living spaces, it took just three weeks
to construct, but the pine cladding means it will age
naturally into the garden around it. Inside, white walls
provide hanging space for the artist's paintings, while huge
windows look out on the garden – without even a glimpse
of the client's home.

Architects: Camps Felip Arquitecturia
Build cost: approx. €32,000/£27,000/
$37,000
Footprint: 80m²/861ft²

The higher ceiling of the central workspace provides the artist with space to work on large canvases, as well as display finished paintings.

ART WAREHOUSE

A creative, concrete workspace in the Mediterranean countryside

BOEOTIA, GREECE

Built as a workshop for painter and sculptor Alexandros Liapis, one of the main requirements for this space was that it should be high enough to accommodate the huge sculptures Alexandros creates. The result, described by the architects as a 'monolithic modern structure' is a curved concrete shell housing a double-height studio space, surrounded by olive, oleander and cypress trees. The south-facing wall is entirely glazed, with the roof and walls extending beyond the glazing to create a sheltered patio. Inside is a huge space for the artist to work, while a set of cantilevered, 'floating' concrete steps lead up to a mezzanine warehouse area for storing finished paintings. The studio's domed shape helps what could have been an imposing structure blend in with the surrounding landscape, giving the sense that it's been there for decades.

Architects: A31 Architecture
Build cost: €70,000/£59,000/$80,000
Footprint: 75m²/807ft²

162

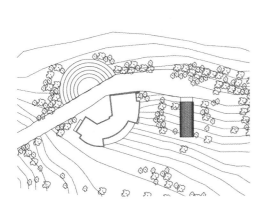

Concrete blocks were sliced from the structure to create a series of horizontal windows following the sun's trajectory: the removed concrete was repurposed to make benches and plinths for the surrounding sculpture garden.

WORK-STATION CABIN

A polygonal pod to use as you see fit

PREFABRICATED IN HUNGARY

Designs for this small wooden pod were in part inspired by the 'tiny house' movement and summer-camp cabins. Initially envisaged as a meeting room for up to six people, the makers say it can also be used as a study, a playroom, a sleeping capsule, a garden room... the list goes on. The complex 15-sided shape, sat on raised legs, looks different from every angle and provides a striking sculptural element to any garden it's placed in. It's also fully insulated and soundproof, even with one of its walls being almost entirely glazed. Prefabricated and assembled onsite with weatherproof wood cladding, it provides a year-round space to enjoy working all-but-outdoors.

Architects: Hello Wood
Build cost: from €37,500/£31,500/
$43,000
Footprint: 8m²/86ft²

ENCHANTED SHED

*An outbuilding transformed into
a workshop and guestroom*

VIENNA, AUSTRIA

This 1930s black timber outbuilding was in bad shape
and at risk of being torn down when, determined to
save it, Franz&Sue architects set about refurbishing it
while retaining many of its original features. Somewhat
unusually for the 'sheds' featured in this book, the
downstairs portion is actually used to store gardening
equipment – but above the twine and plant pots, a brass
trapdoor leads up into an attic space with a treehouse-like
feel where one of the gable walls has been entirely glazed.
The other walls are panelled with varnished grey fir, and
a built-in upholstered seat nestled into a nook can also
function as a guest bed. Though the crumbling building
has been almost completely renewed, the architects note:
'We didn't touch the roof. It is covered in moss – and we
like that.'

Architects: Franz&Sue
Footprint: 30m²/323ft²

169

The top-floor space for work and play gives a magical view of the surrounding treetops, so the clients' children can sit and watch the garden's resident squirrels.

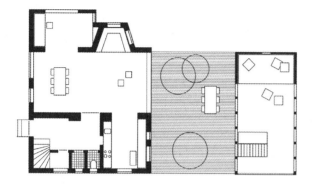

171

SMALL STUDIO FOR DRAWING

An artist's workspace inspired by the camera lucida

VORARLBERG, AUSTRIA

Hugging the angle of the sloped garden in which it sits, this eccentrically-shaped concrete studio features two huge picture windows, one at each end, with extended metal frames intended to offset the views to dramatic effect. Its tilted, light-refracting glazing was inspired by a *camera lucida*: an optical instrument that allows artists to look through a prism so they can draw while observing both their hand and their subject. Moveable exterior screens mean the client can modulate the sunlight and introduce controlled areas of shade. The lower end, which protrudes slightly over the valley below, houses a space for large canvases and sculptures, while a mezzanine level offers a more compact area for sketching and smaller work.

Architect: Christian Tonko
Build cost: approx. €202,000/
£170,000/$231,000
Footprint: 50m²/538ft²

174

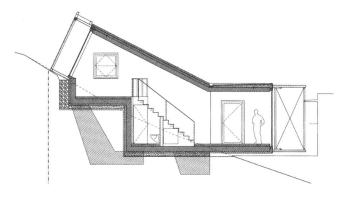

The structure of the drawing studio is formed from cast concrete: exposed on the interior, but outside clad in weathered steel.

REMISEN-PAVILLON

A perforated brick outhouse with multiple uses

LOWER SAXONY, GERMANY

'Actually, it was only supposed to be a garage,' the architects of this project admit – but the build seemed to take on a life of its own, and in the end became much more than just storage space. The materials used have a fascinating history: the bricks, which have been arranged in a delicate perforated pattern that looks almost like lace, were reclaimed from a burned-down farmhouse, while the wood that was used for the huge floor-to-ceiling doors came from an old oak tree that had been struck by lightning 15 years before and had stood dead on the land ever since. The resulting structure was so appealing that it is now used as a summer house for work and leisure, as well as a reception space for garden parties, with the unusual brickwork keeping it cool and light. In winter however, it can still take on its intended role of a wood store and a parking space for tractors.

Architects: Wirth Architekten
Footprint: 42m²/452ft²

177

The pavilion is built within a
traditional farm complex in
northern Germany: its architects
sought to give it the feel of an
modernised outbuilding through
their use of scale and materials.

ÖÖD OFFICE ROOM

An almost-invisible mirrored pod

PREFABRICATED IN ESTONIA

The concept of the ÖÖD was to create a design that would blend into its surrounding environment as seamlessly as possible. Once inside its mirrored glass exterior, the ÖÖD Office Room offers up panoramic views of whatever landscape it's been placed in. With a focus on Nordic minimalism, these structures are all clean lines and smooth surfaces, letting their users escape into the outdoors while staying warm and dry. Made from steel, insulated glass and wood, the prefabricated ÖÖD takes just hours to put up, and can even be dismantled and moved to a new location. They also make bedroom versions, which have been used for everything from hiking cabins to luxury hotel rooms.

Architects: ÖÖD
Build cost: £67,200/$91,400
Footprint: 18m²/194ft²

The ÖÖD interacts uniquely
with its environment: the more
beautiful its surroundings,
the more beautiful it looks.

12

A music studio stacked on top of a ceramics workshop

HELSINKI, FINLAND

The shape of this timber-clad build on the Jollas peninsula is rather hard to pinpoint: it looks different from every angle. The rectangular ground floor houses a ceramics workshop, while – balanced on top, slightly askew – is an asymmetric structure containing a music studio, the irregular lines of which enhance its acoustics. The clients also wanted the space to function as a guesthouse and, ultimately, a home for one of their young daughters, so the architects incorporated a bathroom and kitchen into the design, too. With eco-friendly construction a priority, the structure was built on the existing foundations of an old garage, and the irregular roof designed to slope towards the south to catch the sun on its solar panels, which power the heat pump for the main house. The whole thing is clad in exposed timber, inside and out: on the exterior, this will fade and silver with time, merging with the surrounding trees.

Architects: ORTRAUM
Build cost: approx. €222,000/
£187,000/$254,000
Footprint: 72m²/775ft²

The structure's timber frame was erected on top of the existing concrete foundations in just one day, avoiding groundwork on site completely and minimising disruption to the neighbourhood.

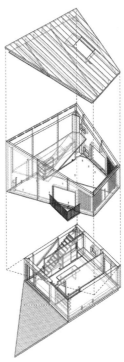

BARN HOUSE

A two-storey activity space for a creative couple

LILLEHAMMER, NORWAY

As they approach retirement, the clients who commissioned this barn, Kristin and Ruth, are anticipating having more time to spend on their hobbies: Ruth is a painter and sculptor, while Kristin loves to make things and is a keen cross-country skier. The Barn House was designed to provide them with a place to create as well as some much-needed storage space. It replaced a previous outbuilding, which was all but falling down, but kept the old structure's position and proportions and the architect used a traditional post-and-beam wood construction to give the feel of a classic Norwegian barn. Downstairs is a workshop for Kristin and a garage, while the upstairs space, with its large double windows, makes an ideal art studio for Ruth. The addition of a sink, a hob and a bathroom mean it can also double as a guesthouse when their children and grandchildren come to stay.

Architect: Jon Danielsen Aarhus
Build cost: approx. £166,000/$226,000
Footprint: 16m²/172ft² (upper floor: 44m²/474ft²)

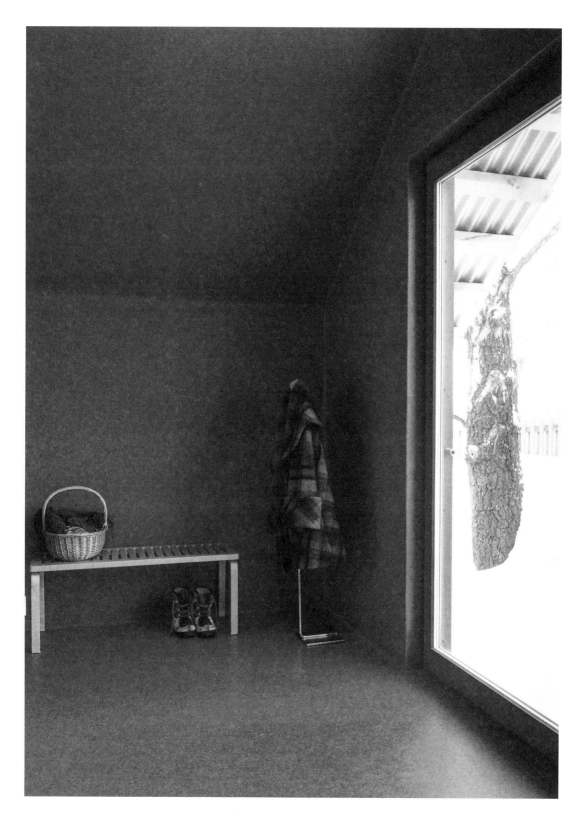

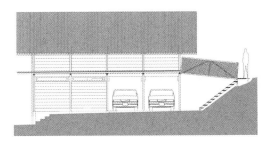

The ground-floor workshop
doubles as a place for Ruth,
a keen gardener, to propagate
plants over winter.

WRITERS' COTTAGE

Escape to the country without leaving the city

OSLO, NORWAY

The clients who commissioned this 'cottage' wanted a place to work and write that had the feel of a country bolthole – something of a challenge in a suburban garden next to a railway line and a carpark. The resulting annexe's design was dictated by providing the clients with as much of a view as possible, with one entirely glazed façade. The structure, coated in a high-gloss black paint more commonly used for boats, rises in height towards the south to allow natural light in over the neighbour's hedge. Inside, the walls are dark-stained timber and a staircase that doubles as a bookcase leads up to a small mezzanine level where a sheepskin-lined relaxation nook looks out over the landscape.

Architects: Vigsnæs+Kosberg++Arkitekter
Build cost: £41,500/$56,500
Footprint: 15m²/161ft²

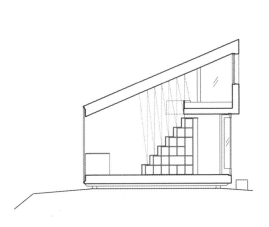

The architects' addition of a glass desk ensures the clients' all-important view is completely uninterrupted.

STUDYPOD

A futuristic, multi-use cube

PREFABRICATED IN NORWAY

With its minimalist design, rounded corners and black-tinted glass, the sight of a Studypod dropped into a natural landscape gives a slightly sci-fi feel. Although designed primarily as a home office (the pod comes with an optional, detachable desk), it can also be used as a mini yoga studio, a kids' playroom or even a spare bedroom (if you want to put nothing but a bed in it, that is). Inside, oak laminate flooring provides an attractive finish, but the pod is practical, too: there's even the option of mounting it on heavy-duty lockable wheels so that it can be manoeuvred around at will. With a comparatively tiny footprint, it's suitable for compact spaces, making a home office a possibility even for those with just a tablecloth-sized garden.

Architects: Livit
Build cost: from £10,100/$13,700
Footprint: 3.6m²/39ft²

GARDEN STUDIO

An asymmetric office in a family garden

TORONTO, CANADA

Like many who choose to 'work from shed', architect Oliver Dang needed extra space, but couldn't afford to move due to rising house prices. With a young family, he was also keen to be at home as much as possible, so this shed-office was the perfect solution. Keen to make it feel like a cohesive part of his home, Oliver clad the structure in strips of cedar, using the same wood for the decking and fencing in the garden to visually link it with the main house. The pitched roof follows the line of the mature maple tree above while maximising sunlight from the south. The birch plywood-lined interior is true to its shed-like origins, with exposed studs that double up as shelving, but there is still space left over for both standing and sitting desks. The finishing touch is a slab of salvaged marble marking the entrance, adding an element of grandeur to the humble space.

Architects: Six Four Five A
Build cost: £11,750/$16,000
Footprint: 9.3m²/100ft²

The exposed stud shelving maximises this shed's small footprint, providing storage for books, files and periodicals without taking up any extra floor space.

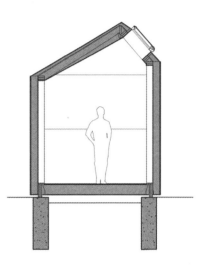

WRITING PAVILION

A tiny, pine-clad space for big ideas

NEW YORK, USA

Designed as a retreat for an artistic couple to write and
draw in, this black-stained-cedar shed sits on a concrete
plinth behind their home. With the aim of minimising
distractions, Architensions clad the interior entirely in
pine plywood, adding an angled skylight to fill the space
with natural light and a small window over the desk
looking out over the enclosed garden. By day, the pavilion's
dark exterior provides a striking contrast to the colours
of the garden; by night, it melts away into the darkness.
It's minimally furnished, too, with just a folding desk and
a chair: its simple form is intended to allow the clients'
imaginations to run wild.

Architects: Architensions
Footprint: 4.6m²/50ft²

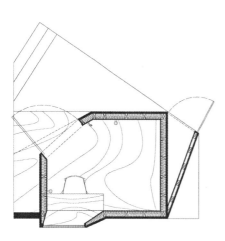

The roof of this shed was conceived as 'a large sloping lightwell', and its walls were carefully angled to let in as much sunlight as possible.

LONG STUDIO

A barn-like structure celebrating modest materials

MAINE, USA

Eric Reinholdt, founder of 30x40 Design Workshop, built this multifunctional studio in the grounds of his home in Mount Desert Island to be used as an office, a gathering space and a place to demonstrate the appeal of a clean, simple aesthetic to new clients. White aluminium-clad external walls, minimal wood interiors and a brutally simple form makes for a rather unassuming structure, where natural light is the star of the show. An array of windows give differing, controlled views of the studio's glorious surroundings; small windows look out on the tree canopy to the north and south, while the eastern wall is almost entirely glazed and, on the western wall, horizontal slot windows offer different views depending on whether you sit or stand. Above all of this, skylights show the island's changing weather and, outside, an aesthetically pleasing log store means an after-work campfire is never too far away.

Architects: 30x40 Design Workshop
Footprint: 36m²/384ft²

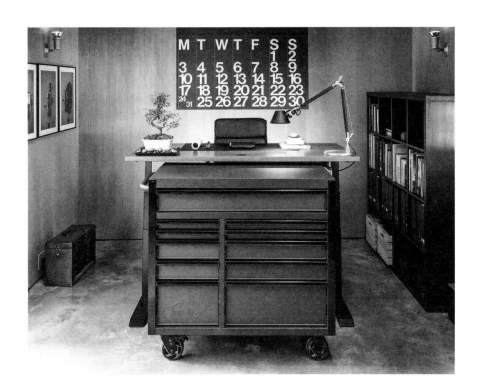

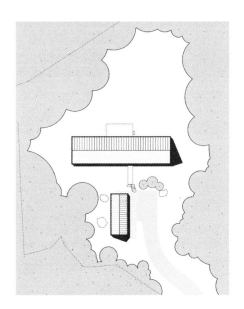

The studio's design intends to demonstrate that accessible, unassuming materials can be made to feel expensive if thoughtfully combined: it's a manifesto for authentic, affordable architecture.

BLACK BOX

A surreal 'floating' box on an LA hillside

CALIFORNIA, USA

Seeming to hover above the main residence on a steep, leafy slope, this aptly named 'Black Box' provides a workspace for a technology author and columnist. The structure, made of blackened steel and dark-stained redwood cladding, is dominated by a huge picture window that looks out over the valley. The interior is minimally furnished: letting the view create the space's focal point. To access the studio, you have to climb a set of steps in the hillside, emerging through the tree canopy and entering via a sliding glass door. This, the architects say, provides an important separation between work and home life – it's hard to imagine many better commutes.

Architects: ANX
Build cost: approx. £44,000/
$60,000
Footprint: 18.5m²/199ft²

This hillside studio's picture window frames a panoramic view of Griffith Park in the Santa Monica Mountains.

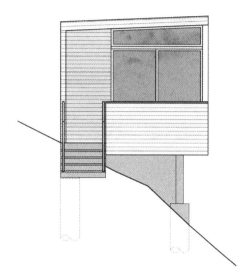

POLYGON STUDIO

A sculptor's retreat on the banks of Lake George

NEW YORK, USA

With its zig-zagging, double-gabled roof and steel-and-cedar cladding, this multifunctional space was designed primarily as a sculpture studio, for which vertical space was a priority, but also serves a second role as a guest bedroom. To meet both needs, the interior is double-height, with a small mezzanine loft at one end to accommodate guests. The loft leads out to a balcony overlooking the lake, while downstairs, large glass doors let in both light and natural vistas. One exterior wall is clad in galvanised steel, which extends up on to the roof, while the others are finished in red cedar. The cedar continues inside, making the studio feel truly nestled among the trees.

Architects: Jeffery S. Poss/WORKUS Studio
Build cost: approx. £85,000/$115,000
Footprint: 38m²/409ft²

217

Located in the steep grounds of a lakefront residential property, the studio was placed at the site's highest point to maximise views over the water.

THE SHED

A simple yet striking utility space

MISSOURI, USA

Used to store maintenance equipment, this project is a shed in the truest sense of the word: yet its elegant, steel-framed structure, clad in white oak, elevates it beyond simply storage space. Its architects wanted to explore the possibilities of a prefabricated assembly kit, using modular wooden wall components put together onsite. The timber wraps uninterrupted around the roof and sides, while both gable ends are covered in translucent polycarbonate to allow daylight to filter through. Huge, fully mechanised doors take up the whole of one side, allowing large-scale machinery to fit into the space. Fluorescent lighting is built in to the steel rafters, and at night the shed's glowing gabled form looks almost like a chapel. It's not hard to imagine it being used as a rather spectacular workshop space. Practical? Eminently. Beautiful? Undoubtedly.

Architects: Hufft
Footprint: 59m²/635ft²

WRITER'S STUDIO

A poet's forest escape made from stone, oak and glass

CONNECTICUT, USA

Retired banker and published poet John Barr was looking for a calming space to read, write, and store his 1,700-volume poetry collection. The result is this beautifully finished structure clad in irregular stone, which both evokes the traditional dry-stone walls seen throughout Connecticut and gives the impression that the studio is almost growing out of the rocky landscape. A large, glazed section cantilevers over the hillside so that from within the structure seems to float among the trees. The interior walls are lined with oak bookshelves, while a wooden staircase leads up to a compact roof terrace: a spot for quiet contemplation. The studio intends to cause minimal disruption to the surrounding area, so as to encourage local wildlife to wander past.

Architects: Eric J. Smith Architect
Footprint: 60m²/646ft²

SHED
NO. 8841

*An ingenious solution to a
shortage of water and space*

ARIZONA, USA

Water is a valuable resource in the desert town of Tucson, and local architect Ben Lepley had long wanted to put together his own water tower to irrigate his fruit trees. Finding himself also in need of a workshop and tool room, Ben began to put his plans into action. He tore down an old garage and put aside the timber and steel roofing to use in his new build, then bought a 900-gallon water tank on Craigslist. Inspired by industrial buildings he'd seen in India, he opted for a louvered metal façade, which allows for natural ventilation and light without overheating. The water tower sits in one corner, forming a support for the rest of the shed, and the whole thing is clad in uncoated Cor-Ten, which has weathered to its current shade. The finishing touch was a door made from an old picket fence. With minimal outlay and predominantly recycled materials, Ben now collects more than 10,000 gallons of rainwater per year.

Architects: Tectonicus
Build cost: £11,200/$15,000
Footprint: 37m²/398ft²

SHED-O-VATION

Once a shed, now a home office and gym

WASHINGTON, USA

For this shed renovation (or Shed-O-Vation), the architects expanded an existing storage shed that they had previously built for the client, transforming it into a multifunctional office and gym while retaining its original wooden siding and sloping roof. Inside, the floor and part of the walls are covered with black rubber, and useful hooks allow the client to hang bikes in one corner. A plywood cabinet conceals a seafoam-green office space that can be packed away when not in use, while further cabinets offer essential storage (including a generous wine rack). A large accordion window with a concrete bench beneath opens up on to the garden, allowing the clients to also use the space as a tranquil yoga studio.

Architects: Best Practice
Footprint: 20m²/215ft²

GRASS-HOPPER STUDIO

*A single structure that transforms
a family's living space*

WASHINGTON, USA

This studio in Seattle was commissioned in response to
the city's housing shortage: significantly expanding and
enhancing the clients' living space without the need to
move. The studio itself features floor-to-ceiling glazing,
behind which sits a lounge area for work or relaxation
and a library with plywood and repurposed-MDF shelving.
It's connected to the main house by a raised, covered
walkway that also serves as a seating area (although the
family's children have since co-opted it as a stage for
putting on impromptu plays). The design also creates a
partially enclosed courtyard between the main house
and studio, at the centre of which a silk tree provides
shelter and shade. Inspired by ancient Chinese courtyard
housing, here Wittman Estes show that, with creative
thinking, a garden can truly be an extension of the home.

Architects: Wittman Estes
Build cost: approx. £44,000/
$60,000
Footprint: 33m²/355ft²

The studio's roofing extends to the rear, creating space for both an outdoor workshop and a covered parking space.

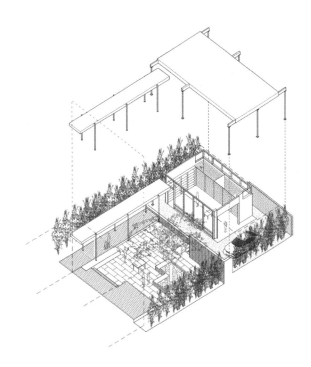

LA POTTERY STUDIO

A tree-top space to show off ceramics

CALIFORNIA, USA

When ceramicist Raina and her partner Mark, an architect, moved into their new home, they discovered this small treehouse in the sloping backyard. Seeing its potential as a unique space in which to showcase Raina's pottery designs, they set to work transforming it into a display studio. Accessed by wooden steps and a bridge, the exterior is clad in exposed fir in homage to its surroundings. Inside, minimal interiors offset the maximalist nature of Raina's ceramics: with plywood walls and a large, simple, circular table. Expansive windows provide views over the treetops, while Raina's creations are displayed on a set of shelves made from wood salvaged from old shipping crates and branches cut from the surrounding woodland.

Architects: Raina Lee and Mark Watanabe
Footprint: 6.3m²/68ft²

The treehouse was originally built for the children of a previous owner: now it brings to life the organic forms of Raina's work.

HERALD GARDEN STUDIO

*A simple, natural studio
creating more family space*

WELLINGTON, NEW ZEALAND

The clients for this studio, who live in a compact
two-bedroom cottage in the suburbs of New Zealand's
capital city with their two young sons, were keen to
create more room for their family without having to
relocate. This studio was the answer, providing a versatile
space that can be variously used as a playroom, study,
peaceful retreat and guest accommodation. The main space
offers room for work or play, with a bathroom and storage
at the rear, while a ladder leads up to a mezzanine loft
with room for a bed. The studio is raised from the ground
on timber supports, and has timber decking at the front
facing towards the house – cut around an established olive
tree and covered with a pergola to provide a sheltered
outside space. Floor-to-ceiling glass doors blur the line
between inside and out, while the interior walls are
lined with eco-friendly strandboard for an unfussy,
hardwearing finish.

Architects: Parsonson Architects
Build cost: £51,400/$70,000
Footprint: 172m²/1,851ft²

ARROW STUDIO

An uniquely formed garden art gallery

VICTORIA, AUSTRALIA

This chevron-shaped structure was created for a client who wanted a space in which to display his late wife's paintings. Concerned about security, he asked the architects to keep windows to a minimum, and position them in such a way that it would be very hard to break in. After some deliberation, they created this arrow-like design that extends inward at one end and outward in the other. These protruding sections are covered by timber slats, protecting the windows behind them. With a limited budget, they opted for a plywood structure clad in galvanised metal, and the result, the architects say, looks like 'a random piece of space junk has fallen into a back garden'. Built in just ten days, the space now serves as a studio for the client as well as providing him with a precious space in which to remember his wife. At night, light flows through the slats, illuminating the garden like a patterned lantern.

Architects: Nervegna Reed and pH architects
Build cost: approx. £26,000/$35,500/AUD $50,000
Footprint: 32m²/344ft²

LIGHT SHED

A serene studio tailored to a photographer's needs

KANAGAWA, JAPAN

As its name suggests, this project was all about light –
in particular, the soft, natural light required by the client,
a photographer. The architects created this minimalist
open-plan studio with an asymmetrical, multifaceted
gable roof, delivering a large vertical space without
the need for horizontal beams. The exterior is clad in
translucent polycarbonate panels, which reveal the
timber frame and give a 'behind the scenes' feel. Inside,
a large, frosted-glass skylight at a 45-degree angle floods
the space with diffused light and simple, white walls
and a grey concrete floor create a blank canvas for the
photographer's work.

Architects: FT Architects
Footprint: 33m²/355ft²

The wide, minimally-framed
window was designed to make
this studio feel like an extension
of the client's garden.

TINY ATELIER

*A converted barn that marries
old and new materials*

KURASHIKI, JAPAN

Sitting on a mountainside overlooking a green valley, this small studio is the workspace of a designer who makes accessories using dried flowers, which she grows in her adjacent garden. The architects converted an 80-year-old barn to create the space, retaining many of its original features – including the traditional tiled roof – while revitalising its structure and aesthetic. The exterior is clad in vertical wooden boards, and the door finished with the same boards placed diagonally. A large window wraps around one corner, providing views over the valley. Inside, the white painted walls contrast with the timber-lined ceiling and original beams, and wooden shelving provides space to display the designer's floral creations.

*Architects: Ryuji Kajino and
Malubishi Architects
Build cost: £40,000/$54,000
Footprint: 12m²/129ft²*

The barn's original tiled roof matched those of the long-standing buildings surrounding it: the architects were determined to keep this history and continuity.

A–Z BY COUNTRY

A–Z BY ARCHITECT

253

IMAGE CREDITS

12 (pp.184–187) images by Marc Goodwin (Archmospheres); A Room in the Garden (pp.2–3 and pp.46–49) images by Ben Tynegate; Abandoned Trailer (pp.142–145) images by FELT; Arrow Studio (pp.242–243) image by Sam Reed + Toby Reed; Art Warehouse (pp.162–165) images by Yiannis Hajiaslanis; Artist's Studio (pp.158–161) images by José Hevia Blach; Barn House (pp.188–191) images by Knut Bry; Bert's Boxes (pp.122–125) images by Beth Davis; Black Box (pp.212–215) images by Brian Thomas Jones (Project Team: Aaron Neubert (Principal), Jeremy Limsenben, David Chong, Xiran Zhang / Structural Engineer: FJ Engineering / General Contractor: Doug Dalton / Steel Windows and Doors: John Dunne / Millwork: Dan Taron); Cedar Cabin (pp.38–41) images by Jack Hobhouse; Claire & Tom's Garden Studio (pp.67–69) images by Tom Cronin (architects: Zminkowska De Boise Architects); Clerkenwell Road (pp.92–95) images by The Modern House; Cork Study (pp.78–81) and Writer's Shed (pp.24–27) images by Wai Ming Ng; Daniel Heath's Garden Studio (pp.43–45) images by Daniel Heath / Carmel King; Decorated Shed (pp.16–19) images by Julian Abrahams (styling by Emilio Pimentel-Reid); Dwelling Unit for Musicians (pp.98–101) images by NAARO; Enchanted Shed (pp.168–171) © Franz&Sue/ Andreas Buchberger; Escape Pod (pp.134–137) images by Tim Brotherton; Faye & Daniel's Place (pp.30–33) and Greenwich Garden Studio (pp.54–55) images by FRENCH+TYE; Forest Pond House (pp.126–129) images by Ben Blossom; Garden Office (p.5 and pp.120–121) images by Hugh Metcalf; Garden Room (pp.147–151) images by Tim Van de Velde; Garden Studio (pp.198–201) images by Ashlea Wessel; George Bernard Shaw outside of his shed (p.8) © Keystone Features / Stringer; Grasshopper Studio (pp.232–235) images by Nic Lehoux; Herald Garden Studio (p.240) image by Paul McCredie; Holloway Lightbox (pp.28–29) image by Jon Holloway; LA Pottery Studio (pp.236–239) images by Philip Cheung; Light Shed (pp.244–247) images by Shigeo Ogawa; London Townhouse Shed (pp.96–97) image by Matt Clayton; Long Studio (p.206, pp.208–9, p.210 and p.211, bottom right) images by Trent Bell; Long Studio (p.211, top) image by Eric Reinholdt; Manbey Pod (pp.60–61) image by Taran Wilkhu; Minima Moralia (pp.90–91) and My Room in the Garden (pp.62–65) images by Boano Prišmontas; Myrtle Cottage Studio (pp.138–141) images by Jo Chambers; Nestle Studio (pp.56–59) © Tim Crocker; ÖÖD Office Room (pp.180–183) images by Oliver Soostar; Polygon Studio (pp.216–219) images by Jeffery S. Poss, FAIA; Potting Shed (pp.82–85) images by Adam Scott Images; Reed House: Garden Studio (pp.130–133) images by The Modern House; Remisenpavillon (pp.176–179) images by Christian Burmester; ROOM (pp.103–105) images by Tim Denton; ROOM CGI visualisation (p.256) by Andy Butler (www. infinite-images.co.uk); Rug Room (pp.74–77) images by Damian Griffiths; Sculpture Cabin (pp.112–115) images by Edvinas Bruzas; SE5 Garden Library (pp.86–89) images by Adam Scott (architects: Turner Architects Ltd); Shed No. 8841 (pp.226–227) image by Benjamin Lepley; Shed-O-Vation (pp.228–231) images by Rafael Soldi; Shoffice (pp.12–15) images by alanwilliamsphotography.com; Small Studio for Drawing (pp.173–175) images by Eduard Hueber; Studypod (pp.196–197) image by Livit Terrazzo Studio (pp.71–73) images by Sarah Burton; The Bunker (pp.20–23) images by Edmund Sumner; The Forest House (pp.152–153) image by Maxime Leyvastre; The Light Shed (pp.50–53) images by Chris Snook Photography; The Shed (p.4 and pp.220–223) images by Mike Sinclair; The Studios (pp.110–111) image by Peter Cook; The Writing Room (pp.34–37) images by Rory Gardiner; Tini Office (pp.155–157) images by Imagen Subliminal (Miguel de Guzmán + Rocío Romero) @imagensubliminal; Tiny Atelier (p.7 and pp.248–251) © Yasushi Okano; Two Pavilions (pp.116–119) images by Johan Dehlin; Workstation Cabin (pp.166–167) image by Zsuzsa Darab; Writer's Studio (p.6 and pp.106–109) images by dapple photography; Writer's Studio (pp.224–225) image by Durston Saylor; Writers' Cottage (pp.192–195) images by Jonas Adolfsen; Writing Pavilion (p.202–205) images by Cameron Blaylock.

254

Work from Shed
First edition

Published in 2022 by Hoxton Mini Press, London
Copyright © Hoxton Mini Press 2022
All rights reserved

Introduction by Rowan Moore
Shed descriptions by Tara O'Sullivan
Design by Daniele Roa and Friederike Huber
Copy-editing by Florence Filose
Production and project management by Anna De Pascale
Production support by Becca Jones

A CIP catalogue record for this book is available
from the British Library.

ISBN: 978-1-914314-12-4

Printed and bound by FINIDR, Czech Republic

Hoxton Mini Press is an environmentally conscious
publisher, committed to offsetting our carbon footprint.
This book is 100% carbon compensated, with offset
purchased from Stand For Trees.

For every book you buy from our website, we plant a tree:
www.hoxtonminipress.com

*Pictured overleaf: A CGI visualisation
of Tim Denton's ROOM (p.102) shows
the possibilities of this prefab office.*